GW01081544

# URBAN AUSTRALIA

Planning Issues and Policies

# URBAN AUSTRALIA

## Planning Issues and Policies

edited by

Stephen Hamnett and Raymond Bunker

An Alexandrine Press Book

Mansell Publishing Limited, London and New York
Nelson Wadsworth, Melbourne, Victoria

First published 1987 by Mansell Publishing Limited
(A subsidiary of the H. W. Wilson Company)
6 All Saints Street, London N1 9RL
950 University Avenue, Bronx, New York 10452

First published in Australia 1987 by Nelson Wadsworth
Thomas Nelson Australia, 480 La Trobe Street, Melbourne, Victoria 3000

This book was commissioned, edited and designed by
Alexandrine Press, Oxford

**British Library Cataloguing in Publication Data**

Urban Australia: planning issues and policies.
 1. Urban policy—Australia
 I. Hamnett, Stephen   II. Bunker, Raymond
711'.4'0094   HT149.A8

ISBN 0-7201-1843-3

**National Library of Australia Cataloguing in Publication Data**

Urban Australia: planning issues and policies.
 Includes bibliographies and index.
 ISBN 0 17 007166 9
 1. Cities and towns—Australia—Growth.
 2. City planning—Australia.
 3. Urban policy—Australia.  4. Urban economics.
 I. Hamnett, Stephen.  II. Bunker, Raymond, 1929–.
307.7'6'0994

**Library of Congress Cataloging in Publication Data**

Urban Australia.
 Includes index.
 1. City planning—Australia.  2. Urbanization—
Australia.  I. Hamnett, Stephen.  II. Bunker, Raymond C.
HT169.A8U73  1986     307.1'2'0994     86–23762
ISBN 0–7201–1843–3

Typeset by Katerprint Typesetting Services, Oxford
Printed and Bound in the United Kingdom by The Alden Press

# CONTENTS

# NOTES ON THE CONTRIBUTORS

**Stephen Hamnett** is Associate Professor and Head of Planning at the South Australian Institute of Technology in Adelaide.

**Raymond Bunker** is a Senior Lecturer at the South Australian Institute of Technology and is Deputy Chairman of the South Australian Planning Commission.

**Chris Maher** is a Senior Lecturer in the Department of Geography at Monash University in Victoria.

**David Rich and John Langdale** are Senior Lecturers in Human Geography in the School of Earth Sciences at Macquarie University, Sydney.

**Richard Cardew** is a Senior Lecturer in the Centre for Environmental and Urban Studies at Macquarie University, Sydney.

**Toni Logan** is a member of the Victorian Planning Appeals Board.

**Chris Paris** is a Principle Lecturer at the Canberra College of Advanced Education.

**Derek Scrafton** is Director-General of Transport for South Australia.

**Margaret Starrs** is a consultant with the firm of Travers Morgan in Sydney. She was formerly Senior Research Economist in the South Australian Department of Transport.

**Leonie Sandercock** is Professor of Urban Studies in the Centre for Environmental and Urban Studies at Macquarie University, Sydney.

**Peter Melser** is a Post-Doctoral Fellow in the Centre for Environmental and Urban Studies at Macquarie University, Sydney.

**John Minnery** is a Lecturer in Planning in the School of the Built Environment at the Queensland Institute of Technology in Brisbane.

**David Wilmoth** is Head of the Central Policy Division, New South Wales Department of Environment and Planning.

## ACKNOWLEDGEMENTS

The editors are grateful to Alexandrine Press for permission to use the papers by Chris Maher, Chris Paris, Raymond Bunker, Leonie Sandercock and Peter Melser, and John Minnery which originally appeared in *Built Environment*, 1985, Volume 11, number 2, but have been revised for publication in this volume.

The editors are also grateful to Pion Ltd, for permission to reproduce the paper by Toni Logan, which originally appeared in *Environment and Planning A*, 1984, Volume 16, pp. 1041–54.

# Introduction

STEPHEN HAMNETT and RAYMOND BUNKER

Twenty years ago Donald Horne wrote a book about Australia which he called *The Lucky Country*. The phrase quickly passed into everyday language, even though many people who used it were perhaps not familiar with the rest of Horne's book which contained an attack on what he perceived as the mediocrity of much of Australian intellectual, political and cultural life. Horne's thesis was that Australians in the mid-1960s were enjoying high standards of material prosperity and an enviable quality of life despite their efforts rather than because of them.

The quality of life for most Australians remains high today. By international standards Australia is still an affluent and well-housed society. Recent years, however, have seen the decline of Australian manufacturing industry and the growth of unemployment in the face of competition from developing countries with lower labour costs. Housing costs have risen in such a way as to place home-ownership – the Great Australian Dream – out of the reach of many young or single-income families and the gap between owners and renters has widened. Cuts in public expenditure have been felt across a wide range of community facilities. Four or five years ago many people were confident that a new era of economic prosperity would follow from the exploitation of Australia's great natural mineral wealth, but to date the 'Resource Boom' has not arrived. For an increasing number of Australians the luck seems to have run out.

This collection of essays, which has been compiled primarily for students of planning and urban studies, and others interested in these areas, explores a number of aspects of life in urban Australia in the mid-1980s – almost two hundred years since the first white settlers landed at Sydney Cove. Maher's chapter provides an introduction to the history of the Australian urban system and, in particular, to the spatial effects of recent structural economic change. Australia's vast empty spaces and the popularity of works which romanticize rural life and the values of 'The Bush' have created an image of Australia overseas which diverts attention from an understanding of how urban a nation Australia is. Yet, as Maher emphasizes, since the beginnings of white colonization, Australia has had a predominance of urban dwellers and, indeed, has consistently had a higher proportion of its population in towns and cities than any other Western industrialized nation. The concentration of the Australian population began under nineteenth-century colonial capitalism when the dominance of the major port cities became established. The harsh physical environment constrained economic activity to a small coastal portion of the land area, and the adoption in 1901 of a federal political system reinforced the separateness of the major cities and their primacy within the new states.

Maher describes how the concentration of population and economic activity continued after the Second World War until the early 1970s, as industrial output expanded and new immigrants from overseas settled in the cities. In the past ten years, however, economic and demographic conditions have changed markedly. Shifts in the investment pattern of public and private capital and changes in the distribution of the population through internal migration are bringing about changes in the nature of the space economy which are illustrated by recent patterns of urban growth. Maher discusses, in particular, changes in the traditional distribution of economic functions between the two major cities of Melbourne and Sydney; the success of the previously peripheral areas of Brisbane and Perth in capturing a growing proportion of the slowing population growth of the country (which has led some commentators to point to superficial similarities between this trend and the 'Sunbelt' phenomenon in the United States); and the significance of the recent incidence of net migration losses from the major cities to the non-metropolitan areas of their states in apparent reversal of previous trends.

The next three chapters explore further the economic processes which are transforming the nature of Australian urban development and consider, in different ways, the attempts of urban policy-makers and the planning systems to cope with this transformation. The chapter by Rich, Cardew and Langdale analyses the recent effects of financial, organizational and technological change on urban development in Australia, with specific reference to Sydney. The authors examine, firstly, the role of domestic and international capital flows and the activities of the finance sector on metropolitan Sydney's physical development, in particular through the channelling of overseas investment funds into property development. Secondly, they examine the physical consequences of major changes in the organization of business, focusing especially on the increasing domination of the economy by a small number of large firms and the growing spatial concentration of control of economic activity in Sydney. The third part of the chapter looks at the spatial consequences of recent technological change and, in particular, at the current and likely impacts of new information technologies on urban development. Rich, Cardew and Langdale then assess critically the history of post-war attempts to regulate and guide Sydney's development through a series of regional schemes and plans. They conclude that, as late as the beginning of the present decade, Sydney's planners were developing plans which were not based on an understanding of the underlying processes of economic and technological change shaping the development of the metropolitan area.

Logan's comparative study of urban and regional planning in New South Wales and Victoria lends support to the argument that planning is still wedded to outdated concepts and has failed to respond to the new urban policy issues which characterize the 1980s. She argues that until recently the rationale for planning has rested on implicit assumptions of continued economic growth and that planning was primarily concerned with negative regulations intended to check the physical expansion of cities. Her study notes the contrasting administrative styles of planning in the two major states of New South Wales and Victoria – a centralized managerial and political style in New South Wales and an apolitical and decentralized style in Victoria – but provides evidence of convergence in styles in the face of economic recession, with both states currently competing for development and showing a willingness to disregard or by-pass planning legislation in the process.

The traditional concern of planning with the control of urban growth is still very much on the agenda in Australia in the 1980s, even so. The air traveller coming in to land at the airport of a major Australian city will see a scene which does not differ greatly from one city to another. In the centre of the city are clustered the high-rise reflective glass and concrete towers which have sprouted in the business districts in the last decade or so, more likely than not funded by foreign investors. And beyond the city centre is suburbia – mile after mile of coloured corrugated iron or tiled roofs stretching away almost to the horizon, sometimes, as in Brisbane and Adelaide, clinging to forested hillsides, but more often spilling formlessly across the plains, cross-cut by roads and railways and relieved, here and there, by the green of parks and race courses and the tiny dots of blue which are the backyard swimming pools. Around the edge of the urban area the suburbs peter out into small farms, each with its dam and pond, but it will be clear from the evidence of new dirt roads that some of this farmland is about to be subdivided for more housing. The low-density sprawl of the Australian city is the dominant image which such an aerial view provides.

Bunker's chapter reviews the efforts which have been made in recent years in three Australian cities – Sydney, Melbourne and Adelaide – to check the sprawl of the urban area and to achieve 'urban consolidation'. Although the containment of urban sprawl is not a new idea in Australia, urban consolidation policies have been given priority recently, in part as a consequence of economic recession and the fiscal crisis of state governments, which have led to a concern to achieve greater efficiency in the spending of scarce capital funds on urban infrastructure, and in part through making fuller use of inner-city facilities, which are underused as a consequence of the decline or changed composition of inner-city populations. Other arguments for urban consolidation relate to rises in liquid fuel costs, fears of fuel shortages and the belief that a more compact city form would be more efficient in transport terms and more able to survive any future dramatic change in the availability of fuel. A third set of arguments has more to do with equity than efficiency considerations – the need to create a better match between the requirements of households for shelter and the nature of the dwelling stock; and, in particular, to meet the need for accommodation in inner and middle suburbs from aged persons and small households.

Bunker examines these arguments and shows clearly that some of their assumptions relating to land or cost savings from consolidation policies are rather simplistic and not founded on detailed analysis of the nature of trends in metropolitan development or of the likely impact of specific policies. The general conclusion is that urban consolidation policies are likely to have little significant influence on the overall characteristics of population distribution in Australian metropolitan areas in the short-term. There is, however, a need to provide more housing choice by location, by type of dwelling and by tenure, and this might best be achieved in inner areas by the adoption of consolidation policies.

The chapter by Chris Paris looks in more detail at housing issues and policies. Paris identifies the central issue in housing in Australia today as the contrast between the well and cheaply-housed majority and the less-well and expensively-housed minorities. He reviews the development of post-war housing policies by federal and state governments and discusses, in particular, the continuing crisis of private tenants and the limited achievements in recent years of public housing policies and of government attempts to increase home-ownership in an increasingly difficult economic context. Paris suggests that tenure has become increasingly class-divided during the post-war period, although the category of class needs to be redefined to take account of the particular problems of women and the elderly in the housing market. He also points to the inadequacy of data on obsolescence in the Australian housing stock and argues that there is an urgent need for a systematic housing survey.

The chapter by Scrafton and Starrs looks at transport issues and shows that Australian cities are kept going largely by use of the private car and truck, operating on road networks built and maintained by local and state governments using money from all three levels of government. Despite oil price shocks, vehicle usage expressed in terms of kilometres per annum has increased at a faster rate than vehicle ownership over the decade from 1971 to 1981. Not unexpectedly, there is evidence that the level of service provided by arterial roads in the largest cities of Melbourne and Sydney is not as good as it is in the smaller capital cities. Sydney's peak hour traffic conditions are poor. One indication of this is that the average distance travelled each day on arterial roads per person in Sydney is lower than that of any other capital city except for the smallest – Hobart. Another is the comment that when a car breaks down in the peak hour on the Harbour Bridge, it would be cheaper to tip it immediately into the Harbour, rather than to retrieve it.

Local traffic networks are used both to carry traffic and to provide access to property. Planning for new areas and traffic management schemes in established localities increasingly try to resolve this conflict.

Almost all urban freight transport is carried out by private companies, but public passenger transport, largely by bus, is provided by both the public and private sectors. Suburban rail networks are important in Sydney and Melbourne, and Melbourne also has a large tram system serving the inner suburbs. Public transport is heavily subsidized and, while the poor, young, elderly and disadvantaged benefit from this, so too do well-to-do white collar workers on commuter services to the central areas of the capital cities.

Scrafton and Starrs discuss a number of important issues regarding transport in Australia's cities. Two are particularly significant. The first is the obvious and growing problem of large deficits on urban public transport. These may be even more severe than indicated in this chapter – some recent estimates have suggested that the level of cost recovery obtained from fares is much lower, once account is taken of hidden subsidies and concessions. The scale of these growing deficits may mean that the use of taxis and vehicle-sharing become more common, together with such measures as changed work practices to ease the public transport task.

A second issue is more fundamental and continuing. This is the compartmentalization and segregation of different aspects of transport planning, as well as insufficient attention to the broad relationships between population distribution and transport services in metropolitan planning. Scrafton and Starrs see the main impediments to progress in these areas as political and institutional. The practices of management and unions, for example, in the Victorian transport industry, have been the subject of continuing adverse public comment. With less money around to spend on transport, as the chapter indicates, public policy-making and planning for transport are unlikely to become easier in the future.

Much has been written in the recent past about international economic restructuring and about the consequent 'deindustrialization' of Australia. Sandercock and Melser provide a vivid illustration of what these processes mean for the inhabitants of one town – Wollongong. Home of what was proudly described in the 1960s as the 'biggest steelworks in the British Commonwealth' and with coal mining as another important employer,

Wollongong has suffered severely in recent years from the decline of these industries. Unemployment increased from 7,700 in early 1982 to 21,000 by the end of 1983. The length of time that people stay unemployed is increasing, younger workers in the manufacturing sector are hardest hit, prospects for school leavers are severely limited and there is considerable hidden unemployment among women. Sandercock and Melser have interviewed unemployed workers and their families in Wollongong and their chapter shows what unemployment means for some of these people.

The authors then look at the various programmes, initiatives and dogmas which have comprised the response to restructuring and unemployment to date. They are unimpressed by the fragmented and unco-ordinated nature of federal government employment and retraining programmes and justifiably sceptical about the scope for revitalizing Wollongong through high technology or tourist development. They argue, instead, for a new look at manpower planning, education, training and skill formation processes; for learning the lessons from those countries like Sweden and Japan which have used economic restructuring as the opportunity to introduce effective retraining for workers; for tackling the need to reform the education system so that it is not only seen as a preparation for jobs that are no longer there; for facing tough decisions about how to distribute work and income when there are no longer enough jobs to go around; and, overall, for 'hard-headed yet visionary and holistic thinking about coherent alternatives to the present mish-mash of *ad hoc* responses to Australia's economic transformation'.

There is an enormous gulf between the sort of thinking which Sandercock and Melser call for and the 'Deep North' attitudes which Minnery describes in his chapter entitled 'Queensland: Planning on the Fringe'. Minnery points out that generalizations about Australia need to be qualified at some point by an understanding of the differences in issues and policies between states. Queensland, with a small and weak manufacturing sector, has in recent years gone wholeheartedly in pursuit of an economic growth strategy based on the exploitation of its mineral resources, primarily with the assistance of foreign-owned mining corporations. Through case studies of sand-mining and the destruction of tropical rainforest, Minnery illustrates the weakness of the conservation movement in a state where the style of government is one of 'political authoritarianism, socially-repressive fundamentalism and hillbilly panache' (Mullins, 1980).

Minnery also discusses some of the difficulties of pursuing policies at Federal level in a system where 'States' Rights' remain important constitutionally and electorally.

The final chapter by David Wilmoth contains an account of the current state of the art in planning for metropolitan Sydney. Several of the themes of previous chapters are picked up and interwoven in this account and it provides an applied case study, exemplifying and relating the planning and policy issues discussed in this book. As the largest city in Australia, and the home of over 20 per cent of the population, Sydney's development is the nation's biggest urban planning challenge.

Wilmoth is head of the Central Policy Division of the New South Wales Department of Environment and Planning. His account is very much one of work in progress on a heroic canvas. As he points out, this work is producing a third regional plan for Sydney. The first, in 1948, was much influenced by British practice of the time, laying down a land-use planning framework to order and structure the growing urban area within a green belt to contain sprawl. It under-estimated the rate of population growth. The 1968 Sydney Region Outline Plan sought to manage growth by co-ordinating investment in urban facilities and infrastructure, particularly at the fringe of the extending metropolitan area. It over-estimated the rate of population growth. The present work is meant to build a *strategy* defined as a structure plan associated with a series of supporting policies. The plan is both implemented by those policies and a product of them. The process seeks to capitalize on the fact that the state government of New South Wales provides and operates the main elements and controls of urban development.

Sydney is under the influence of rapidly changing economic, demo-graphic and social circumstances, and as Wilmoth says, a new approach is needed as well as a new plan. That new approach is to associate physical development more closely with structural change and economic develop-ment, access to shelter, effective communication, environmental manage-ment and social change. It is also apparent that close monitoring of trends in these fields is necessary to allow for adjustments and amendments to the broad strategy informing metropolitan growth and change. It is all diffuse, complex and relevant. The attention to implementation and uncer-tainty is refreshing. The various suites and dimensions of actions can-vassed are remarkable. Here is the ultimate challenge. Can large cities like Sydney be guided to reflect and accommodate considerable growth and substantial change? Does history fix them too powerfully? Are institutional processes and practices adequate? Is there sufficient understanding? Power? Resources?

Wilmoth identifies the economic future of Sydney as the most important variable with which a metropolitan strategy must deal. The Australian economy is becoming much more open, particularly in its relationship to the Asia-Pacific region. Sydney will play a key role in this evolution and integration. An important feature of future economic growth is how far manufacturing employment will continue to decline. But economic growth cannot be left to exogenous factors. Economic development policies have to be developed together with those concerning employment distribution, location, and degree of concentration in centres.

Sydney's population growth has slowed, but is still formidable with another million people expected over the next quarter of a century. Wilmoth argues that Sydney's future should be part of an even-handed state development strategy with adequate attention to the environmental impacts of this growth. With this last issue, as with others, land-use planning will need to be matched with appropriate use of technology, sufficient deployment of resources and suitable social controls. Often the mix of these can be varied, but the role of physical planning is crucial.

Fitting in all these people will be possible, as Wilmoth demonstrates with some deft arithmetic. But the management of urban expansion in new areas in terms of location, amount, timing and extent of housing choice is a vital planning instrument – as is the degree of urban consolidation it may be possible to achieve in the existing developed area.

Wilmoth concedes that this work has concentrated on population characteristics, economic development, employment distribution and environmental issues. Alternative transport arrangements, energy and resource use and other variables are also important. But one remains impressed by the need to select leading variables in the construction of a metropolitan strategy, in the attempt to manipulate and orchestrate them. Complex and diverse the task is, but as Wilmoth's chapter concludes, so are the needs and hopes of the people of Sydney, and indeed of urban Australia as a whole.

REFERENCES

Horne, D. (1965) *The Lucky Country*, 2nd ed. Sydney: Angus and Robertson.

Mullins, P. (1980) Australian urbanisation and Queensland's underdevelopment: a first empirical statement. *International Journal of Urban and Regional Research*, **4**, pp. 212–38.

# Chapter 1

# The Changing Character
# of Australian Urban Growth

CHRIS MAHER

The space economy of a nation, as reflected in its settlement system, is the outcome of a complex set of processes. The nature of population distribution and urban functional character results from a continual interplay of social and economic forces, the particular character of the local environment, and the current urban pattern as it has developed in the past. The length of time over which development has taken place, the influence of various technologies, and the degree of openness or closure in the national economy are all factors which have an impact on such development. Australia provides a good example of the manner in which the conditions and timing of development can have a profound impact on the nature of the physical outcome. An examination of changes in the spatial expression of development, and particularly that of the urban system, can also highlight the manner in which physical pattern is responsive to broader social, economic and political forces. The purpose of this chapter is to discuss the historical basis of white settlement in Australia, to outline the current situation with respect to urban population distribution in particular, and to examine the effect of recent macro-economic changes on the way in which the urban system is evolving.

In many ways, the settlement pattern of Australia is typical of the development which occurred in new world countries. The imposition of colonial administration, the development of resources for export back to the old world, and the gradual extension of settlement into lands previously occupied by indigenous peoples which occurred in Australia soon after the advent of white colonization are similar to the experience of countries such as Canada, the United States, New Zealand, Argentina and South Africa. Common features include the absence of previous permanent settlement, the dependent status of the fledgling colonies, and the strong orientation of economic activity from points of contact in the new nation toward the colonial power. Further features which distinguished Australia were the particular resource base, the timing at which the settlement took place and thus the available technology to affect development, and the conditions of the local environment.

Although Australia was first seen only as a depository for the undesir-ables of British society, the resource potential soon became apparent. Wool and wheat and gold all provided initial stimuli for the development of the countryside and thus for the investment in infrastructure to enable the exploitation of those resources. Much of this investment went into the establishment of urban facilities through which the goods could be channelled.

The timing of development proved crucial to the spatial expression of settlement. Although white settlement in Australia dates back to 1788 and the first landing in Sydney Cove, the great majority of development, at least in terms of the establishment of permanent structures, did not take place until the middle of the nineteenth century. At this stage a new economic order based on the emergence of capitalism was being estab-lished, at the same time that the effects of the industrial revolution were being widely felt. The effects of both these processes were crucial in establishing the pattern of settlement in the new territory.

## The Development of the Urban System

The local environment, characterized by vast distances, and harsh condi-tions in all but a relatively small coastal zone, superimposed upon the more general conditions of economic potential and emerging administrative structures based on the initial colonial configuration, created a settlement system which focused on a very few sites. Each of these emerging settle-ments quickly dominated the commercial, administrative, and distributive sectors for the surrounding territory and each tended to develop somewhat independently from the rest. By confederation in 1901, Australia was a nation of urban dwellers. At that stage 52 per cent of the population resided in centres populated by 2500 or more (Logan et al., 1981, p. 19). This degree of urbanization was higher than any comparable country, and has since increased.

The reasons for such concentration are largely historical. As a great deal has already been written on this topic (McCarty, 1974; Jackson, 1977; Logan et al., 1981) there will only be a brief discussion here. In many ways the urban pattern that has evolved in Australia is the classic illustration of the spatial imprint of post-1800 capitalism, mediated by a federal political system, and implanted in a harsh and constraining physical environment which limited settlement to a few widely separated regions. Driven largely by the demands of an external power, the economy of the country, and thus the spatial expression of development, began and has continued to grow in a rather unique manner. This uniqueness is reflected both in the degree to which the settlement system of Australia has been responsive to external influences throughout the period of its development, and in the physical expression of development which has been brought about.

The timing of white settlement in this country has been very important in determining the manner in which urbanization has occurred. Colonization was very much a function of the outward expansion of the European world economy, and the emergence of an integrated world industrial system. The absence of any permanent pre-industrial settlement meant that the pattern which emerged was unconstrained by any prior decisions, and thus was a direct response to the demands of the developing international economy.

The extent of external influences worked in other ways as well. The production of a limited range of staples, as well as the potential for further development, was able to generate considerable capital inflows to the country. This was directed largely to the port cities, the points of contact between the European world and the extensive farming and grazing areas of rural Australia. With some differences, this pattern of external investment in resources and primary production has continued to be very important in the development of the character of the Australian settlement system.

The fact that the external points of contact, the port cities, also became the administrative centres for each of the six separate colonies which made up the country until federation in 1901, and thereafter, the six states, has also contributed to the nature of urbanization. The degree of independence exhibited by each colony, together with the vast distances between them, meant that each state developed a substantially separate settlement system centred on and dominated by the port city. This separate development was enhanced by such measures as the establishment of customs posts between the colonies, and by the introduction of different rail gauges. Only much more recently has the extent of national integration expanded to the point at which it is realistic to speak of an Australian urban system, rather than a set of regional systems.

The impact of the commercial and administrative dominance exhibited by each of the capitals, together with the somewhat limited range of alternative sites for competing major settlements, resulted in a marked primacy being exhibited by each capital city within its own state. This is evidenced in the proportion of each state's population in the major metropolitan area outlined in table 1. The occurrence of such dominance prompted Rose (1966) to argue that although at a national level there was very little evidence of primacy in the distribution of settlement sizes, the situation for each state was the more appropriate pattern to observe and

Table 1.    Capital city as proportion of state population, 1851–1981.

| | New South Wales | Victoria | Queensland | South Australia | Western Australia | Tasmania |
|---|---|---|---|---|---|---|
| 1851[1] | 28 | 38 | — | 28 | — | — |
| 1861[1] | 27 | 23 | 20 | 28 | 33 | 28 |
| 1871[1] | 27 | 26 | 13 | 27 | — | 25 |
| 1881[1] | 30 | 31 | 14 | 33 | 30 | 23 |
| 1891[1] | 35 | 41 | 24 | 37 | 32 | 22 |
| 1901[1] | 37 | 40 | 24 | 39 | 33 | 20 |
| 1911[2] | 47 | 45 | 23 | 41 | 38 | 21 |
| 1921[2] | 49 | 51 | 28 | 50 | 47 | 25 |
| 1933[2] | 51 | 54 | 32 | 54 | 39 | 27 |
| 1947[2] | 55 | 60 | 37 | 59 | 54 | 30 |
| 1954[2] | 54 | 62 | 39 | 61 | 54 | 31 |
| 1961[3] | 55 | 65 | 41 | 61 | 57 | 33 |
| 1971[3] | 59 | 71 | 44 | 69 | 62 | 33 |
| 1976[3] | 58 | 68 | 44 | 69 | 64 | 33 |
| 1981[3] | 56 | 67 | 41 | 69 | 64 | 31 |

*Source:* 1. Logan *et al*, 1981.
    2. Bunker, 1965.
    3. Australian Bureau of Statistics. *Persons and Dwellings in Local Government Areas and Urban Centres.*

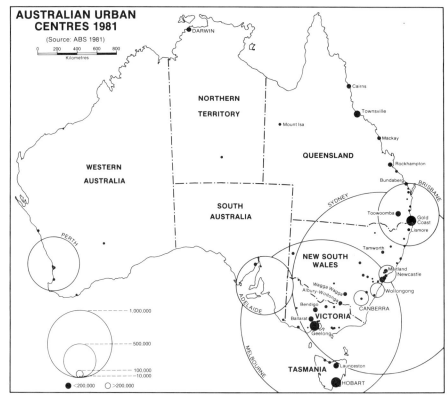

Figure 1.

that these did exhibit an extreme primacy which, Rose argued, was in fact the 'normal' state.

As well as the prominent degree of metropolitanization, there also developed a distinctive locational pattern. The combination of the commercial and administrative roles and port functions with the limited range of available sites through environmental constraints, has resulted in a predominantly coastal location for all cities. More specifically, the locations overwhelmingly favour the south-east of the country. The locational pattern of settlement, as well as the predominant stature of the large cities, is illustrated in figure 1.

The turn of the century saw the creation of a national identity for Australia, although the heritage of the separateness of development which had been a characteristic of development up to that point has, in many ways, remained. The new federal government gradually moved to establish its authority, and although interrupted by a world war, and a major depression, strove to broaden the economic base of the entire nation. With a growing domestic population creating larger markets, with some impediments to interstate trade being removed, and with the adoption of a nationwide protectionist policy, industrialization was begun in earnest. Again, because of the existing infrastructure, the population concentrations already in place, and the focus of transport facilities, the development of manufacturing added to the existing urban dominance. The majority of manufacturing was established in the states of New South Wales, Victoria and South Australia, and it was in these areas that the degree of metropolitan dominance grew to the greatest extent.

## The Urban System 1947 to the 1970s

*Industrialization*

The peak of metropolitan dominance in Australia coincided with the long economic boom which followed the Second World War. Much of the growth was associated with the industrialization which occurred in this period (Logan *et al.*, 1981). In the 1930s, 16 per cent of Australia's GDP and 21 per cent of the workforce were accounted for in the manufacturing sector; by 1950 these figures had increased to 28 per cent of GDP and 25 per cent of the labour force. The peak of employment in manufacturing as a percentage of the total workforce was recorded in the 1954 census, at 27.8 per cent. Manufacturing growth saw this figure sustained through to 1966 when it was still 27 per cent. Subsequent structural change has altered the workforce composition markedly however, such that by 1981 the figure had dropped to 17.7 per cent.

The growth in the manufacturing sector was largely engendered by domestic tariff policy, by import control, and by growing local demand arising from a rapidly expanding population (Linge, 1979). Even in this period when the local economy was developing and consolidating, it was still very much influenced by external events. Overseas investment in manufacturing, and particularly the establishment of some of the very large international firms such as General Motors, Ford, Shell, ICI and BP continued the tradition of external sources of expertise and finance which had been apparent since the beginning of economic development. In the 1950s much of the investment which was brought in by these and other firms was oriented toward import-substituting manufacturing activity (Adrian and Stimson, 1984) and concentrated very much on Sydney and Melbourne. Only later, with economic downturn and structural change apparent, has there been a change from this pattern of concentration of investment and economic activity.

The development of manufacturing in the post-war period was very influential in the manner in which population distribution occurred. Each state sought to achieve a widely-based industrial structure, although the costs of such an exercise were often never revealed or even considered. The real establishment costs and the running costs were frequently disguised by the manner in which the enterprises were encouraged by loans and grants, by the provision of infrastructure, and by the promise of government contracts (Linge, 1979). Some attempt was made in most cases to diminish the effect of overconcentration in the metropolitan areas through incentives to locate elsewhere. Although there was some demonstrable degree of success in that between 1947 and 1966 there was a slight tendency for manufacturing employment to grow faster in non-metropolitan areas (apart from Melbourne), the effect was generally one of a fairly fragile and highly protected industrial structure. Even before the events of the 1970s there were powerful forces in train which would have led to drastic change in the structure of manufacturing industry in Australia. The greatest spatial changes at this stage have occurred within the major metropolitan areas where the older inner-city industrial areas have undergone considerable depletion in activity. The rather dismal prospects for the domestic manufacturing sector, with growing competition and internationalization of activities, are likely to affect those areas which have hitherto been most shielded. Many of these areas are those which have taken the incentives to locate outside the major cities. Thus future changes in manufacturing, although likely to affect all activity, may well have a more serious impact in terms of population distribution on the areas already experiencing difficulty in attracting or holding population.

*Immigration*

Associated with the post-war recovery and industrialization of the Australian economy, a further external input was of great importance in the growth and character of the Australian population: that of immigration. The character of Australia's population from the beginning was significantly shaped by the extent and nature of immigration. In a country whose history of white settlement is not yet 200 years old, there has been a strong dependence on the intake of population from external sources as a means of population growth. Although immigration was important from the time of first white settlement, the period following the Second World War saw the greatest influx of migrants. By 1981 20.6 per cent of Australia's resident population had been born overseas; between 1947 and 1971 42 per cent of population growth was directly attributable to external sources (Burnley, 1976, p. 24); and one-third of the net gain in the period 1976–81 was likewise attributable (Australian Council on Population and Ethnic Affairs, 1983). Even these figures greatly underestimate the impact which such movements have had. The migrants, many of whom have been of child bearing age, have contributed further to population growth through adding to the natural increase. Burnley (1976) estimates that if the children of migrants were added to the immigration intake, then 60 per cent of the population rise between 1947 and 1971 could be seen as a function of immigration.

More significantly in terms of the character of urban Australia, the immigrants have shown a marked tendency to agglomerate in urban rather than rural areas. While 58 per cent of the total population of Australia in 1981 resided in the urbanized fractions of the six state capitals and Canberra, these same cities contain 75 per cent of the overseas born. The highest proportion of a capital's population having been born overseas is the 31.2 per cent in Perth. Sydney, Adelaide, and Melbourne (the last mentioned having the highest representation of non-English speaking migrants) all have in excess of 27 per cent.

In recent years, immigration has been particularly important as a component of population growth in the metropolitan areas, particularly in Sydney and Melbourne. With a falling rate of population growth stemming from the fact that the net reproduction rate of population (an index which takes into account fertility and mortality) fell below replacement level in the late 1970s, and with a net loss of Australian-born from the major capitals to other parts of the country through internal migration (Burnley, 1980), the growth of Sydney and Melbourne in the last decade or so has been almost entirely a function of their immigration intake. The role of immigration in the maintenance of urban dominance was something never conceived of, nor acknowledged, in the setting of immigration policy.

*Concentration and Its Problems*

By the early 1970s, Australia's settlement system was thus characterized more than anything else by concentration both of population and of economic activity. It was in the thirty years leading to this period that industrial output expanded most; that immigration, encouraged largely to fulfil the demand for labour, was concentrated on the major cities; and that public investment in infrastructural, cultural and educational facilities was expanded. Each of these elements fuelled the process of circular and cumulative growth focusing on the major areas (Stilwell, 1980). Capital favoured the cities because of the ease of access to labour and markets as well as to capitalize on the obvious cost savings associated with communication; governments, despite rhetoric to the contrary, encouraged concentration through their own locational behaviour and investment decisions; there were few other options for labour; and even on non-economic criteria the cities were more attractive, with a more varied social and cultural environment.

The concentration took two forms: firstly, there was the overwhelming dominance of urban over rural settlements; and secondly, urban population was located in a few metropolitan centres rather than being more dispersed among smaller cities or towns. The nature of the current urban settlement system is depicted in tables 2 and 3. Table 2 shows the manner in which the country's population is accommodated in a three-level settlement hierarchy; major urban (a population in excess of 100,000), 'other' urban (between 1,000 and 99,999), and rural. It shows that from 1961 to 1976 the previous pattern of metropolitan dominance continued, with the rural component in particular falling off. Since 1976 however (and earlier in some states), both 'other' urban and rural populations have shown some recovery at the expense of the major urban areas. The current disposition of urban centres by size class is shown in table 3. Despite a slight slackening in the degree of concentration, the size distribution of towns is still dominated by the very large, with few centres in the intermediate size ranges. Thus, despite the image of the continent as one with vast open spaces and having strong rural roots, there is, and always has been since colonization, a predominance of urban dwellers. In fact, Australia has consistently had a higher proportion of its population in towns and cities than has any other western industrialized nation.

By the 1970s, Australia's cities had taken on many of the characteristics of large metropolitan areas rather than those of the country town from which they had begun. Increasingly by this time there was also a recognition that there were costs involved in such concentration – not only the costs associated with the large urban areas, but also those associated with the difficulties of adequate service provision for non-metropolitan areas.

The period 1969–72 was in many ways a turning point. Leading up to the federal election of 1972, urban problems and settlement policy came to the fore for the first time as a federal issue. Although urban affairs is constitutionally a state responsibility, it was perceived by the Australian Labor Party under the leadership of E. G. Whitlam that the pattern of urban

Table 2. Distribution of state and territory population in urban hierarchy, 1961–81.

| | Year | New South Wales | Victoria | Queensland | South Australia | Western Australia | Tasmania | Northern Territory | Australian Capital Territory | Australia |
|---|---|---|---|---|---|---|---|---|---|---|
| Major urban | 1961 | 65.4 | 65.3 | 40.9 | 60.7 | 57.0 | 33.1 | — | — | 58.8 |
| | 1966 | 67.1 | 68.7[a] | 43.2 | 66.7 | 59.8 | 32.2 | — | — | 61.4 |
| | 1971 | 69.1[b] | 71.7 | 44.8 | 69.0 | 62.3 | 33.3 | — | 97.8 | 64.5 |
| | 1976 | 67.9[c] | 71.1 | 48.4[c] | 68.9 | 63.9 | 32.6 | — | 98.4 | 64.6 |
| | 1981 | 65.9 | 70.6 | 47.0 | 68.7 | 63.5 | 30.7 | — | 99.0 | 63.5 |
| Other urban | 1961 | 19.7 | 19.5 | 35.0 | 18.1 | 16.2 | 37.3 | 39.5 | 95.9 | 22.9 |
| | 1966 | 19.3 | 16.8[a] | 33.2 | 15.7 | 15.9 | 38.1 | 53.4 | 96.1 | 21.5 |
| | 1971 | 19.5[b] | 16.1 | 34.6 | 15.6 | 19.2 | 40.9 | 64.1 | — | 21.1 |
| | 1976 | 20.8[c] | 16.7 | 31.8[c] | 16.0 | 19.6 | 42.3 | 66.4 | — | 21.4 |
| | 1981 | 22.2 | 17.4 | 32.2 | 16.1 | 20.8 | 44.5 | 74.2 | — | 22.2 |
| Rural | 1961 | 14.9 | 15.2 | 24.1 | 21.2 | 26.8 | 29.6 | 60.5 | 4.1 | 18.3 |
| | 1966 | 13.6 | 14.5 | 23.4 | 17.6 | 24.3 | 29.7 | 46.6 | 3.9 | 17.1 |
| | 1971 | 11.4 | 12.3 | 20.6 | 15.4 | 18.5 | 25.8 | 35.9 | 2.2 | 14.4 |
| | 1976 | 11.3 | 12.2 | 19.8 | 15.1 | 16.5 | 25.7 | 33.6 | 1.6 | 14.0 |
| | 1981 | 11.9 | 12.0 | 20.8 | 15.2 | 15.7 | 24.8 | 25.8 | 1.3 | 14.3 |

(a) Affected by Geelong classified as major urban for first time.
(b) Affected by Queanbeyan classified as part of urban Canberra for first time.
(c) Affected by Gold Coast (part) classified as major urban for first time.
Source: Australian Council on Population and Ethnic Affairs, 1983, p. 14.

Table 3. Urban centres by size class 1981, state/territory.

| Size | New South Wales | | Victoria | | Queensland | | South Australia | | Western Australia | | Tasmania | | Australian Capital Territory | | Northern Territory | | Total | |
|---|---|---|---|---|---|---|---|---|---|---|---|---|---|---|---|---|---|---|
| | No. | Cum % | No. | Cum % | No. | Cum % | No. | Cum % | No. | Cum % | No. | Cum % | No. | Cum % | No. | Cum % | No. | Cum % |
| 1 million + | 1 | 56.1 | 1 | 67.3 | — | — | — | — | — | — | — | — | — | — | — | — | 2 | 37.4 |
| 500,000–999,999 | — | 56.1 | — | 67.3 | 1 | 41.1 | 1 | 68.7 | 1 | 63.5 | — | — | — | — | — | — | 3 | 55.5 |
| 100,000–499,999 | 4 | 66.0 | 1 | 70.6 | 1 | 47.0 | — | 68.7 | — | 63.5 | 1 | 30.7 | 1 | 98.9 | — | — | 8 | 63.1 |
| 50,000–99,999 | 2 | 68.1 | 3 | 74.0 | 3 | 55.7 | — | 68.7 | — | 63.5 | 1 | 46.1 | — | 98.9 | 1 | 45.8 | 10 | 67.0 |
| 10,000–49,999 | 24 | 78.1 | 12 | 79.2 | 10 | 66.2 | 5 | 75.7 | 8 | 74.4 | 2 | 56.1 | — | 98.9 | 1 | 60.7 | 62 | 75.5 |
| 1,000–9,999 | 158 | 88.0 | 109 | 87.7 | 96 | 79.0 | 43 | 84.7 | 41 | 84.3 | 23 | 74.3 | — | 98.9 | 8 | 74.2 | 478 | 85.6 |

Source: Australian Bureau of Statistics, Persons and Dwellings in Local Government Areas and Urban Centres. Catalogues 2402.0–2408.0.

development was having a marked redistributive effect on certain elements of the population. Given that the two major cities of Sydney and Melbourne were forecast to reach a population of 5 million by the turn of the century, the Labor party argued that national action was necessary. Whitlam was an articulate advocate of a less concentrated and fairer settlement pattern, and on his election in 1972 created a new Department of Urban and Regional Affairs (DURD). This body undertook a number of programmes requiring substantial capital investment, as well as attempting to provide a means of co-ordinating much of the decision-making relating to urban administration and development.

The efforts of DURD were concentrated in two particular areas. The first related to the planning and provision of resources and facilities in those parts of the largest urban areas which had traditionally been very poorly served. The second was the development of a set of policies encouraging or implementing the decentralization of activity away from the state capitals. The initiatives involved the federal government in areas previously the realm of state and local government, and as a result there was widespread resistance to the measures. Despite the lack of co-operation, there were some achievements. Most notable of these was the success of the venture to expand the Albury-Wodonga region as a decentralization exercise. Located on the New South Wales-Victorian border, the development was funded in association with both state governments and has been successful in attracting both population and economic enterprise.

While the programmes were innovative and undoubtedly necessary, the timing proved unfortunate. Soon after the accession of the Whitlam government, the environment within which the proposals had evolved changed markedly. The rationale underlying the experiment to change both the nature of the settlement system and the social conditions within the urban areas, was that the fruits of the economic growth which had been experienced in the previous twenty years should be shared more equitably while the problems of overconcentration should be directly confronted. This involved the creation of genuine alternatives in terms of cities in different locations and of different sizes, and of the correction of the inequalities which were seen to pervade the existing settlements. Yet the mid-1970s saw the onset of a recession which cut economic growth and made questions of equity a much less potent force.

The timing of the policy initiatives was unfortunate in another way as well. Whereas population growth had been sustained by high rates of both natural increase and immigration up to the 1970s, in 1975 the Report of the National Population Inquiry identified for the first time a drastic downward trend occurring in growth rates. Thus, much of the ground upon which decentralization in particular was based suddenly disappeared. Meanwhile, the government was faced with a number of other pressing problems relating to the nature and direction of economic development and control which took attention away from the urban initiatives. In 1975, following a constitutional crisis precipitated by the conservative Federal Upper House, the government was dismissed and the initiatives foundered. By the late 1970s, a whole new set of conditions had emerged. The energy crisis, unemployment, inflation, high interest rates, and demographic changes were starting to have an effect on the nature of the urban system and on the ability of the government to influence it. The most recent phase in Australia's urban development then, while still very recent, is quite distinguishable.

## Towards the 1980s: The Decline of Dominance

The conditions under which the Australian urban system has evolved, and particularly those conditions which created the greatest degree of metropolitan concentration in the nation's history by the 1970s, have undergone considerable change more recently. The metropolitan concentration of population was based largely on a pattern of development which had emphasized industrial growth through the protection of the manufacturing sector, while maintaining the traditional commercial, distributive, and administrative control functions governing rural enterprise. Through sustained economic growth, full employment, high population growth rates and a steady investment in physical and social facilities, metropolitan dominance continued to expand until the 1970s.

In the past ten years however, both economic and demographic conditions have changed markedly. The long economic boom of the 1950s and 1960s has been replaced by the deepest recession the country has experienced since the 1930s. Associated economic conditions of high inflation and the realignment of international currencies have engendered a process of structural change which is having an impact on the nature and distribution of Australia's population and the nature of economic endeavour (Linge and McKay, 1981). At the same time there have been important changes in the demography of Australia. Birthrates have fallen, the population is ageing, and both the rate and composition of immigration streams have varied substantially from previous periods. These changed conditions have affected the basis upon which metropolitan concentration was built. Shifts in the investment pattern of both public and private capital, and changes in the distribution of the population through internal migration are bringing about changes in the nature of the space economy and this is reflected in recent patterns of urban growth.

Changes in the growth rates of the major metropolitan areas in the post war period can be seen in table 4. In that period there has been a consistent decline in the annual rate of growth at a national level. However, it is at the level of individual urban areas that the uneven spatial impacts of such processes are most apparent. As the table shows, until 1971 the growth rate of all the urban areas with the exception of Hobart was at or above the national average. However, the rate of growth in these areas halved in the

Table 4.   Population growth rates – capital city statistical divisions (annual average percentage change).

|           | 1966–71 | 1971–76 | 1976–81 | 1981 Population |
|-----------|---------|---------|---------|-----------------|
| Sydney    | 2.1     | 0.6     | 1.1     | 3,204,211       |
| Melbourne | 2.3     | 0.8     | 0.9     | 2,722,541       |
| Brisbane  | 3.7     | 2.0     | 1.4     | 1,028,289       |
| Adelaide  | 3.0     | 1.3     | 0.7     | 931,341         |
| Perth     | 5.9     | 2.8     | 2.2     | 898,918         |
| Hobart    | 1.6     | 1.1     | 0.8     | 168,359         |
| Canberra  | 8.9     | 6.6     | 2.4     | 221,210         |
| Australia | 2.2     | 1.4     | 1.2     | 14,576,330      |

Source: Australian Bureau of Statistics, Census of Population and Dwelling Units.

1971–76 period and in most cases fell below that of the national average. Thus for the first time in the short history of the country, there are indications that the degree of metropolitan dominance may have begun to ease.

The individual cities have been affected in quite diverse ways. Canberra, although showing a substantial fall in its growth rate since the 1966–71 period, is still expanding faster than any other city. The continued growth of Canberra reflects its special position within the Australian urban system. As the national capital much of the growth to the present day relates to the continued relocation of administrative units, or to the expansion of government functions. In many ways this city is sheltered from the forces of economic change which are affecting the other areas.

Other areas to show relatively consistent growth are Perth and Brisbane. Even though these too have been affected by the general population downturn described above, they have been able to attract population at a rate greater than the other areas. Throughout the 1970s in particular these two cities have been in receipt of substantial numbers of people migrating from elsewhere in Australia, and particularly from New South Wales and Victoria (Jarvie, 1984).

The two dominant cities of Sydney and Melbourne on the other hand have had a relatively weak growth performance despite their position as the preferred destination for a large proportion of overseas migrants. In fact, if it were not for the addition of immigrants to the population, there would have been an absolute population loss as both cities are experiencing significant outward migration to elsewhere in Australia.

Of the other centres, the position of Adelaide has eroded in the latest period and in fact is showing the lowest rate of growth of any city. Internal migration is again largely responsible for this pattern, with Adelaide losing population to all other centres. Even Hobart, which has traditionally been the poorest performer of the state capitals, is not losing population to such a spread of locations as is Adelaide.

The population trends enumerated above are in fact evidence that there is something of a turnaround occurring in the nature of population distribution both between urban areas, and amongst urban and rural regions. Much of the redistribution is from the capital city statistical division to the 'rest of state' – a term used to describe the non-metropolitan settlement component made up of smaller urban areas, as well as rural regions. While the magnitude of the net migration losses from the cities is not great, it does represent a dramatic reversal of earlier trends. The magnitude and rate of the most recent internal migration figures (1980–81) are contained in table 5.

While there is a danger in reading more into the results of a one-year span in migration figures than may actually be there, the figures do show consistency with previous figures for the 1975–76 period (Maher, 1986).

Table 5. Internal migration by capital city and rest of state, 1980–81.

|  | Net change | In-rate | Out-rate |
|---|---|---|---|
| Sydney | −28203 | 2.07 | 2.96 |
| Rest of New South Wales | 13059 | 4.34 | 3.65 |
| Melbourne | −13990 | 2.00 | 2.51 |
| Rest of Victoria | −1390 | 3.89 | 4.02 |
| Brisbane | 10851 | 4.50 | 4.41 |
| Rest of Queensland | 24383 | 6.29 | 4.26 |
| Adelaide | −2437 | 2.84 | 3.10 |
| Rest of South Australia | −2762 | 4.67 | 5.49 |
| Perth | 3866 | 3.90 | 3.47 |
| Rest of Western Australia | −1639 | 6.68 | 7.14 |
| Hobart | −1969 | 4.13 | 5.32 |
| Rest of Tasmania | 993 | 3.79 | 3.40 |
| Darwin | 2202 | 15.27 | 11.37 |
| Rest of Northern Territory | −1868 | 11.08 | 14.55 |
| Australian Capital Territory | −1096 | 6.82 | 7.32 |

Source: Australian Bureau of Statistics, Internal Migration. Unpublished Matrix Tape 184.

The largest gainers in absolute terms are the non-metropolitan areas of New South Wales and Queensland. This growth is occurring largely in the coastal areas of northern New South Wales and southern Queensland, associated with resort and tourist developments which are springing up in these areas. Another component of New South Wales growth is the over-spill from the Sydney metropolitan area. Brisbane itself is also gaining considerably from the trends in population redistribution, as are Perth and Darwin.

In terms of rates of change which are standardized by the size of the population, both Darwin and the Northern Territory are exhibiting very high rates of turnover, a situation not uncommon in a frontier type region. The high rates exhibited by Western Australia are likewise related to the nature of opportunities arising in a region undergoing rapid development.

Sydney, Melbourne and Adelaide on the other hand all have very low rates of turnover. Their population loss is likely to be more a function of a diminished ability to attract population, particularly given their lower rate of employment opportunities in a period of structural adjustment.

Whether the population changes, which occur both through differential population growth figures and through the redistribution of population by internal migration, represent a significant change in the spatial outcome amongst urban regions, or whether it is a relatively temporary pause in metropolitan growth, is too early to ascertain at this stage. However, it does seem clear that there are substantial changes to the context in which metropolitan growth is occurring in Australia.

## The Resource Boom and Structural Economic Change

The recent changes to the Australian space economy represent a set of responses to processes of economic restructuring which have originated in shifts in the nature of economic organization at a global level. Australia, through its abundant natural resources, has always relied on external contacts to sustain a high standard of living. Until the late 1960s these resources were predominantly agricultural, although after that the country's mineral wealth was recognized. In the period 1977–78 primary products made up nearly 90 per cent of foreign exchange earnings (Fagan et al., 1981, p. 26). The significance of the primary export sector of course makes the country very vulnerable to fluctuations in external economic conditions, a situation which in some form has always determined local development.

Following the discovery of considerable mineral wealth in the last fifteen years, particularly of oil and gas, bauxite, coal, iron ore and uranium, the economic future of the country at the end of the 1970s looked assured. There was considerable debate at that time over issues of ownership and control of the resources, but not over the expected benefits which it was assumed would accrue to the country as these resources were developed. The 1970s saw something of a scramble for investment, particularly as state governments competed to attract largely international companies to provide both the capital and technical expertise through which development could proceed. For many politicians at least, the prospect of being able to compensate for the difficulties being experienced in the manufacturing sector, by stimulating jobs in the resources sector, was very attractive. For the two resource-rich states, Queensland and Western Australia, there was another prospect at least as exciting – the chance to pull some of the growth and investment away from the dominant cities of Sydney and Melbourne.

While there have been shifts in both the focus of economic activity in some sectors, and in the movement of labour to the growth areas, it has not occurred in the manner or at the rate that some expected it might. Investment capital, both foreign and domestic, did move away from its traditional locations as the need for the expenditure of vast sums to develop the minerals took precedence over other forms of investment. However, the uncertainty of the world economy, and particularly a decline in demand from Japan, has caused the expectations to be revised. At the same time there has been considerable questioning of the extent to which there are likely to be benefits of the nature envisaged, either at the regional level (Harman, 1982) or even at the national level (Stilwell, 1980). The location of the control functions for many of the developments is still remote from the resources themselves, the developments are highly capital intensive and thus are not likely to generate large numbers of jobs on a long-term basis, and because many of the developments are controlled by multi-national enterprises the benefits may not stay in Australia anyway. Despite the doubts about the long-term effects of changes in the economy it is apparent that, at least in demographic terms, there has been something of a population turnaround through which the previously peripheral areas of Brisbane and Perth have been able to capture a growing proportion of the slowing population growth of the country. Whether this will translate into a broader economic base for these areas, through the addition of both manufacturing and service functions for both producers and consumers, is a question which will require detailed scrutiny.

Changes within the urban system in recent years have not been confined to the spatially remote areas or to a distinction along metropolitan versus non-metropolitan lines, however. As a result of many of the macro-economic changes stemming from restructuring, from the role of inter-national capital, and from political decisions with respect to the regulation or deregulation of financial markets in Australia, there are also significant changes occurring at the top end of the urban hierarchy. The relative position of Sydney *vis à vis* Melbourne, the two dominant cities which between them have traditionally shared many of the control functions in the Australian economy, is also undergoing some potentially far reaching changes (Daly, 1984; O'Connor, 1984). While Melbourne has been the city which has hosted the head office of a number of Australia's largest firms, there has been a marked preference of many newer enterprises to locate in Sydney. This is particularly apparent in the areas of finance, property and business services, where changes in the Australian financial scene have resulted in a rapid expansion in Sydney both in employment and invest-ment. Recent trends suggest that the roles of the two cities are changing. As the dominant contact with the Pacific rim, having both the major international airport and the functions most finely attuned to external events in the financial field, Sydney seems to be exerting a dominance which may well define for it a role distinct from that of Melbourne. The latter city, while well placed to maintain some of the internal functions which rely on distribution and contact, cannot compete in the international sphere.

## Overview

It appears that there are some quite profound and far reaching changes occurring in the settlement system of Australia. The outcomes of the past 150 years of urban development, where there has been a steadily increas-ing proportion of population in the major urban areas, and where the two dominant centres of Sydney and Melbourne have vied with each other and with the rest of the system, seem to have altered in the past decade. These changes have been brought about largely through the fact that Australia continues to be very responsive to world economic events, and that recently economic conditions have undergone great changes, reflecting the worst recession in fifty years. Through a growing internationalization of the world economy, into which Australia has been drawn, the outcomes of urban development and change in this country are increasingly the product of external events. While this situation is nothing new, the nature and direction of the change being experienced is.

While the nature of the changes outlined above is very much a product of the conditions of recession, the structural economic responses to those conditions are likely to create a set of conditions which make a return to the previous trends, if and when the economy recovers, extremely unlikely. The combination of a reorientation of position and role within the urban system, as is happening with Sydney and Melbourne; the development of certain functions related to the servicing of a resource rich area which is happening in a limited way with Perth and Brisbane; the loss of population and economic functions which is occurring in Adelaide and Hobart; and the growing differential between metropolitan, other urban and rural growth rates, are all trends which are creating a spatial outcome somewhat different from that which has been the norm. Once having had a spatial impact of course, the very result itself becomes an element in further change by providing conditions of opportunity or constraint. To this extent, the macro-economic forces which have made themselves felt recently, are likely to have a long lasting effect on the character of the Australian settlement system.

REFERENCES

Adrian, C. and Stimson, R. (1984) *Capital City Impacts of Foreign and Local Investment in Australia*. Canberra: AIUS Publication No. 120.

Australian Council on Population and Ethnic Affairs (1983) *Population Report 7: Population Change 1976–81*. Canberra: A.G.P.S.

Bunker, R. (1965) Australia since the war: a study of economic growth and physical planning. *Town Planning Review*, **35**, pp. 311–28.

Burnley, I. H. (1976) *The Social Environment*. Sydney: McGraw Hill.

Burnley, I. H. (1980) *The Australian Urban System*. Melbourne: Longman-Cheshire.

Daly, M. (1984) The revolution in international capital markets: urban growth and Australian cities. *Environment and Planning A*, **16**, pp. 1003–20.

Fagan, R., McKay, J. and Linge G. J. R. (1981) Structural change: the international and national context, in Linge, G. J. R. and McKay, J. (eds.) *Structural Change in Australia*. Canberra: Research School of Pacific Studies, Australian National University.

Harman, E. (1982) The city, the state and resource development in Western Australia, in Williams, P. (ed.) *Social Process and the City*. Sydney: George Allen and Unwin.

Jackson, R. V. (1977) *Australian Economic Development in the Nineteenth Century*. Canberra: Australian National University Press.

Jarvie, W. (1984) The Turnaround in Australia: Changes in Interregional Migration 1966–71 to 1971–76. Unpublished Ph.D. thesis, Flinders University of South Australia.

Linge, G. J. R. (1979) Australian manufacturing in recession: a review of the spatial implications. *Environment and Planning A*, **11**, pp. 1405–30.

Linge, G. J. R. and McKay, J. (eds.) (1981) *Structural Change in Australia*. Canberra: Research School of Pacific Studies, Publication HG/15, Department of Human Geography, Australian National University.

Logan, M. I., Whitelaw, J. S. and McKay, J. (1981) *Urbanization: the Australian Experience*. Melbourne: Shillington House.

McCarty, J. (1974) Australian capital cities in the 19th Century, in Schedvin, C. B. and McCarty, J. (eds.) *Urbanization in Australia: The 19th Century*. Sydney: Sydney University Press.

Maher, C. A. (1986) Macro-economic forces and urbanisation in Australia, in Bourne, L. S., Cori, B. and Dziewonski, K. (eds.) *Progress in Settlement Systems Geography*. Milan: Franco Angeli.

O'Connor, K. B. (1984) Urban and regional change in Australia: an empirical introduction. *Environment and Planning A*, **16**, pp. 993–1002.

Rose, A. J. (1966) Dissent from down under: metropolitan primacy as the normal state. *Pacific Viewpoint*, **7**, pp. 1–27.

Stilwell, F. J. B. (1980) *Economic Crisis, Cities and Regions*. Sydney: Pergamon.

*Chapter 2*

# Urban Development and Economic Change: The Example of Sydney

DAVID C. RICH, RICHARD V. CARDEW and
JOHN V. LANGDALE

Historically, urban development has been substantially influenced by economic processes. Such processes and their urban impacts are complex and poorly understood. One reason is that the nature of these processes has changed markedly over recent decades, with developments in the financial system, the organization of businesses and technology particularly important. The complexity also derives from the fact that these processes have international as well as Australian-specific dimensions. Global economic forces are becoming increasingly important influences upon urban development. This reflects, in part, the internationalization of production in a number of industries, particularly those in the information services area, such as banking and finance, advertising and computer services, as well as in manufacturing. Still further complexity results from the fact that many of these processes have lagged and often indirect impacts on the pattern of urban development.

This chapter examines the impact of economic processes, especially financial, organizational and technological change, upon Sydney's development. Sydney is an interesting case study, given its key role within Australia and its important function linking the country with the international economic system. However, because of Sydney's unique position, some of the impacts of economic change upon it are different from those experienced in other metropolitan areas. The chapter begins by outlining Sydney's changing physical structure, then considers the nature of contemporary economic change, and finally explores the extent to which governments have responded to metropolitan change, both to stimulate it and to manage its impact.

## Sydney's Post-War Development

Like most major cities, Sydney has expanded massively since the Second World War. Population has almost doubled from 1.70 million in 1947 to 3.39 million in 1985. Employment has increased commensurately. The built-up area has grown threefold to over 1,200 square kilometres.

In the same period, Sydney's geographical structure has changed considerably. In the 1940s it was a single-centred city, with most activity focused on the central business district and surrounding areas, while in the 1980s the suburbs have acquired an increasingly important role. The CBD and surrounding areas have undergone considerable change in the interim. The mix of economic activities has changed, with rapid declines of employment in manufacturing, wholesaling and retailing and a growing specialization in office-based industries, notably finance and property, public administration, and community and business services (Neutze, 1977). Such trends have been accompanied by massive physical restructuring of the inner city, with the amount of office space increasing by more than 50 per cent between the late 1950s and mid-1980s. The CBD remains Sydney's most important single centre and has a more significant role than, for example, in many large US cities. The transport system is essentially radial and focuses on the city centre. The CBD is still by far the largest concentration of office activities and plays a dominant role in the emerging information economy.

Nevertheless, the suburbs are now vastly more important than they were forty years ago. No longer are they essentially residential dormitories. They contain a growing proportion of all economic activity, especially manufacturing and retailing, but also wholesaling and office activity. As one example, as late as 1954 the then City of Sydney accounted for 45 per cent of all manufacturing jobs in the metropolitan area, whereas by the early 1980s the (slightly smaller) City accounted for under 18 per cent. Along with the decentralization of economic activity has come the rise of major suburban nodes as centres of economic activity. However, an important characteristic of most activities is that they are quite widely dispersed across the suburbs, rather than being concentrated in a few nodes. Although suburban centres such as Parramatta and Chatswood have become very important and a few others such as Epping and perhaps Burwood are of rising significance, none is likely to challenge the CBD as Sydney's most important concentration in the foreseeable future.

The Sydney economy has undergone very substantial change since the 1940s, reflecting the restructuring of the national and international economies and Sydney's position within them. Some crude indication of recent development is given by data on changes in employment in Sydney's industries between 1971 and 1981 (table 1). By far the most expansionary sectors have been Community Services (such as health, education and

Table 1. Employment change in the Sydney metropolitan area,[1] 1971–1981.

| Industry | Employment 1971 | 1981 | Change Absolute | % | Percentage of total 1971 | 1981 |
|---|---|---|---|---|---|---|
| Agriculture, forestry and fishing | 11,922 | 10,871 | −1,051 | −8.8 | 0.9 | 0.7 |
| Mining | 5,587 | 6,264 | 677 | 12.1 | 0.4 | 0.4 |
| Manufacturing | 359,822 | 294,610 | −65,212 | −18.1 | 27.9 | 20.3 |
| Electricity, gas and water | 23,666 | 28,534 | 4,868 | 20.6 | 1.8 | 2.0 |
| Construction | 91,611 | 84,974 | −6,637 | −7.2 | 7.1 | 5.9 |
| Wholesale and Retail | 251,687 | 265,292 | 13,605 | 5.4 | 19.5 | 18.3 |
| Transport and Storage | 72,075 | 85,511 | 13,436 | 18.6 | 5.6 | 5.9 |
| Communication | 27,080 | 31,952 | 4,872 | 18.0 | 2.1 | 2.2 |
| Finance and business services | 121,460 | 169,690 | 48,230 | 39.7 | 9.4 | 11.7 |
| Public administration and defence | 70,011 | 76,120 | 6,109 | 8.7 | 5.4 | 5.2 |
| Community services | 131,883 | 207,521 | 75,638 | 57.4 | 10.2 | 14.3 |
| Recreation, personal and other services | 69,165 | 79,357 | 10,192 | 14.7 | 5.3 | 5.5 |
| Other[2] | 57,521 | 111,328 | 53,807 | 93.5 | 4.4 | 7.6 |
| Total | 1,293,490 | 1,452,024 | 158,534 | 12.3 | 100.0 | 100.0 |

Notes:
1. The metropolitan area is defined as the Sydney Statistical Division, as expanded in 1976.
2. Includes unclassifiable and not stated.
Source: 1971 and 1981 Census of Population and Housing.

welfare) and a range of Finance, Property and Business Services. Employment also increased noticeably in Transport and Storage, in Recreation, and in Wholesale and Retail Trade, though in the last case it was insufficient to keep up with general employment growth. Manufacturing suffered by far the greatest employment decline of any industry, reflecting the massive restructuring the industry has undergone nationally and Sydney's disproportionately rapid decline as a centre of manufacturing production. Such figures are very important because they represent some of the direct human consequences of economic change – shifts in the sorts of activities that employ most people. However, they mask many other important features such as the type of work done and the hours worked. Likewise, they reveal only in an indirect manner information about the processes of economic change which have moulded Sydney's development.

## Urban Development and Economic Change

Urban development is affected by economic conditions at local, national and international levels, and the interdependencies between these levels need to be recognized. Sydney plays an important part in and is in turn much influenced by the Australian economy. At the same time, Australia's position in the international economy and Sydney's gateway role in linking the two are becoming increasingly significant influences on the pattern of urban development.

Six related developments with important implications for Australia have characterized international economic change over the last two decades (Fagan et al., 1981). First is the progressive internationalization of industrial production, to add to the long established pattern of international trade, portfolio investment and other financial flows (Hymer, 1975; Perrons, 1981). Second is the growing economic domination of transnational corporations, mostly based in the United States, Western Europe and Japan (Barnet and Muller, 1974; Hood and Young, 1979). The third feature is the rapid industrialization of certain Third World countries and their increasing emphasis on high technology and/or capital intensive activities such as steel and electronics (Frobel *et al.*, 1980). Next is the impact of technological change on production, employment structure and information transfer (Freeman, 1974). Fifth, fluctuating energy prices have affected industrial economies dependent on imports of oil, especially Japan and Western Europe, leading to a rationalization of energy intensive production in those countries. The final development is the very rapid growth of international banking and the rise of large-scale international monetary transfers (Daly, 1984).

Australia's international economic position has long been somewhat ambiguous (Taylor and Thrift, 1981*b*). The country is prosperous and industrialized, but it relies heavily on primary production and is dependent on imports of capital and technology to sustain growth. These characteristics persist, but there have been changes in Australia's role in the world economy and a reorientation of its international contacts. Australia's trade with Japan, Asia and the Middle East has expanded while that with Western Europe and the United States has stagnated. Exports of agricultural commodities and associated processed goods have declined in significance, while minerals and part-processed materials have become more important (Fagan *et al.*, 1981, pp. 30–31).

Likewise, partial reorientation of manufacturing away from import-competing and durable goods production towards mineral processing, energy intensive production and related activities is a product of Australia's evolving role in a changing world economy (Rich, 1987). Three important components of Australian and international economic change are worthy of special consideration. These are, first, the role of domestic and international capital flows and the activities of the finance sector; second, the changing nature of business and government organizations together with their evolving economic roles and locational requirements; and third, the impact of technological change.

## Finance and Urban Development

The last two decades have seen a burgeoning of international money supply (stimulated by demands of expanding transnational corporations, deficit financing and regulatory practices of US governments, and surplus funds accruing to OPEC countries) and the emergence of new institutions, such as international banks and the Eurodollar market to handle it (Daly, 1984). Consequently, very large volumes of funds now circulate internationally in search of investment opportunities in resource development, commerce, property, government and speculative outlets of one sort or another. Australia has been dependent on inflows of capital for investment throughout European settlement, and periodically for balance of payments purposes (Butlin, 1964; Cochrane, 1980). The global developments described above have vastly increased the funds available but flows have become much more volatile.

London and New York dominate the world financial system. Tokyo is growing rapidly in importance and is likely to rival them within a few years. It is difficult to rank other major financial centres, but cities such as Los Angeles, Chicago, Paris and Zurich as well as offshore financial centres like Hong Kong and Singapore are important (Reed, 1981).

Diversification and the growing sophistication of the Australian financial system have accompanied these developments. Building societies, finance companies and credit unions have expanded much more quickly than conventional banking activities (Taylor and Hirst, 1984), thus tapping the higher disposable incomes brought by economic growth. Finance companies have also expanded rapidly, many of them linked to the major banks; indeed, trading banks have reacted to increasing competition and changing circumstances by diversifying and internationalizing their activities (Hirst and Taylor, 1985). The short-term money market has grown particularly rapidly because of the need of businesses to maximize their use of funds in an inflationary and competitive environment. Borrowing provisions of government, particularly relating to utilities such as water or electricity supply, have been liberalized to enable them to seek funds from a wider range of sources. These utilities are often active sources of funds in the short-term money market.

Deregulation of the banking sector and floating of the Australian dollar in the 1980s have led to several important changes. The Australian economy has become much more open to international trends. Increased uncertainty and high interest rates have been among the most widely publicized effects, but improved scope for moving Australian money offshore and provision of corporate finance by foreign banks are other significant effects. Coupled with changes in tax legislation the pattern of investment opportunities has changed substantially.

While Sydney is a comparatively small financial centre in international terms, it occupies a significant position in the Western Pacific region. Developments in the financial system and the entry of foreign banks and financial institutions have strengthened its position as an international and domestic financial centre, while Melbourne has gained to a much lesser extent (Daly, 1984). Of the seventeen foreign banks recently given permission to operate in Australia, Sydney has eight of the head offices, and Melbourne has five (two banks have a joint Sydney/Melbourne head office). Furthermore, Sydney was already the head office of two foreign banks. Sydney dominates the head office locations of merchant banks in Australia with 73 per cent of the total; Melbourne has 25 per cent (Peat Marwick Mitchell, 1983, p. 64). However, the fourteen largest merchant banks, which account for approximately 65 per cent of the market, have their head offices evenly divided between the two cities and have offices in both (Henderson, 1983, p. 46).

Changes in the financial system have had major consequences for the physical development of the metropolitan area. Perhaps the most important has been the channelling of overseas investment into property. The most spectacular evidence for this was the surge of office construction in the CBD in the late 1960s and early 1970s, partly a product of constrained investment opportunities in the United Kingdom (Balchin and Kieve, 1982). In more recent times there has been a resurgence of overseas funds, although this has been constrained by Foreign Investment Review Board restrictions on portfolio investment. Increasingly this money has come from South East Asia and has gone into property, with some recent emphasis on hotels and tourist projects.

Increasing quantities of domestic capital have also gone into the property sector through conventional financial institutions such as finance companies, superannuation and pension funds, but also through property trusts and directly through developers. Some property developers see their role more as putting investment packages together than building and development of property. These funds were particularly significant in stimulating construction of retail and industrial property (Cardew and Rich, 1982).

Many developments have been created simply as investment packages, bringing the rapid spread of leasehold tenure to all major property sectors with the exception of the residential sector. Firms can occupy premises that are larger or otherwise more suited to modern modes of operation, and at the same time release capital from fixed assets in property to increase working capital for plant and machinery. Leasehold tenure has also facilitated higher mobility of most businesses and so encouraged the rapid dispersal of economic activity across the metropolitan area.

Restructuring of financial systems together with taxation changes have had major impacts on the housing sector. In the late 1960s and into the 1970s there was a surge of money from mainly personal investors into financial intermediaries such as building societies and finance companies, who in turn lent the money at often very favourable rates on land and housing. This trend contributed to one of the greatest property booms in Sydney's history (Daly, 1982). In the aftermath of this boom the cost of housing finance increased substantially, but to a large extent property prices adjusted to this so that the real cost of housing fell, only to rise again with another upward trend in the property cycle.

More recently very high interest rates and partial deregulation of housing finance have reduced the level of subsidy in the housing sector but may have increased the quantity of money available for house purchase. Increases in interest rates have been related to the nation's balance of payments and the role of foreign investment in covering current account deficits. Taxation changes relating to negative gearing and depreciation allowances have created uncertainty for investors in residential property and may lead to a shift in investment to commercial property (Wilson, 1986).

## Organizational Change

Closely related to developments in the financial sector have been major changes in the organization of business. Most important has been the increasing domination of the economy by a few large firms. Concentration of ownership and control has increased markedly in recent times and is high by world standards. About 260 firms account for half the value added and 42 per cent of employment of the 34,800 manufacturing enterprises in Australia (Rich, 1987). The level of concentration appears to be highest in those activities most strategic to the future direction of the economy (Fagan et al., 1981, p. 34). Increases in concentration have been associated, in part, with the emergence of transnational corporations and growing foreign investment in Australia. In the early 1980s roughly half of mine output and one-third of manufactured goods were produced by foreign owned companies.

Large firms are important products of economic change but they also initiate and control further change. They play a major role in directing worldwide and Australian economic trends; they wield considerable influence on government and to a large extent define the working environment for small firms. Penetration of Australia by foreign firms transfers some control of the economy to overseas interests and increases its vulnerability to secular and cyclical shifts in international economic conditions. Large firms determine much of the demand for capital flows into and within Australia and, in the case of transnational corporations, form one medium through which the transfer of funds takes place.

One feature of the increasing dominance of large firms is the growing spatial concentration of control in international and national economies. Such spatial concentration is important because of its implications for numbers and types of jobs, demand for office space and influences upon economies of other areas. In Australia control has been progressively more concentrated in Sydney and Melbourne. These cities accommodate the great majority of the headquarters of Australian firms and Australian head offices of transnational corporations; there is evidence that Sydney is usurping Melbourne's traditional role as pre-eminent control centre (Taylor and Thrift, 1980, 1981a; O'Connor and Edgington, 1984), yet they are both part of an interlocking worldwide set of economic decision-making centres dominated by cities in the United States, Western Europe and Japan.

It is important not to over-emphasize the centralization of control of the Australian economy in Sydney and Melbourne. Organizations differ widely in the degree to which control is centralized in the head office. Some organizations have used new information technologies to centralize control, while others have used them to decentralize decision-making. Still others, and this may be quite common, have centralized corporate policy-making and financial matters at the head office (whether it be in New York or London for a transnational corporation, Sydney or Melbourne for a national firm), while decentralizing production and marketing decisions to be more responsive to the market (Langdale, 1985, p. 30–31).

Concentration of head offices in Sydney has stimulated growth of business service firms (accounting, legal, financial and advertising), institutions facilitating the operation of markets (stock and futures exchanges), and federal and state government agencies regulating firms' activities. The greater the concentration of head offices in a city, the more specialized the set of associated organizations (Cohen, 1979). Traditionally, these organizations have clustered in the CBD to communicate easily with each other; more recently there has been decentralization of both major offices and service firms to suburban locations.

Large firms have many other impacts on urban structure. One of the most obvious relates to decisions about investment in production and distribution facilities. Large new projects help mould the pattern and speed of growth, while closure or changed use of existing facilities may have equally significant adverse effects. Both directly and through the effects on linked firms, there is an impact on the volume and spatial pattern of economic activity and employment, which in turn may influence demand for housing, transport and urban infrastructure.

The impact of organizational change on urban development is clearly seen in the distribution sector with the movement of warehousing to the suburbs and the integration of office and sales functions with warehousing in individual establishments (Nugent et al., 1982). The competitive strategies of large retailers, the packaging of retail development in planned shopping centres, and the expansion of direct trading by manufacturers and wholesalers have influenced the character and distribution of retail facilities.

## Technological Change

Much technological change has occurred in response to the desire of producers and consumers for lower costs and better products, and is characterized by reduced requirements for one or more factors of production for each unit of output. Large firms in particular are both a product of and a stimulus to new production and distribution techniques and improvements in transport and communications. In particular, advances in computer communication systems, together with falling transmission costs, are essential to the effective coordination of national and international networks of offices and plants of large firms, and so underpin projects such as General Motors' world car scheme. But technological change increasingly affects the operations of even the smallest firms; indeed smaller firms in some situations are among the most innovative technologically.

Technological change has many effects on the urban environment, but the details of these are poorly understood, partly because of the difficulty of tracing the indirect impacts of technological change through the economy. It is clear, though, that technological change has encouraged the relocation of factories and warehouses out of cramped inner-city sites to the middle and outer suburbs (Cardew and Rich, 1982; Nugent et al., 1982).

An important component of technological change is in the information technology area. New information technologies are having a major impact on Sydney's international and national role as well as on the nature of its intra-urban linkages. Sydney is Australia's international telecommunications gateway (Langdale, 1982). This role is becoming more significant as Australia becomes more tightly linked to the international information economy.

Sydney's role as an international and a domestic financial centre is closely related to the introduction of new information technologies. Most foreign banks recently granted licences to operate in Australia have linked their Australian branch offices into their sophisticated international telecommunications networks (Langdale, 1985, pp. 80–81). Australian banks have also rapidly expanded their domestic and international communications networks. The increasing diversity of corporate and retail banking services relies heavily on these electronic funds transfer networks. At an intra-urban level the rapid diffusion and acceptance of automatic teller machines and point of sale terminals are likely to have an important impact on shopping trip behaviour and on the number of suburban bank branches.

New information technologies are also influencing the design of office buildings. New buildings will require extensive cabling below each floor to enable the establishment of complete workstations at any point in the building. Already the effect of computer technology has been to generate a significant increase in the demand for office space.

The impact of technological change on employment and the distribution of employment opportunities is a subject of much debate. As yet the trends are not entirely clear. Whilst employment has been reduced as a result of technological change in particular industries such as banking, insurance, printing, wholesaling and retailing, its effect on the overall economy is uncertain. Very few studies have attempted to measure the indirect employment impacts resulting from the adoption of new technologies.

## Planning in Sydney

Government actions impinging on urban development are many and varied, in part reflecting the plethora of bodies involved. All three levels of government take part and virtually all departments, statutory authorities and advisory bodies have direct or indirect impacts. Linge (1971) identified more than sixty federal and state instrumentalities which influenced the development decisions in the local government area of the City of Sydney. It is not surprising that conflicts and contradictions between government agencies abound.

Virtually all government policies have some urban impact. There is no clear distinction between urban policy and other policy relevant to urban development (Neutze, 1978; Painter, 1979). In practice there is a gradation from urban planning (dealing with land-use zoning, development control and the management of urban expansion), through policies whose focus is not explicitly urban (housing, banking deregulation), to foreign affairs, where any urban influence is indirect and often unintended. It is thus better to consider the urban dimension of public policy than focus simply on urban policy (Neutze, 1978).

Nevertheless, urban planning is the most obvious example of government influence on urban development. In broad terms, urban planners have two roles. One is to prepare plans and procedures to manage patterns of urban development from the local government level to metropolitan regional scale. Their less obvious but most time consuming role is development control, involving assessment of development applications usually within the context of existing planning instruments.

There have been attempts at both metropolitan and local scales throughout the post-war period to influence urban development. In many respects, though, these attempts have not been very effective, partly because of a degree of ignorance and lack of analytical expertise on the part of planners. Both market forces and other aspects of government policy have had a greater impact.

The first metropolitan planning documents were prepared by the Department of Main Roads in 1945 (NSW. DMR, 1945) and were largely incorporated in the County of Cumberland Planning Scheme (CCC, 1948). The Scheme proposed a greenbelt to restrict metropolitan expansion, satellite towns to accommodate growth, and an increase in the range of jobs and facilities in the suburbs.

In 1968 a new and different type of plan, was published (NSW. SPA, 1968). In contrast to the County Scheme, it was a strategic plan: it provided a broad outline of future growth corridors with a general indication of the planning of development rather than the detailed prescription of land uses. It sought to provide an orderly approach to urban expansion with more emphasis than previous plans on the coordination of public expenditure. Among its principal concerns were to maintain Sydney as Australia's major city, accommodate substantial population growth, ensure an adequate and well located supply of industrial land, retain a strong CBD, but to decentralize jobs and reduce traffic congestion.

Economic, demographic and political conditions changed rapidly during the 1970s, confronting planners with a new range of problems and producing a reassessment of the fundamental nature of metropolitan planning. The Review of the Outline Plan published in 1980 (NSW. PEC, 1980) represented one stage of that reassessment. It recognized that the issues confronting planners had widened to include social, environmental and additional economic considerations. Several objectives of the Outline Plan were modified while others were added. Greater emphasis was now placed on heritage issues, influencing land prices, extending housing choices and managing urban change to make the most effective use of existing resources.

There have been two developments in urban planning since then, one politically unsuccessful and the other yet to fulfil its promise. The first was the development of financial programmes to identify comprehensively the cost and pattern of urban expenditure by government. This has run into the problem mentioned earlier, namely that urban policy *per se* is hard to define and implement. Also, attempts to integrate the urban dimension of all public policy tend to usurp the function of the Treasury department, which carries far more political status.

The second development is the use of policies and directives as strategic planning instruments. These were facilitated by important legislative changes enacted in 1979 (NSW, 1979). Two of the more important policies covered urban consolidation (increasing the density of residential areas) and office location (in the form of a centres policy). Again these policies have been of questionable merit. The urban consolidation policy had to be withdrawn in the face of public opposition and may not, in any case, have achieved the gains expected (Stone, 1985; Cardew and Pratt, 1984). The centres policy has yet to be given formal legal status but has been informally adopted by the Department of Environment and Planning (DEP). It is a narrowly conceived policy that attempts to confine office development to selected suburban shopping centres. This fails to acknowledge adequately market trends, specifically the dispersal of office development to industrial estates and business parks, and the appeal of suburban centres other than those nominated by the DEP. The Victorian government also tried a centres policy, but quickly modified it after representations from the development industry and business. The NSW centres policy is much more generally worded, in some respects so generally that it is likely to be ineffective.

There have been major changes in the demographic, political and economic environments affecting urban development. In some ways metropolitan planning has evolved to reflect such changes, but often adjustment has lagged far behind, and frequently there has been little real recognition of the potential impact of changing conditions. Planners were very slow to recognize the decline in the CBD workforce, the dispersal of office jobs to suburban centres and industrial estates, the reasons behind the surge of retail development in the 1970s, the changing requirements of industrial land uses and the voracious appetite of urban population growth for housing land.

Population change has been a particular problem for planners. The County Scheme was based on a population projection of 2.3 million in the 1970s (in context of an expectation that Australia's population would stabilize at 9 million). The Sydney Region Outline Plan was based on a population projection of 5.5 million for a somewhat larger Sydney region, but with the publication of the Borrie Report in 1975 (Australia. National Population Inquiry, 1975) and the dramatic economic and social changes of the 1970s, planners first revised downwards the forecasts and then more recently adopted a different strategy. Now the approach is to plan for a population in Sydney of 4.5 million but be non-committal on when that population will be achieved, perhaps the second decade of the next century. This strategy may be realistic in recognizing the difficulty of population projection but ignores a trend within government service instrumentalities to have better estimates of growth trends in order to assess the feasibility and cost recovery mechanisms associated with public expenditure.

The political environment has likewise undergone many changes. The County Scheme reflected the optimism and idealism of the early post-war years; it was strongly imbued with a sense of social justice and equity in line with the philosophy of governments of the day (Alexander, 1981). Economic efficiency was also seen as desirable but was a secondary objective. In contrast, the Outline Plan was concerned primarily to achieve a more efficient urban structure and accommodation of growth; again this appeared to reflect the ideals of the Coalition state government of the day, as well as the Labor opposition. Similarly, the review reflected a more recently declared political ethos of efficient use of resources, tempered with a concern for social and environmental issues. Perhaps understandably, planning appears to be more sensitive to political circumstances than to other aspects of contemporary conditions. In extreme cases, planning has been viewed as little more than the desire to legitimate the capitalist system and reinforce existing order and the distribution of wealth (Sandercock, 1975). While sensitivity to political conditions and governmental requirements is understandable, rapid changes in political philosophy or governing party make for major changes in planning priorities or funds available, as evidenced at a federal level by the rise and fall of urban concerns during the 1970s.

Economic conditions have a major impact on urban development, but this has not been clearly recognized in metropolitan planning. Reflecting prevailing conditions, the Outline Plan interpreted the economy as prosperous, growing strongly and distributing benefits to all (the latter perhaps one reason for the lack of concern with equity issues); market forces, where recognized at all, were viewed as largely irresistable and adequately reflecting community preferences. But while economic buoyancy was recognized, the Outline Plan was based on little real analysis of the mechanisms underpinning economic change and their impact on the city. Gradually there has been a growing recognition of the importance of such mechanisms. The interrelation of macroeconomic and urban issues was reflected in the establishment at a federal level of a Department of Urban and Regional Development. Later in NSW growing economic problems demanded an increasing awareness of the impact of economic change. Such awareness grew during the 1970s and meant that the Outline Plan Review recognized phenomena such as the unprecedented level of activity in property development, deterioration of economic conditions, and reduced government funding for urban programmes, as well as other changes such as the new planning system in NSW and growing community involvement in planning issues (NSW. PEC, 1980).

Despite such growing awareness, those formulating the Review have failed to recognize the crucial importance of issues such as the extent of dispersal of economic activity, rapid change in business organization, growing significance of the financial sector, major change and rapid expansion of the communications sector, and the full extent of the urban planning conflicts engendered by technological and economic change, for example in the transport field. Each of these has major impacts on the nature of urban development, the lives of Sydney's inhabitants, the performance of business, and so on. Each needs to be examined carefully and its implications fully probed in designing future metropolitan plans.

NOTE

This chapter is a revised version of 'Themes in urban development and economic change', in Cardew, R. V., Langdale, J. V. and Rich, D. C. (1982) *Why Cities Change: Urban Development and Economic Change*. Sydney: George Allen and Unwin, pp. 17–41.

REFERENCES

Alexander, I. (1981) Post-war metropolitan planning: goals and realities, in Troy, P. N. (ed.) *Equity in the City*. Sydney: George Allen and Unwin, pp. 145–71.

Australia. National Population Inquiry (the Borrie Report) (1975) *Population in Australia: A Demographic Analysis and Projection*. Canberra: Australian Government Publishing Service.

Balchin, P. N. and Kieve, J. L. (1982) *Urban Land Economics*, 2nd ed. London: Macmillan.

Barnet, R. J. and Muller, R. E. (1974) *Global Reach: the Power of the Multinational Corporations*. New York: Simon and Schuster.

Butlin, N. G. (1964) *Investment in Australian Economic Development 1861–1900*. Cambridge: Cambridge University Press.

Cardew, R. V. and Pratt, I. (1984) *Urban Consolidation in the Illawarra*. Sydney: Department of Environment and Planning.

Cardew, R. V. and Rich, D. C. (1982) Manufacturing and industrial property development in Sydney, in Cardew, R. V., Langdale, J. V. and Rich, D. C. (eds.) *Why Cities Change: Urban Development and Economic Change in Sydney*. Sydney: George Allen and Unwin, pp. 115–34.

CCC (1948) *The Planning Scheme for the County of Cumberland*. Sydney.

Cochrane, P. J. (1980) *Industrialization and Dependence: Australia's Road to Economic Development*. St Lucia: University of Queensland Press.

Cohen, R. (1979) The changing transactions economy and its spatial implications. *Ekistics*, **46**, pp. 7–15.

Daly, M. T. (1982) *Sydney Boom Sydney Bust: the City and Its Property Market, 1850–1981*. Sydney: George Allen and Unwin.

Daly, M. T. (1984) The revolution in international capital markets: urban growth and Australian cities. *Environment and Planning A*, **16**, pp. 1003–20.

Fagan, R. H., McKay, J. and Linge, G. J. R. (1981) Structural change: the international and national context, in Linge, G. J. R. and McKay, J. (eds.) *Structural Change in Australia: Some Spatial and Organisational Responses*. Canberra: Publication HG 15, Department of Human Geography, Australian National University, pp. 1–49.

Freeman, C. (1974) *The Economics of Industrial Innovation*. Harmondsworth: Penguin.

Frobel, F., Heinrichs, J. and Kreye, O. (1980) *The New International Division of Labour: Structural Unemployment in Industrialised Countries and Industrialisation in Developing Countries*. Cambridge: Cambridge University Press.

Henderson, C. G. (1983) *Foreign Banking in Australia*. Unpublished BA Hons. Thesis, School of Earth Sciences, Macquarie University.

Hirst, J. and Taylor, M. J. (1985) The internationalisation of Australian banking: further moves by the ANZ. *Australian Geographer*, **16**, pp. 291–5.

Hood, N. and Young, S. (1979) *The Economics of Multinational Enterprise*. London: Longman.

Hymer, S. (1975) The multinational corporation and the law of uneven development, in Radice, H. (ed.) *International Firms and Modern Imperialism*. Harmondsworth: Penguin, pp. 37–62.

Langdale, J. V. (1982) Telecommunications in Sydney: towards an information economy, in Cardew, R. V., Langdale, J. V. and Rich, D. C. (eds.) *Why Cities Change: Urban Development and Economic Change in Sydney*. Sydney: George Allen and Unwin, pp. 77–94.

Langdale, J. V. (1985) *Transborder Data Flow and International Trade in Electronic Information Services: an Australian Perspective*, Report to the Department of Communications. Canberra: Australian Government Publishing Service.

Linge, G. J. R. (1971) Government and spatial behaviour, in Linge, G. J. R. and Rimmer, P. J. (eds.) *Government Influence and the Location of Economic Activity*. Canberra: Publication HG 5, Department of Human Geography, Australian National University, pp. 25–52.

Neutze, G. M. (1977) *Urban Development in Australia*. Sydney: George Allen and Unwin.

Neutze, G. M. (1978) *Australian Urban Policy*. Sydney: George Allen and Unwin.

NSW (1979) *Environmental Planning and Assessment Act*, Sydney.

NSW. DMR (1945) *Main Road Development Plan for Sydney and the County of Cumberland*. Sydney.

NSW. PEC (1980) *Review: Sydney Region Outline Plan*, Publication 80/5. Sydney.

NSW. SPA (1968) *Sydney Region: Outline Plan 1970–2000 A.D. A Strategy for Development*. Sydney.

Nugent, E., Rich, D. C. and Simons, P. L. (1982) Organisational and locational change in Sydney's wholesaling industry, in Cardew, R. V., Langdale, J. V. and Rich, D. C. (eds.) *Why Cities Change: Urban Development and Economic Change in Sydney*. Sydney: George Allen and Unwin, pp. 135–50.

O'Connor, K. and Edgington, D. (1984) Tertiary industry and urban development: competition between Melbourne and Sydney, in Adrian, C. (ed.) *Urban Impacts of Foreign and Local Investment in Australia*. Canberra: Publication 119, Australian Institute of Urban Studies, pp. 93–110.

Painter, M. (1979) Urban government, urban politics and the fabrication of urban issues. The impossibility of urban policy. *Australian Journal of Public Administration*, **38**, pp. 335–46.

Peat Marwick Mitchell (1983) *Sydney: Financial Growth Centre for the Pacific*, a study on behalf of the NSW Department of Industrial Development and Decentralisation. Sydney.

Perrons, D. C. (1981) The role of Ireland in the new international division of labour: a proposed framework for regional analysis. *Regional Studies*, **15**, pp. 81–100.

Reed, H. C. (1981) *The Preeminence of International Financial Centres*. New York: Praeger.

Rich, D. C. (1987) *The Industrial Geography of Australia*. London: Croom Helm.

Sandercock, L. K. (1975) *Cities for Sale*. Melbourne: Melbourne University Press.

Stone, C. (1985) Urban consolidation: problems and prospects, in Burnley, I. and Forrest, J. (eds.) *Living in Cities: Urbanism and Social Change in Metropolitan Australia*. Sydney: George Allen and Unwin, pp. 215–22.

Taylor, M. J. and Hirst, J. (1984) Environment, technology and organisation: the restructuring of Australian trading banks. *Environment and Planning A*, **16**, pp. 1055–78.

Taylor, M. J. and Thrift, N. J. (1980) Large corporations and concentrations of capital in Australia: a geographical analysis. *Economic Geography*, **56**, pp. 261–80.

Taylor, M. J. and Thrift, N. J. (1981*a*) Spatial variations in Australian enterprise: the case of large firms headquartered in Melbourne and Sydney, *Environment and Planning A*, **13**, pp. 137–46.

Taylor, M. J. and Thrift, N. J. (1981*b*) Some geographical implications of foreign investment in the semiperiphery: the case of Australia. *Tijdschrift voor Economische en Sociale Geografie*, **72**, pp. 194–213.

Wilson, J. (1986) Review of recent changes to taxation law. *The Valuer*, **29**, pp. 96–99.

*Chapter 3*

# Urban and Regional Planning in a Federal System: New South Wales and Victoria

TONI LOGAN

In Australia it is the states that have legislative control over land, so there are really eight separate systems for urban and regional planning (including those of the two territories). When planning was accepted as a legitimate function of government, largely as a result of a federal Labor government initiative in the 1940s, the differences between the planning systems were slight because, essentially, they were derived from the same English model. But as planning slowly matured, the contrasts became sharper, reflecting varied ideologies and administrative styles. Yet there have been few comparative studies of planning in Australia. The more notable exceptions, Stretton (1970), Sandercock (1975*a*), Harrison (1978), and Bowman (1979), tend to draw out common features rather than to focus on the differences. It is with the latter emphasis that I review recent major changes to planning in New South Wales and Victoria.

Although these two states have different planning systems they are confronting substantive issues that are remarkably similar. Both have large populations on Australian standards (in 1981, New South Wales had a population of 5.2 million and Victoria one of 3.9 million). Each has a primate coastal city of similar size (in 1981, Sydney had a population of 3.3 million and Melbourne one of 2.8 million), which functions as the administrative, cultural, commercial, and industrial core of its state and which has a pronounced pattern of social segregation, with concentrations of low-income groups living in the deprived western suburbs (Logan *et al.*, 1975). The hinterlands of these cities are occupied predominantly by sparse agricultural activities, but there are secondary industrial centres: Newcastle and Wollongong in New South Wales, and Geelong and the towns of the

Latrobe Valley in Victoria. Both states have been traditional leaders in manufacturing and, during the 1970s, felt the sharp impact of structural change (Linge and McKay, 1981). This decline in manufacturing employment was partly counterbalanced by growth in the tertiary sector, especially in financial, administrative, and community services, all of which are highly concentrated in the two capital cities. However, there is mounting concern that the growth in tertiary employment is unlikely to be sustained. Overall unemployment rates have followed a similar path: both states had 1.6 per cent and 5.6 per cent of the workforce unemployed in 1971 and 1981, respectively.

Apart from these marked parallels in resource disposition and patterns of structural change, each state functions within the context of a national economy which has become increasingly integrated and increasingly internationalized since World War II. The expanding role of federal government policies of economic management has had a fairly uniform impact on New South Wales and Victoria, which have been treated as wealthy states from which to redistribute revenues to the less wealthy (Stilwell, 1980). Further, the escalated inflow of transnational capital, with its tendency to locate head offices in Sydney and Melbourne, treats Australia as a single market rather than in terms of the common pre-war conception of a set of fairly distinct subnational markets (McKay and Whitelaw, 1977). Yet, with the exception of brief periods of Labor office in the 1940s and early 1970s, federal governments have been explicitly disinterested in urban and regional planning, which they have seen as a state preserve (Logan, 1979); and the recently elected Hawke Labor Government has taken no initiatives in this direction. Nevertheless, other federal policies do have important effects on urban and regional development. The impact of tariff reductions on manufacturing industries in the early 1970s is one example, as was the Fraser Liberal-Country Party Government's policy of public-sector restraint, which meant major cuts in grants for service and works programmes at the state level.

My purpose in this chapter is to explore the ways in which similar physical and economic contexts have generated different administrative arrangements and policy emphases for urban and regional planning. These variations illustrate how, in a period of rapid economic change, the function of planning has become less certain. Until recently the rationale for planning has rested on implicit assumptions of continued economic growth, so the aim was to develop mechanisms for controlling the direction of physical expansion in the cities and regions. But with the onset of a major economic recession during the 1970s, these packages of negative regulations have become increasingly irrelevant. Planning agencies at state and local levels have few resources to allocate, and so find it difficult to adopt a more positive stance, unlike the powerful functional authorities that deal with transport, electricity, and public housing, for example.

Consequently, planning has tended to stress its potential for coordinating public investment, but here, too, state governments are developing other agencies, linked to the premier's department or to the budgeting department, which can fulfil this function more effectively. So planning, a relatively new addition to the responsibilities of government, continues to seek legitimacy.

## Institutional Frameworks for Planning

### A Prime Role for Local Government

Both states introduced planning legislation at the end of World War II: Victoria passed its *Town and Country Planning Act* in 1944 (TCPA, 1944), and, in the following year, New South Wales inserted Part XIIA (Town and Country Planning) into its *Local Government Act* (LGAA, 1945). As frequently happens in the transfer of a policy from one environment to another, the model was applied without much adjustment to its new context. In the two-tier government structure of England, town planning was seen as a logical extension of controls over building and sanitation so local authorities were permitted to prepare planning schemes, with zones allocated for specific types of land use, and were given powers to ensure new developments conformed to the scheme after its approval by a central agency. Such a distribution of responsibilities was not particularly relevant to Australia where local government is relatively weak (Bains *et al.*, 1979) and where population is highly concentrated in a few coastal cities.

### State and Metropolitan Agencies

Paradoxically, in view of the primary role assigned to local government, the states believed that in each metropolitan area planning would achieve coordination between the large number of statutory works authorities. So the New South Wales Premier, McKell, argued that a master plan for Sydney would eliminate the disconnected 'jabs and stabs at public works' (quoted in Sandercock, 1975a, p. 177), and in Melbourne it was admitted that public bodies were 'making decisions from day-to-day without any attempt at co-ordination' (VPD, 1944, p. 841). Yet the respective planning legislation focused on coordination among municipal authorities which have only a minor role in public works. Victoria's Town and Country Planning Board (TCPB) was to advise the Minister for Local Government on the adequacy of planning schemes: in New South Wales, the Town and Country Advisory Committee (TCAC) fulfilled this role. In neither case could these bodies exert much influence on the major public works programmes, which were largely undertaken by *ad hoc* authorities (Holmes, 1978; Wilenski, 1978).

In Melbourne very few of the forty-one local councils (now fifty-two) responded to the new permissive planning powers, so in 1949 the Melbourne Metropolitan Board of Works (MMBW), an *ad hoc* authority providing hydraulic services, was given the task of preparing and, later, of implementing a citywide scheme. Thus there emerged a dual organizational structure for planning in Victoria, which has been characterized by tension and rivalry between the TCPB and the MMBW and by major disagreements on policy issues (Logan, 1981). In New South Wales, because of pressure from local government to restrict ministerial powers (Harrison, 1972), a regional planning body for Sydney was established at the outset. This Cumberland County Council (CCC) was essentially a second tier of local government, but with planning powers only, its members being elected by the thirty-nine municipal councils in the metropolitan area (now forty-one).

Successive decades saw a variety of attempts to grapple with the design of organizations to increase coordination. New South Wales demonstrated greater structural fluidity and a strong centralization drive. In 1963 the CCC was replaced by the State Planning Authority, whose members included representatives from public utilities, though it had a reduced local government component, and whose ambit widened from the metropolitan area to the entire State. A further change in 1974 created the Planning and Environment Commission, in which local government influence again was reduced and the pollution-control function brought under a Minister for Planning and the Environment. In 1980 the centralizing process was completed by the establishment of the Department of Environment and Planning, finally bringing planning directly into the mainstream of government from the periphery of statutory authorities. The current Wran Labor government appears to emphasize coordination at the heart of political power, at cabinet level, where, in effect, key planning policies, such as metropolitan land release and urban consolidation, are implemented.

Victoria's progress towards a centralized solution has been more hesitant. In 1968 the State Planning Council, comprising representatives from sixteen public agencies, was established to assist the Minister of Local Government (who at that time was responsible for planning) in preparing and implementing statements of planning policy. But at much the same time, increasing concern for environmental issues spawned a new crop of statutory authorities to deal with issues like pollution control and preservation of historic buildings. And, although a Ministry for Planning was set up in 1973, it had a small staff and did little to encroach on the independence of the TCPB or of the MMBW. The trend was thus one of increasing complexity and dispersal of planning responsibility, 'preventing the formulation of a comprehensive integrated set of policy objectives and in their absence consistent decision-making . . . was unlikely' (Bland, 1974, p. 8). Despite further organizational experiments, it was not until 1981 that the

Victorian government took more direct responsibility for planning, merging the TCPB and the Ministry for Planning to establish the Department of Planning. But the problem of a dual structure remains, and this Department has considerably less responsibility for metropolitan planning than its counterpart in New South Wales. The current Cain Labor government so far has not stressed the role of cabinet in the coordinated implementation of planning policies.

At the beginning of the 1980s, both states had new planning departments designed for more effective corporate management, with a relatively short chain-of-command compared to the elongated vertical hierarchies that typify more traditional bureaucracies (Paterson, 1980). In structuring the two departments, the intention was to integrate better the policy and control functions, but there is a pronounced contrast in the role assigned to policy research. The New South Wales Department of Environment and Planning has six divisions, one of which is devoted to policy research, and, in early 1983, this included a broad range of issues: metropolitan land release, urban consolidation, employment policy, and a review of the metropolitan strategy. The research arm of the Victorian Department of Planning is relatively weak. Initially there was a small unit for policy analysis and development attached to the Chief Planner, but within a year this unit had disappeared. Policy research resources were incorporated into the two major regional directorates of Country Victoria and the Port Philip District (including Melbourne), a dichotomy abandoned by New South Wales in the late 1970s (Paterson, 1980).

*The Scope of Planning*

Institutional definitions of planning were slower to change than organizational structures. Until recently the legislative provisions defining the ambit of planning continued to focus heavily on the physical aspects of land use. For example, the Third Schedule of Victoria's *Town and Country Planning Act* (TPCA, 1961) still lists the matters that may be included in planning schemes, which basically relate to the reservations of land for public use and for vehicular and pedestrian thoroughfares, the provision of utilities, controls over private development, and, since the early 1970s, the conservation of buildings or sites. After a long gestation period, begun under a conservative Liberal government and completed by a Labor government, New South Wales recently achieved a comprehensive revision of its legislation which included a wider definition of planning as 'protecting, improving or utilising, to the best advantage, the environment' (EPAA, 1979, section 26). Despite a number of attempts, Liberal governments in Victoria have not comprehensively revised the planning legislation, but the current Labor government has initiated such a review aimed at simplifying the development control system to make it more comprehensible and accessible to the general public.

With hindsight, these state responses were surprisingly tardy and small, given the way community views of planning developed during the 1970s. Again, a federal Labor government took the initiative, through its Department of Urban and Regional Development, to broaden the scope of planning to include policies directed explicitly at achieving greater equity. It saw the need to free planning from the physical bias and technocratic or design approaches characteristic of the traditionally dominant professions of engineering, architecture, and surveying in order to achieve better integration of economic, social, and environmental policies by infusing planners with a social science orientation (Sandercock, 1983). The levels of integration achieved by the Whitlam Labor government in its three-year term were not major, but the policies did generate debate within the community and did broaden perspectives on planning. Very little of this increased awareness filtered through into revisions of state planning legislation, which aimed more at an efficient management structure rather than at explicitly incorporating a redistributive philosophy.

The current economic recession has accelerated moves towards streamlining procedures for planning in both states. Specifically, considerable attention has been given to defining mechanisms that reduce delays in the approval of major projects by regulatory agencies. Informal networks have always existed for this purpose, but they emerged overtly in response to aluminium and coal production proposals in the late 1970s, when the respective premiers of each state negotiated directly with transnational companies on packages of subsidies. Since then the approach has been institutionalized in legislative forms. The New South Wales 'hot-line' has been used to approve a regional shopping centre, and Victoria's 'fast-track' has been applied to allow the setting up of an offensive industrial zone and the development of a major shopping centre. Such mechanisms have been felt necessary despite the substantial ministerial powers already existing, in New South Wales to direct public authorities and local councils (EPAA, 1979, Section 117), and in Victoria to determine certain appeals (PABA, 1980, Section 41). Clearly the centralizing tendencies manifest in organizational structures are also reflected in the increasing power of ministers to negotiate or to determine outcomes of development proposals.

*Moves to Strategic Planning*

Since the late 1960s there has been an emphasis in both states on strategic planning – the formulation of policies or strategies to achieve specified goals or objectives. This trend reflects a concern by planning authorities to be seen to be acting rationally in their approach to long-term decision-making, as well as a response to demands from an increasingly critical public for more rigorous justification of planning decisions. The Sydney Regional Outline Plan (NSWSPA, 1968, p. 5) illustrates the trend clearly by its move away from the traditional metropolitan planning scheme to a statement of 'principles, policies and broad strategy', with proposals shown in a 'semi-diagrammatic way'. The proposals were to be translated into detailed planning schemes by local councils. This approach closely resembles the English 'structure' plans and followed the appointment of an English senior planner to the State Planning Authority. Melbourne's planners retained the concept of a statutory metropolitan scheme, although successive reports accompanying scheme revisions do use the vocabulary of strategic planning: objectives, alternatives, framework plan (MMBW, 1967; 1971; 1981b).

In Victoria the prime thrust towards strategic planning took a different form. After 1968 the Minister of Local Government could prepare statements on planning policy which were to guide local and regional authorities in their scheme preparation. Nine of these policies were approved in the 1970s, mainly relating to areas of land-use conflict at the metropolitan fringe, but outside the ambit of the MMBW. Since then the output of statements of planning policy has dried up, largely because their generalized form was difficult to translate into statutory schemes (Faubel, 1981). Although the statements could 'have regard to demographic, social and economic factors' (TCPAA, 1968, Section 7A(3)), the Third Schedule of the Act excludes such issues from planning schemes. More recently, New South Wales has adopted a similar approach, whereby state environmental planning policies may be prepared on any significant matter (EPAA, 1979, Sections 37–39). In contrast to Victoria, these state policies have concerned quite specific land uses, such as housing for the aged and disabled, and medium-density housing, and therefore offer more chance of effective implementation.

Despite the long-term move towards the design of strategies to achieve defined goals, it is only recently that the goals themselves have been given some legal standing. Victoria now allows a statement of objectives to be included in a planning scheme (TCPGAA, 1979, Section 9(2)(c)), whereas New South Wales requires its inclusion in all plans (EPAA, 1979, Section 25).

*Regional Planning*

Outside the metropolitan areas, regional planning organizations have received more attention in Victoria. Partly this emphasis reflects the dual administrative structure; because the MMBW has the major responsibility for planning Melbourne, the TCPB focused its energies on the rest of the state. Here, regionalism was an obvious response to the government's inability to overcome the relatively greater fragmentation at local level (Bains *et al.*, 1979). Victoria achieved a complete coverage of local authorities by the 1870s, but the ease with which communities could petition for urban and rural councils resulted in a large number of small units. Since then the system has ossified: there have been few boundary changes, despite a number of inquiries into local government calling for amalgamations (Bowman, 1981). It is in the larger provincial towns that this legacy militates against effective planning. The Ballarat urban area, for example, has a population of about 70,000 and is dissected into six municipalities. There are wide variations in property tax rates and service provision, as well as serious policy conflicts when some of the outer shires compete to attract growth away from the central city (Neilson, 1980). The local government system in New South Wales has been more adaptable. A comprehensive network of municipal authorities was finally imposed in the early twentieth century, but since then a series of amalgamations has resulted in generally larger units and the absence of the Ballarat type of problem (Bains and Miles, 1981).

During the 1970s Victoria experimented with regional forms and functions; however, regional planning here has none of the economic policy overtones of aid to lagging areas, which is common in western Europe. Rather, it has evolved simply as land-use planning at a scale larger than a single municipality. The first batch of regional planning authorities (Westernport, Geelong, and Loddon-Campaspe) were very much creatures of local government. Their members were all municipal councillors and their function was to prepare statutory planning schemes. But problems of dual control (regional and local), restrictive composition, and insufficient public access (Logan, 1981) led to a modified approach incorporating a strategic function, a wider membership, and requirements for greater public involvement (exemplified by the Upper Yarra Valley and Dandenong Ranges Authority). Towards the end of the decade, local councils resisted the state's attempt to create two more regional bodies, fearing a loss of autonomy and an increased financial burden. Currently the Cain government is reviving the regional planning authority concept, which forms part of the Labor party commitment to reducing inequalities between regions and to decentralizing administration.

Regional planning in New South Wales has followed a different path. In the early post-war period, the CCC's arrangements for planning metropolitan Sydney were duplicated for the nearby secondary centres of Newcastle and Wollongong. But with the advent of the centralized State Planning Authority, regional planning was taken out of the ambit of local government. This trend has continued, so that in the recent restructuring of the planning system it is the Department of Environment and Planning that is responsible for preparing regional environmental plans.

What emerges from the review of institutional frameworks for urban and regional planning in the two states are major contrasts in the degree of centralization, the rate of systemic change, and the influence of local government. Nevertheless, during the late 1970s, the administrative structures at state level have moved closer together. The discussion now focuses on the types of policies produced by these institutional frameworks, both for metropolitan and for non-metropolitan areas.

## Metropolitan Policies

Policy responses for Sydney and Melbourne appear very similar: a first round of plans emphasized containment, a second round promoted radial corridor growth, and a third is stressing urban consolidation. This cycle, as Sandercock (1975a) points out, relates closely to broad national economic trends of recession and prosperity. However, a careful analysis of metropolitan planning reveals significant differences in approach for the two cities.

*First-Round Plans*

In the early post-war period, planners assumed that the cities would continue the low growth rates of the depression and war years. For both cities, prevention of low-density sprawl was perceived as a major problem, and a specific non-urban zone with minimum subdivision sizes was the device for containment: in Sydney it was a greenbelt and in Melbourne a rural zone. But within that framework there was a distinct contrast in objectives.

The Sydney plan had a pronounced concern for the social benefits of bringing residences and employment closer together: 'shorter travelling times, reduced fares and relief from the strain of daily travelling under conditions of intense crowding' as well as bringing employment opportunities closer to married women (CCC, 1948, p. 62). So the metropolitan city was divided by a network of open spaces into fourteen urban districts to encourage largely self-sufficient communities, with retailing and industrial employment as well as higher order educational and recreational facilities. Melbourne's planners also opted for decentralization of activities within the metropolitan area, but more on grounds of efficiency than of equity. 'The purpose of this planning scheme is to find out what is efficient and what is not, to show how faults can be remedied and the city made more pleasant, more convenient and more efficient' (MMBW, 1954, p. 3), although the policies for five district business centres and a dispersal of new industrial zones, is also closely linked to civil defence (1954, p. 4). Alexander (1981) argues convincingly that the equity stance of the Sydney planners was reflected in policy implementation. A greater degree of territorial justice in access to large retail centres, to industrial jobs, and to open space was achieved during the following decade in Sydney than in Melbourne.

*Second-Round Plans*

Towards the late 1960s, the context for metropolitan planning had become one of high economic and demographic growth assumptions. How to accommodate so many people at the low densities they seemed to prefer, and how to service them with roads that could cater for the large and rapidly increasing number of carowners, were the key problems perceived by planners. The cities were to expand by radial linear extensions, with a considerable emphasis on more growth in the less attractive western suburbs (MMBW, 1967; NSWSPA, 1968). At much the same time, metropolitan transport studies concluded that massive investment in the construction of inner suburban freeways was necessary (MTC, 1969; SATS, 1974). Thus on two grounds it can be argued that planning in both cities was now deficient in terms of equity considerations.

These policies were implemented with varying degrees of success. At the metropolitan fringe, using a combination of zoning, subdivision standards, developer contributions to service costs, and the designation of priority servicing areas, it was relatively easy for planning authorities to direct urban expansion. It is in this part of the city that, in a period of rapid growth, the regulatory or negative planning systems have most chance of success. But there was also an example of positive planning. Since the 1960s, state planning agencies in New South Wales have had development powers, unlike other Australian metropolitan planning bodies, except in the national capital of Canberra. Under a conservative government, the State Planning Authority and its successor, the Planning and Environment Commission, acquired and developed land in the west and southwest of Sydney (Harrison, 1978). This commitment to public intervention in the urban land market remains strong. So although a federal programme funding land commissions collapsed with the demise of the Whitlam government, the policy has been sustained by strong support in New South Wales, whereas in Victoria it plays a very minor role.

Freeway plans were implemented only partially. Ensuing years witnessed a series of sometimes violent confrontations between road authorities and antifreeway groups (Sandercock, 1975a). By the mid-1970s the states were forced to scale down their inner freeway projects, but the residue of this conflict can still be seen in Melbourne's unconnected strips of freeway, which cause serious congestion in the intervening residential areas, and in inner Sydney's stark row of untopped freeway pylons. For both cities the emphasis has shifted towards improving public transport, yet the long-standing dichotomy between land-use and transport planning remains.

During the 1960s, office-type employment increased substantially, mostly concentrated in the central areas of both cities (Alexander, 1979), where glass towers replaced historic buildings, created unpleasant micro-climates for pedestrians and generated much traffic congestion. Sydney's second plan identified the increasing concentration of employ-ment as 'the biggest single urban problem' and proposed the development of a few substantial countermagnets in the suburbs (NSWSPA, 1968, p. 17). The policy was not followed through, partly because the planning body lacked the powers and resources for implementation, but also because of a downturn in the demand for office space. Melbourne's second plan vaguely mentioned 'growth centres . . . offering a full range of employment opportunities' in each radial corridor, but simultaneously advocated employment growth in the central business district (MMBW, 1971, pp. 7–8).

The 1970s saw a major change in people's awareness of planning. Until then few understood the intricate statutory system (Paterson *et al.*, 1976) and its essentially technocratic approach, which was remote from the political arena. But planning decisions increasingly were challenged by conservationists and by more general demands for public participation. There were many instances of highly vocal well-organized pressure groups that opposed the destruction of historic buildings, the alienation of park-land, the pollution of coastlines and the lack of resident involvement in redevelopment projects (Sandercock, 1975*b*). It was in Sydney, though, that this kind of protest first developed into a unique coalition, between middle-class residents and a radical trade union, for the imposition of the first 'green ban' (Roddewig, 1978). Authorities in both cities are now more conscious of the political nature of planning and of the conflicting interests involved. Nevertheless, as Sandercock (1975*b*) explains, the growing con-cern for public participation largely serves middle-class residents and has little impact on the poor, the migrants, the very young, and the very old. Despite its important ideological role in presenting planners as 'caring for the community', most participation has tended to legitimize the planners' plans.

*Third-Round Policies*

By the end of the 1970s the effects of a major economic recession and a decline in population growth rates generated a metropolitan policy stress-ing the desirability of some degree of urban consolidation. This policy is directed to increasing the number of dwellings or the size of the population in the existing urban area. The main way that this can occur is to expand the supply of medium-density housing in middle-ring suburbs, which at present have high accessibility to jobs and facilities but relatively low residential densities (Roseth, 1982). A number of reasons indicate why such a policy became attractive at this time. Reflecting the tight financial situation of the states, which partly resulted from the federal monetarist policy, a prime concern was to reduce infrastructure investment in new outer suburbs. However, in both cities, claims of excess infrastructure capacity for the inner and middle suburbs have been seriously questioned (Nicholls, 1979; Orchard, 1982). There was also emphasis on the need for greater diversity of residential types to cater for the increasing number of smaller and poorer households for whom the standard detached house was not appropriate or no longer achievable.

For Sydney, another major policy objective, articulated strongly by the Minister for Environment and Planning (Bedford, 1981, p. 2.), was 'that of reducing the cost of housing, or at least the rate at which this cost is rising'. It is on this issue that the ensuing public debate has focused. Empirically based studies suggest that medium-density dwellings in middle-ring suburbs will cost more than an average suburban house (Cardew, 1982; de Monchaux, 1982), largely because these are the areas in which many local authorities are opposed to further medium-density development and have used exclusionary control devices such as minimum allotment-size and flat-size, parking and landscaping requirements, and height and setback provisions (Reid, 1982). One senior planner maintains that much of the debate has been motivated by desires to protect privileged local environments, rather than 'equity considerations [which] are at the very heart of urban consolidation policies' (Wilmoth, 1982, p. 17).

In Melbourne, equity considerations were a late addition to policy objectives (MMBW, 1979a; 1979b). Nevertheless, there was long-standing concern for rising unemployment levels and the belief that 'a more contained metropolitan structure may assist in the provision of more personal service jobs to offset the loss of manufacturing employment opportunities' (MMBW, 1979b, p. 21). This proposition has been subject to much criticism. Wyatt (1982, pp. 24–25), for example, argues that it was based on 'impressionistic overseas knowledge' and 'dateless misassertions'. Over time the consolidation thrust has weakened, but it remains part of the 'incremental growth strategy', which incorporates slower fringe growth, the designation of fourteen-or-more district centres, a vigorous central area, as well as revitalization of the inner and middle suburbs (MMBW, 1981b).

New South Wales has taken a firm line on implementation, almost provocatively so. There have been several initiatives in relation to housing submarkets, which move towards reducing the exclusionary development controls in many Sydney municipalities (Wilmoth, 1982). Dual-occupancy provisions have been introduced to encourage conversion of an existing house into two dwellings. Statements of environmental planning policy promote the location of group homes and housing for the aged and disabled in residential rather than in institutional zones. The Task Force on Rental Accommodation is examining ways of increasing the supply of rental accommodation. A draft policy on medium-density housing indicates that developments incorporating three-or-more town houses, villa units, or flats may be permitted in areas where they are currently prohibited by restrictive local codes. And to implement this draft policy, the Department of Environment and Planning is negotiating with local authorities on targets for medium-density dwelling completions.

Melbourne's incremental growth strategy has been translated into a formal draft amendment to the metropolitan planning scheme. Amendment 150 to the scheme (MMBW, 1981*a*) will introduce as-of-right dual-occupancy provisions in residential zones, but, under existing arrangements, further measures to promote diversity and higher density housing will depend upon municipal councils choosing to prepare a local development scheme. Only then can they be compelled to implement the metropolitan housing objectives. At this stage there is no indication that the metropolitan authority is prepared to confront restrictive local controls as in Sydney.

Amendment 150 for Melbourne also includes the designation of fourteen district centres to have concentrations of employment and of private and public facilities. Here the objectives are to improve accessibility and to promote the viability of public transport (MMBW, 1981*b*). But mere designation is insufficient. Private and public investment funds are scarce and, judging from past experience, the coordination required for such large-scale redevelopment of existing shopping centres appears beyond the capacity of the public sector (Logan and Ogilvy, 1981). In Sydney the policy for subregional centres is seen as distinct from urban consolidation, but, again, New South Wales has grasped the implementation nettle more firmly. Cabinet has agreed to the long-term relocation of a substantial proportion of government office workers from the central area to major suburban nodes in the west and south-west.

Clearly there have been differences in the planning approach in the two cities. For Sydney, equity objectives were articulated more strongly in the first- and third-round metropolitan policies and, certainly for the first-round plan, substantial gains were made in this direction. The New South Wales planning agencies have intervened in the urban land market both under conservative and under Labor governments. As well, the Sydney planners currently are demonstrating a willingness to tackle the parochialism of local authorities where it conflicts with metropolitan objectives. On the other hand, the Melbourne planning authority has been more conservative, both under Labor and under Liberal governments, emphasizing efficiency rather than equity goals. It has been unable or unwilling to confront local authority powers. And, above all, it has not been encouraged to intervene in the urban land market.

## Nonmetropolitan Policies

Among the key problems facing planners for non-metropolitan areas of both states have been the fragmented pattern of local authorities in country towns and the need for controls over rural subdivision in environmentally sensitive areas. I have already referred to the first, arguing that, by its willingness to initiate amalgamations, New South Wales has virtually eliminated marked local disparities in the provision of services, as well as policy conflicts between local governments in a single urban area. For Victoria these difficulties still loom large. Here the planning response has evolved through a series of stages. Early on, local councils in country towns were encouraged to prepare joint planning schemes. Many did, but progress was slow: the Ballarat Joint District Planning Scheme, for example, was begun in 1955 and approved in 1972. After 1968, a larger scale regional approach was tried, but only one provincial centre (Geelong) has produced a regional scheme. More recently, the approach has been for the state agency to persuade and assist councils in a few centres to prepare a 'subregional' strategy, which is then translated into local planning controls. This has been a convoluted planning approach to what is a problem in the structure of government.

Rural subdivision burgeoned in the late 1960s and early 1970s, when rising incomes were reflected in demand for second homes, rural retreats, and hobby farms (Wagner, 1975). Local councils, land developers, and farmers responded enthusiastically, so that when demand faltered there was a marked oversupply of small rural lots, yet subdivision rates remained high, especially in coastal areas and close to larger urban centres (Pollock, 1976). In many cases the scatter of rural residential lots created severe negative externalities on landscapes and agricultural productivity, as well as increasing the servicing costs of rural municipalities. Initially the Victorian planning agency responded by imposing a statewide subdivisional minimum of 16 hectares; but frequently this resulted in larger hobby farms rather than a reduction in rural subdivision (Lennie, 1978). Towards the end of the 1970s a more flexible approach was adopted. The TCPB began to assist local councils in developing more sensitive and effective processes for policy-making and implementation. Its innovative rural land mapping programme shows how relevant data can be assembled and analysed easily to provide a useful basis for decisions on subdivision applications (Shields and Morris, 1978); and this is supplemented by guidelines for the design and siting of buildings in specific landscape types (TCPB, 1978). Throughout much of the 1970s, New South Wales had a blanket minimum subdivision control of 40 hectares, which appears to have stemmed the flow of small rural lots (Boss, 1982). More recently there has been a move towards the Victorian approach of developing techniques to show how local councils can evaluate land for urban or rural purposes (DoEP, 1981).

It is in the non-metropolitan areas that governments of both states have encouraged major industrial projects, largely because the production and export of aluminium and coal were seen as a counter to the decline of traditional manufacturing sectors. Transnational companies in the late 1970s became adept at bargaining for high subsidies, especially on energy costs, from state governments competing to demonstrate to their electorates that they were attracting economic growth. Alumina smelters were to be built in the Hunter Valley in New South Wales and at Portland in Victoria. For such major developments, state premiers negotiated directly with the overseas firms, promising rapid expansion in electricity generation and transport facilities, as well as concessions on land and water costs (Wilkes, 1980; Larcombe, 1980). Obviously these massive investments required a redirection of public funds from other items, so the implications are for greatly reduced expenditure on metropolitan services. In the New South Wales case, it has been argued that Sydney's urban consolidation policy is a direct outcome of resource development promotion: it is a way of reducing the infrastructural costs of urban expansion (Sandercock, 1982). Further, as aluminium and coal prices fall, the financial difficulties of the states worsen. They are left with costly ongoing capital works programmes for industrial projects which have been severely cut back or abandoned altogether.

## Conclusions

In the preceding discussion, I traced the evolution of planning in two Australian states and identified some important contrasts in the planning structures and policies of the two states. In New South Wales the institutional framework for planning has been subject to more frequent and fundamental change. The system has moved consistently to greater centralization and to higher levels of coordination in policy implementation. Victoria's organizational framework for planning has changed less frequently and in a more incremental manner, but the duality of metropolitan and state agencies survives. Its efforts at coordinated policy implementation have been circuitous and relatively ineffective. In terms of metropolitan policy, for Sydney there has been a greater emphasis on equity objectives, on state intervention in the land market, and, more recently, on overcoming specific local obstacles to policy implementation; whereas for Melbourne, planners have been more inclined to emphasize efficiency objectives, being less interventionist and less direct in their approach to implementation. Non-metropolitan policies have received more attention and have been developed more sensitively in Victoria.

These differences appear to reflect varied ideologies of planning, which do not relate simply to the political philosophy of governments in the respective states. Since World War II, New South Wales has had longer periods of Labor office, which might be expected to correlate with the emphasis on equity objectives and public intervention in the land market. But both states had Labor governments when the first metropolitan plans were produced, yet it was New South Wales that stressed equity and Victoria that focused on efficiency. And it was a conservative government that initiated the large-scale land acquisition and development function of the New South Wales State Planning Authority.

Certainly there have been contrasting administrative styles. By its readiness to adopt centralized organizational forms and to restructure local government, the New South Wales bureaucracy has taken a more pronounced managerial stance, but one in which political skills were exercised openly. On the other hand, the Victorian planning administration has clung to an apolitical and decentralized view.

In the longer term the economic variable is growing in significance. During the boom of the 1950s and 1960s the planning systems diverged, with bureaucratic idiosyncracies developing to a major extent. But the current recession is encouraging convergence. The two systems are moving closer together; for example, in their concern to prevent planning controls hampering development and in the large subsidies offered for the industrial projects of transnational companies. Although past experience suggests that considerable variation is possible, in the future it is likely that the common external influence stemming from the global restructuring of capital will force the two planning systems into the same mould.

## REFERENCES

Alexander, I. (1979) *Office Location and Public Policy*. Harlow: Longman.

Alexander, I. (1981) Post-war metropolitan planning: goals and realities, in Troy, P. (ed.) *Equity in the City*. Sydney: George Allen and Unwin, pp. 145–71.

Bains, M., Chambers, P., Power, J. and Fagan, J. (1979) *Final Report of the Board of Review of the Role, Structure and Administration of Local Government in Victoria*. Melbourne: Victorian Government Printer.

Bains, M. and Miles, N. (1981) New South Wales, in Power, J., Wettenhall, R. and Halligan, J. (eds.) *Local Government Systems of Australia*. Canberra: Australian Government Publishing Service, pp. 123–228.

Bedford, E. (1981) A Programme for Urban Consolidation. Paper presented to the Local Government Association Conference, Sydney, 26 October.

Bland, H. (1974) *Second Report of the Board of Inquiry into the Victorian Public Service*. Melbourne: Victorian Government Printer.

Boss, A. (1982) Rural Land Use Planning. Paper presented to the Department of Agriculture Land Use Planning Workshop, Wagga Wagga, 26 October.

Bowman, M. (1979) *Australian Approaches to Environmental Management*. Tasmania: Environmental Law Reform Group, University of Tasmania.

Bowman, M. (1981) Victoria, in Power, J., Wettenhall, R. and Halligan, J. (eds.) *Local Government Systems of Australia*. Canberra: Australian Government Publishing Service, pp. 229–372.

Cardew, R. (1982) Comparative costs of urban consolidation – inner and outer, in Sandercock, L. (ed.) *Urban Consolidation: The Equity Issue*. North Ryde: Centre for Environmental Studies, Macquarie University, pp. 64–80.

CCC (1948) *Report on the Planning Scheme*. Sydney: New South Wales Government Printer.

De Monchaux, J. (1982) Urban consolidation and residential development, in Archer, R. (ed.) *Planning for Urban Consolidation*. Sydney: Planning Research Centre, University of Sydney, pp. 47–64.

DoEP (1981) *Rural Land Evaluation Manual*. Sydney: Department of Environment and Planning.

EPAA (1979) Environmental Planning and Assessment Act *The Statutes of New South Wales* volume 2, number 203. Sydney: New South Wales Government Printer.

Faubel, M. (1981) Implementation of Statements of Planning Policy in Victoria. Master of Town and Regional Planning thesis, School of Environmental Planning, University of Melbourne.

Harrison, P. (1972) Planning the metropolis – a case study, in Parker, R. and Troy, P. (eds.) *The Politics of Urban Growth*. Canberra: Australian National University Press, pp. 61–99.

Harrison, P. (1978) City planning, in Scott, P. (ed.) *Australian Cities and Public Policy*. Melbourne: Georgian House, pp. 141–73.

Holmes, J. (1978) Victoria II, in Ryan, P. (ed.) *Urban Management Processes*. Canberra: Australian Government Publishing Service, pp. 110–18.

Larcombe, G. (1980) The political economy of Newcastle, in Stilwell, F. (ed.) *Economic Crisis, Cities and Regions*. Oxford: Pergamon Press, pp. 146–62.

Lennie, O. (1978). Rural subdivision: an exploration of the issues involved and the planning response of the Town and Country Planning Board. *Reports—Urban Research Programme I*, semester 2, volume I. Parkville: Department of Town and Regional Planning, University of Melbourne.

LGAA (1954) Local Government (Town and Country Planning) Amendment Act *The Statutes of New South Wales*, number 21. Sydney: New South Wales Government Printer.

Linge, G. and McKay, J. (1981) *Structural Change in Australia*. Canberra: Department of Geography, Australian National University.

Logan, M., Maher, C., McKay, J., and Humphreys, J. (1975) *Urban and Regional Australia*. Melbourne: Sorrett.

Logan, T. (1979) Recent directions of regional policy in Australia. *Regional Studies*, **13**, pp. 153–60.

Logan, T. (1981) *Urban and Regional Planning in Victoria*. Melbourne: Shillington House.

Logan, T. and Ogilvy, E. (1981) The statutory planning framework, in Troy, P. (ed.) *Equity in the City*. Sydney: George Allen and Unwin, pp. 172–94.

McKay, J. and Whitelaw, J. (1977). The role of large private and government organisations in generating flows of interregional migrants: the case of Australia. *Economic Geography*, **53**, pp. 28–44.

MMBW (1954) *Melbourne Metropolitan Planning Scheme Report*. Melbourne: Melbourne Metropolitan Board of Works.

MMBW (1967) *The Future Growth of Melbourne*. Melbourne: Melbourne Metropolitan Board of Works.

MMBW (1971) *Planning Policies for the Melbourne Metropolitan Region*. Melbourne: Melbourne Metropolitan Board of Works.

MMBW (1979a) *Alternative Strategies for Metropolitan Melbourne*. Melbourne: Melbourne Metropolitan Board of Works.

MMBW (1979b) *The Challenge of Change*. Melbourne: Melbourne Metropolitan Board of Works.

MMBW (1981a) *Melbourne Metropolitan Planning Scheme Amendment 150*. Melbourne: Melbourne Metropolitan Board of Works.

MMBW (1981b) *Metropolitan Strategy Implementation*. Melbourne: Melbourne Metropolitan Board of Works.

MTC (1969) *Melbourne Transportation Study Volume 3—The Transportation Plan*. Melbourne: Metropolitan Transportation Committee.

Neilson, L. (1980) *The Possible Future Structure and Administration of Geelong, Ballarat, Bendigo*. Melbourne: Victorian Government Printer.

Nicholls, M. (1979) Containment of Melbourne: towards a rational system of 'preferred densification areas'. *Reports—Urban Research Programme I*, semester 2, volume 2. Parkville: Department of Town and Regional Planning, University of Melbourne.

NSWSPA (1968) *Sydney Region Outline Plan*. Sydney: Department of Environment and Planning, New South Wales State Planning Authority.

Orchard, L. (1982) Has the homework been done?, in Sandercock, L. (ed.) *Urban Consolidation: The Equity Issue*. North Ryde: Centre for Environmental and Urban Studies, Marquarie University.

PABA (1980) Planning Appeals Board Act *State of Victoria: The Acts of Parliament*, number 9512, second session. Melbourne: Victorian Government Printer.

Paterson, J. (1980) Sydney's Great Experiment goes into Mass Production. Paper presented at the 16th Biennial Conference of the Royal Australian Planning Institute, Canberra, 21 May.

Paterson, J., Yencken, D. and Gunn, G. (1976) *A Mansion or No House*. Melbourne: Hawthorn Press.

Pollock, D. (1976) Rural Subdivision in Victoria. Research Report, School of Environmental Planning, University of Melbourne.

Reid, H. (1982) Local government regulation of housing development, in Archer, R. (ed.) *Planning for Urban Consolidation*. Sydney: Planning Research Centre, University of Sydney, pp. 37–46.

Roddewig, R. (1978) *Green Bans: The Birth of Australian Environmental Politics*. Sydney: Hale and Iremonger.

Roseth J. (1982) Urban consolidation possibilities in Sydney, in Archer, R. (ed.) *Planning for Urban Consolidation*. Sydney: Planning Research Centre, University of Sydney.

Sandercock, L. (1975a) *Cities for Sale*. Parkville: Melbourne University Press.

Sandercock, L. (1975b) *Public Participation in Planning*. Adelaide: South Australian Government Printer.

Sandercock, L. (1982) Planning in NSW. Urban Development on the Cheap. Paper presented at the Local Government Planners' Association Conference, Sydney, 3 November.

Sandercock, L. (1983) Urban studies in Australia: producing planners or educating urbanists?, in Murray-Smith, S. (ed.) *Melbourne Studies in Education 1982* Parkville: Melbourne University Press, pp. 1–34.

SATS (1974) *Report Volumes I–IV* Sydney Area Transportation Study. Sydney: Department of Transport.

Shields, J. and Morris, W. (1978) *Rural Land Mapping*. Melbourne: Town and Country Planning Board, Ministry for Planning and Environment.

Stilwell, F. (1980) *Economic Crisis, Cities and Regions*. Oxford: Pergamon Press.

Stretton, H. (1970) *Ideas for Australian Cities*. Melbourne: Georgian House.

TPCA (1944) Town and Country Planning Act *State of Victoria: The Acts of Parliament*, number 5043, second session. Melbourne: Victorian Government Printer.

TCPA (1961) Town and Country Planning Act *State of Victoria: The Acts of Parliament*, number 6849, first session. Melbourne: Victorian Government Printer.

TCPAA (1968) Town and Country Planning (Amendment) Act *State of Victoria: The Acts of Parliament*, number 7676, first session. Melbourne: Victorian Government Printer.

TCPB (1978) *Design and Siting Guidelines*. Melbourne: Town and Country Planning Board, Ministry for Planning and Environment.

TCPGAA (1979) Town and Country Planning (General Amendment) Act *State of Victoria: The Acts of Parliament*, number 9364, first session. Melbourne: Victorian Government Printer.

VPD (1944) *Victorian Parliamentary Debates*, number 217. Melbourne: Victorian Government Printer.

Wagner, C. (1975) *Rural Retreats: Urban Investment in Rural Land for Residential Purposes*. Canberra: Australian Government Publishing Service.

Wilenski, P. (1978) New South Wales, in Ryan, P. (ed.) *Urban Management Processes*. Canberra: Australian Government Publishing Service, pp. 74–85.

Wilkes, F. (1980) Alcoa smelter at Portland – the opposition viewpoint. Copy available from the Australian Labor Party, Carlton, Victoria.

Wilmoth, D. (1982) Urban consolidation policy and social equity, in Sandercock, L. (ed.) *Urban Consolidation: The Equity Issue*. North Ryde: Centre for Environmental and Urban Studies, Macquarie University.

Wyatt, R. (1982) Four lessons from the inner-city controversy: Melbourne, Australia: *Ekistics*, **297**, pp. 424–28.

*Chapter 4*

# Urban Consolidation and Australian Cities

RAYMOND BUNKER

In terms of population densities, Australian cities are closer to the North American model than the European. The 1981 census provided data about the residential densities of the capital cities. The urban areas involved are continuous built-up areas within the census definitions and criteria. The areas to which population densities relate are those of broad residential land use. These make the figures comparable between cities. For Sydney they were 3,160 persons per square kilometre, Melbourne 2,537, Brisbane 2,186, Adelaide 2,178 and Perth 1,702 (Forster, 1984, p. 1).

The continuing sprawl of Australia's largest cities is seen generally to have some undesirable features and efforts have been made in recent years to contain and consolidate them. While this concern reflects the changing circumstances of the late 1970s and early 1980s, the issue of low residential densities has been around for a long time: it is these altered conditions that have thrust it to the fore again. This was well put in the title of a recent paper by John Paterson – 'Urban Consolidation: Lovelier the Second Time Round?' (Paterson, 1980).

## Change in Australian Cities since 1971

For much of the post-war period, Australia's cities grew rapidly. In the 1950s, 1960s and the early 1970s, national growth was associated with high levels of immigration, a protracted baby boom (Australian Bureau of Statistics, 1982), the development of manufacturing and service industries, large imports of capital and very low levels of unemployment. Australia was relatively prosperous, although rates of economic growth were, in fact, moderate. Urban planning efforts were directed at organizing suburban development so that services, infrastructure, residential population and jobs grew in a reasonably coordinated and supportive manner. An example of this kind of approach is the Sydney Region Outline Plan of 1968 (State Planning Authority, NSW, 1968). Such plans reflected high levels of home- and car-ownership, the predilection of most Australians for a detached cottage, the needs of the traditional nuclear family, and the expansion of manufacturing industry – particularly in Sydney, Melbourne and Adelaide. These conditions are reflected in the data for 1971 appearing in the tables in this chapter.

In the last fifteen years, these comfortable conditions have changed. Demographic changes have seen a lower birthrate, a smaller family size and an ageing population. Social trends have included a change in the pattern of household formation, with increasing numbers of single- and two-person households. These changing characteristics are reflected in the fall of occupancy rates for dwellings. Economic trends have seen the onset of recession if not depression, a rise in interest rates, increasing cost of shelter, a fall in the proportion of the workforce engaged in manufacturing industry, the state in fiscal crisis, and high unemployment rates – particularly in areas where the deindustrialization process has been concentrated. These trends are represented in the 1981 census figures in the tables. Most of these trends have continued, and some have become accentuated, since 1981.

Tables 1 to 3 represent some of these changing characteristics in Sydney, Melbourne and Adelaide. Table 1 shows the change in family types, and table 2 the kinds of dwellings available to house these families. Two-thirds of these dwellings are detached cottages in Sydney, but the proportion is three-quarters in the lower-density cities of Melbourne and Adelaide. Table 3 shows that the average occupancy rate of dwellings had dropped to below three in all three cities by 1981.

Accompanying these secular trends was a redistribution of the populations of the cities. These movements are illustrated in table 4, which shows the decline of residential population in inner and middle suburban locations with continued growth at the fringe. In the table, Sydney and Melbourne are divided into core, inner, middle, outer and fringe areas, while the smaller city of Adelaide is separated into three parts (see figures 1, 2 and 3 respectively). These subregions represent areas developed at roughly the same time giving areas of roughly similar demographic, land-use and built form characteristics. The basis of differentiation is described elsewhere (Bunker, 1983, pp. 4–5, 112–14).

The dynamics of change in the cities depicted here concern residential populations. Other processes of this kind include the gentrification of some of the inner suburbs (Badcock and Cloher, 1981), and higher rises in dwelling prices in inner suburbs compared with locations further out (Bunker, 1983, pp. 78, 87, 97; Stimson, 1982, p. 137). A good account of

Table 1.   Family types, Sydney, Melbourne and Adelaide, 1976 and 1981.

| Family Type | Sydney 1976 | Sydney 1981 | Melbourne 1976 | Melbourne 1981 | Adelaide 1976 | Adelaide 1981 |
|---|---|---|---|---|---|---|
| | | | *percentage of families* | | | |
| Head only | 22.4 | 25.7 | 20.3 | 23.9 | 19.8 | 23.6 |
| Head and dependants* | 3.7 | 5.1 | 3.3 | 4.6 | 3.7 | 5.4 |
| Head and spouse only | 21.9 | 20.9 | 21.6 | 21.1 | 23.8 | 23.8 |
| Head, spouse and dependants* | 26.5 | 26.6 | 28.6 | 29.0 | 27.3 | 26.4 |
| Head, other adults | 5.4 | 5.3 | 4.9 | 4.7 | 4.5 | 4.5 |
| Head, other adults and dependants* | 1.4 | 1.3 | 1.3 | 1.3 | 1.4 | 1.4 |
| Head, spouse and other adults | 9.5 | 8.0 | 9.7 | 7.7 | 9.5 | 8.2 |
| Head, spouse, other adults and dependants* | 9.1 | 7.1 | 10.3 | 7.8 | 9.9 | 6.9 |
| | 100% | 100% | 100% | 100% | 100% | 100% |

* 'children' in 1976
*Source:* Bunker, 1983, p. 65.

Table 2.   Kinds of occupied dwellings, Sydney, Melbourne and Adelaide, 1971 and 1981.

| Type of Structure | Sydney 1971 | Sydney 1981 | Melbourne 1971 | Melbourne 1981 | Adelaide 1971 | Adelaide 1981 |
|---|---|---|---|---|---|---|
| | | | *percentage of occupied dwellings* | | | |
| Separate house | 66.6 | 66.4 | 73.4 | 75.4 | 76.5 | 76.1 |
| Attached dwelling } | 32.9 | 27.2 | 26.5 | 21.6 | 23.3 | 22.5 |
| Flats of three storeys + } | | 4.5 | | 1.5 | | 0.3 |
| Caravan/houseboat | 0.2 | 0.1 | 0.1 | 0.1 | 0.2 | — |
| Improvised | 0.2 | — | 0.1 | — | — | — |
| Not stated | — | 1.8 | — | 1.5 | — | 1.0 |

*Source:* Bunker, 1983, p. 68.

Table 3.   Occupancy rate of private dwellings, Sydney, Melbourne and Adelaide, 1971, 1976 and 1981.

| | Sydney 1971 | Sydney 1976 | Sydney 1981 | Melbourne 1971 | Melbourne 1976 | Melbourne 1981 | Adelaide 1971 | Adelaide 1976 | Adelaide 1981 |
|---|---|---|---|---|---|---|---|---|---|
| Average number of people per occupied private dwelling | 3.19 | 3.01 | 2.92 | 3.31 | 3.11 | 2.97 | 3.24 | 3.01 | 2.82 |

*Source:* Bunker, 1983, p. 64.

Table 4.   Population changes in the different parts of Sydney, Melbourne and Adelaide, 1971–76 and 1976–81.

| | Core | Inner | Middle | Outer | Fringe |
|---|---|---|---|---|---|
| | *Percentage Change on Base Population* | | | | |
| **Sydney** | | | | | |
| 1971–76 | –9.6 | –2.7 | 3.1 | 4.0 | 25.1 |
| 1976–81 | –3.1 | –1.3 | –1.3 | 6.0 | 28.5 |
| **Melbourne** | | | | | |
| 1971–76 | –16.2 | –11.0 | –6.3 | 16.8 | 40.7 |
| 1976–81 | –5.2 | –3.6 | –3.8 | 7.4 | 29.2 |
| **Adelaide** | | | | | |
| 1971–76 | –4.0 | | –2.0 | 35.6 | |
| 1976–81 | –7.5 | | –2.6 | 19.1 | |

*Source:* Bunker, 1983, pp. 70, 79, 89.

Figure 1.
Classification of
neighbourhoods in
Sydney.

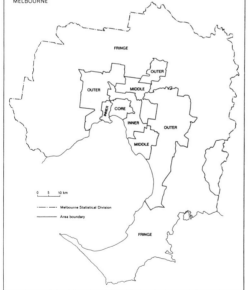

Figure 2.    Classification of neighbourhoods
in Melbourne.

Figure 3.    Classification of
neighbourhoods in Adelaide.

other kinds of change in the cities concerning information handling, office
location and operation, industry, wholesaling, retailing and transport is
contained in a recent study of Sydney (Cardew *et al.*, 1982).

## Recent Imperatives for Consolidation

These secular and fundamental changes to Australian cities caused most central authorities to re-examine the assumptions and processes they had developed to plan and manage the capital cities where most of Australia's people live. In particular, it led to new arguments for containment and consolidation of urban spread. These arguments tended to fall into three categories.

The first of these arose from the rise in liquid fuel prices brought about by OPEC countries. These price increases, and fears of fuel shortage, led to the contention that a more compact city form, minimization of travel by car and intensification of use of land would be an appropriate response (Jay, 1978). In the event, Australia's own oil production has helped the rise in real cost of oil to be contained to moderate proportions; the recession has slowed down the rate of growth of trip-making by car; and adjustments other than to land use have been made in response to rising oil prices such as the use of more fuel-efficient cars and more judicious trip-making (Travers Morgan, 1980). More recently, of course, recent falls in oil prices have further diminished and delayed this argument. The increasing attraction of inner and middle suburbs for living, as shown in the pattern of property price increases in recent years, reflects both a recognition that their locational advantages had been undervalued previously and increased interest in Victorian and early twentieth-century housing stock. Perceptions about future oil shortages and higher prices may have also played a part in this.

The second reason for increasing interest in urban consolidation is the need for efficiency in spending of scarce capital funds on urban infrastructure by state governments. Physical and social infrastructure has sometimes been developed for significantly larger populations than those living in inner and some middle suburbs. In Adelaide, for example, funds had been directed to the rebuilding of inner-area schools and the enlargement of their grounds in the 1970s (Bunker and Orchard, 1982). A few years later enrolments in these schools had dropped substantially, while expensive new schools were still being built in outer areas. By encouraging urban consolidation, it was argued, some of this spare capacity could be utilized, and outer suburban growth slowed.

Again, this contention is disarmingly simplistic. In many cases facilities, services and standards in the inner and middle suburbs are inferior to those now being provided in new residential areas. Much of the physical infrastructure requires major renovation and upgrading. Any increase in residential population could require substantial expenditure and use of land for schools, open space, health and welfare services, and transport. Given the strong case made for saving public costs in urban development by consolidation, it is surprising that so little work has been done to identify the nature of these supposed savings. Little consideration has been given, either, to the running costs of public services after the facilities have been established or upgraded.

A third reason for renewed interest in urban consolidation is some mismatch between the needs of households for shelter and the dwelling stock. The latter is fixed in the short term. High interest rates, strict residential development standards and zoning practices have helped to keep the cost of housing high and restrict the range of choice for housing (Paterson *et al.*, 1976; DEP, 1982). There has been an increasing demand for rental accommodation, whether provided by the public or private sector. There is more need for aged persons' accommodation and the increasing numbers of one- or two-person households could justify the building of more multi-unit dwellings. It was these considerations that led a study of urban consolidation potential in Adelaide to conclude 'that the building of smaller and more densely arranged dwellings, a high proportion of them for public and private rental, in the inner and middle suburbs of metropolitan Adelaide (should) be accelerated over the next decade' (Bunker and Orchard, 1982, p. 67).

## Policy Responses: New South Wales

State governments responded to these issues in different ways and with varying emphases. Urban consolidation has been most vigorously pursued in New South Wales. In the late 1970s, the rate of population growth in Sydney increased. At the same time, in a period of deepening recession, the Fraser government in Canberra wound down many of the urban support programmes developed by the previous Whitlam government. Considerable capital was committed by the state government in New South Wales to the development of coal mines, railways, power stations, ports, coal loaders and other infrastructure to promote the so-called resources boom. By these actions it was hoped to promote coal exports and attract industries, such as aluminium smelting, to sources of relatively cheap power. A fiscal crisis became apparent when the demands for urban infrastructure, and rising expectations of people for adequate social and physical services, conflicted with the need for the capitalist state to provide the necessary conditions for the accumulation and reproduction of capital (Sandercock, 1984, p. 31). In this climate some alarming estimates of the capital costs of providing infrastructure for fringe metropolitan development were generated. It was estimated in early 1980s that the equivalent of A\$13,500 was needed to provide each new household with seven types of public enterprise – schools, technical and further education, child care, community health, hospitals, main roads and water sewerage and drainage. In addition local government services were estimated to cost well over A\$5,000 for each household (Wilmoth, 1982, p. 31). A Housing Balance

Sheet was developed to estimate the demand for housing in Sydney over the next five years. To meet this demand, the government identified a number of instruments it could use, including an Urban Consolidation Program, Urban Development Program and the provision of public housing through the Housing Commission (Reed and Wilmoth, 1983). Some extravagant expectations resulted as to the contribution that could be provided to satisfy housing demand by urban consolidation.

## Policy Responses: Victoria

Victoria was subject to similar pressures and considerations. But much more importance was accorded to the need to develop a more effective housing policy and to increase the diversity of housing types 'at a time when households are becoming more diverse in their housing needs' (Melbourne and Metropolitan Board of Works, 1980, p. 35). A Green Paper on Housing in Victoria (Ministry of Housing, 1980) criticized the opposition of local councils to new forms of development, asked for a reduction in local council discretion in density control, and supported the proposals of the metropolitan planning authority to nominate and strengthen a number of major suburban commercial centres. It is intended to increase housing densities around these centres in the processes of redevelopment, rehabilitation and infill.

Some criteria or guidelines have been established to see how local development schemes relate to these metropolitan housing objectives – hence the importance of 'overall density mix objectives', 'area-wide density control techniques', and 'site density controls' in local development schemes or plans (Melbourne and Metropolitan Board of Works, 1982a). Many local councils are examining their schemes to establish the scope for rezoning and introducing height/density controls of a kind to permit intensification of built form. At the same time the metropolitan planning authority issued a series of papers about Melbourne's development, including statements about what it called the basic structural alternative: increasing spread versus more containment. It concluded that it is necessary to 'facilitate increased residential densities adjacent to centres of commercial and community activity, to parkland and to Port Philip Bay and within . . . areas of high transport accessibility' (Melbourne and Metropolitan Board of Works, 1981, p. 12). A section on public utilities pointed to the heavy infrastructure costs included in servicing low suburban densities and falling population in some established areas.

## Policy Responses: South Australia

South Australian development has been given the name of 'conscious purpose' since the original Wakefield principles of systematic colonization

Figures 4 and 5.    Examples of redevelopment for medium-density housing in Adelaide. The two premises in the photographs are side by side and show the character of the original development compared with the town houses which have replaced it.

were employed in its settlement. Adelaide is a pleasant city. Its recent development has been guided by the Metropolitan Development Plan of 1962 which had suggested that encouraging flats and row (or terrace) house development, together with a reduction in allotment sizes and street widths in developing areas would lead to a more compact metropolitan area (Town Planning Committee of South Australia, 1962). It also commented presciently that 'As the metropolitan area expands, more varied residential buildings will be erected, and the various regulations governing the size, bulk and space around residential buildings may have to be revised' (Town Planning Committee of South Australia, 1962, p. 228).

In 1978 the state government decided that this time had come and that there was a 'need to offer a real alternative to the continued expansion of the fringe areas of Adelaide' (Department of Housing, Urban and Regional Affairs, SA, 1978). The metropolitan planning authority began actively to discourage the practice of 'down-zoning' by local councils. Down-zoning is the process by which residential zones which permitted medium-density housing of various types as of right provided certain standards were observed, were changed to R1 which only allowed detached cottages on separate allotments as of right. This gave more stringent control over medium-density residential development proposals. Adelaide citizens have been sensitive and concerned about the quality of their spacious and pleasant urban environment.

Ironically, more has been achieved in the field of urban consolidation by the South Australian Housing Trust, the public housing authority. About 9 per cent of the total dwelling stock in Adelaide is owned by the Trust. This proportion is higher than in other metropolitan areas. In the middle and late 1970s, the Trust abandoned its policy of building large satellite estates and new towns far out from Adelaide, as at Elizabeth. It bought small areas of land in the city, inner and middle suburbs and built medium-density homes on them. It began a scheme of acquisition of old dwellings in inner and middle suburbs and their restoration and rehabilitation. Significantly, it began the construction of increasing numbers of dwellings for aged people in medium-density attached single-storey units.

## Policy Actions

The actions taken by state governments to promote urban consolidation in the late 1970s and early 1980s fell into two categories. The first was concerned with attempts to increase the density of built form and encourage multi-unit dwelling construction. This was achieved by stopping down-zoning, by seeking to increase the areas where medium- and high-density development and redevelopment could take place, and by trying to relax local planning standards and provisions which inhibited or limited the building of multi-unit dwellings. Such measures included 'dual occupancy' provisions by which additional dwellings could be added to the detached cottage or its curtilage. This could take a variety of forms including the conversion, adaptation or extension of existing dwellings, or the building of an additional dwelling as exemplified and popularized in the 'granny flat' (Melbourne and Metropolitan Board of Works, 1982*b*). Other proposals included a move in New South Wales to allow medium-density housing up to two storeys in height in all residential zones subject to certain standards regarding landscaping, floor area and private open space being satisfied.

These kinds of measures imposed considerable pressure on local councils by metropolitan or state planning authorities. Ideologically, they were part of the 'deregulation' thrust of the early 1980s: the freeing of the market so that the pent-up demand for medium-density housing could take place. Many councils had suffered from insensitive and badly guided multi-unit dwelling development in the late 1960s and early 1970s and fiercely resisted these kinds of proposals. It also became apparent that other factors were involved in the diminution in the numbers of new multi-unit dwellings constructed since then. As one authoritative study put it:

> Any attempt to draw a causal relationship between costs imposed by local governments and the level of commencements is clouded by other significant changes in the entire climate of the housing market. Demographic changes, increased interest rates, periods of tight finance availability, and a decline in the expectation of making substantial capital gains have meant that the production of multi-unit dwellings for large-scale investors has become uneconomic and has virtually ceased (Indicative Planning Council for the Housing Industry, 1980, p. 47).

The second kind of action taken to further urban consolidation was to use public housing authorities in programmes of infill, purchase and rehabilitation of existing dwellings, conversion of cottages to dual occupancy etc., particularly in inner and middle suburbs. As an extension of this, vacant or under-utilized land owned by government authorities was made available for residential development where this was suitable. Usually first refusal for such land was given to the public housing authority, but sometimes land was sold to private enterprise for housing. These kinds of actions, though more limited in scope than those in the first category which were intended to influence the total residential development process over the whole urban area, did demonstrate that residential population could be increased much more effectively by infill housing or the conversion of non-residential buildings to residential use than by redeveloping existing housing stock to medium-density configurations. In Sydney, Melbourne and Adelaide, processes have been established to sell off or lease land surplus to government requirements but again, a number of other factors often inhibit the apparent potential of such land for housing such as poor location, unattractive surroundings, difficult site conditions or the need to use land for public purposes such as open space and community uses.

With a degree of deindustrialization affecting some kinds of manufacturing industry, industrial premises and areas have occasionally become redundant or no longer represent the highest and best use of land. Some rezoning of these areas and their rehabilitation or redevelopment for residential purposes has taken place.

## The Methodologies attending Urban Consolidation

Studies of urban consolidation have been carried out at three levels in Australia. They comprise a review of consolidation policies and issues in Sydney, Melbourne and Adelaide (Bunker, 1983); a study of the potential for urban consolidation in Adelaide and the measures needed to achieve different degrees of consolidation (Bunker and Orchard, 1982); and research to identify the characteristics and dimensions of housing development in Hindmarsh, an inner suburb of Adelaide, following a decision to abandon a transport corridor reservation (Infodec, 1984). These studies involved an assessment of and interweaving of metropolitan-wide and local considerations attending urban consolidation.

The first outcome of this research was the obvious need for a balanced metropolitan policy of development, including urban consolidation and fringe expansion with due consideration to the efficiency and equity aspects of both. In particular, the research showed that the urban consolidation focus on inner and middle suburbs could inflate land values and overtax existing facilities, thereby making access more difficult to low-income earners. It is also unlikely that extensive redevelopment with multi-unit dwellings will lower the cost of housing (Cardew, 1982). Further, it can be demonstrated that a reasonable range of housing types and densities needs to be provided in outer and fringe locations. Ironically, more scope exists to do this in the planning and progressive development of these newer areas than existing suburbs. Substantial investment, both in land and infrastructure, has already been made in many fringe areas and a high rate of development to recoup this is desirable where this has occurred. One researcher concludes that Sydney's inner suburbs are already largely developed for medium-density housing and that there is little capacity for denser residential development (Archer, 1980, p. 9).

To develop, implement, monitor and adjust policies about the distribution of residential population, housing types and densities, an effective information system is needed. It needs to be paralleled by and interwoven with a decision-making system about urban development. These structures would ensure the blending of information concerning trends and policy imperatives in the planning process in the style suggested by Breheny and Roberts (1978, 1980) and Bracken (1982). A range of forecasts could be generated regarding population characteristics. It would include a 'projection' or best estimate of trends under existing policy influences. It would also show alternative 'predictions' of population distribution given the injection of policy thrusts and actions to encourage urban consolidation. The characteristics of such a mixed information and decision-making system are discussed elsewhere (Bunker, 1983, pp. 46–47). The outputs are linked and integrated estimates of future population, dwellings and land development needs for sub-areas of the metropolitan region for varying time periods.

In generating these different predictions and evaluating their public cost, it is necessary to prepare expenditure estimates for parts of the existing urban area and its fringes. Ideally, these calculations should include spending on both physical and social infrastructure and services. Importantly, they should include estimates of the costs of running and operating these public services as well as establishing them. For example, fringe development could take much of the expansion of metropolitan community and social services to the detriment of needs based assessments of what is required in inner areas (Sandercock, 1984, p. 34).

In Australia, these information and policy-generating systems are unevenly developed. In Adelaide, there is a very effective forecasting system with annual revisions of forecasts of population distribution, dwelling demand and distribution of service lots. It takes account of demolition of dwellings, vacancy rates, occupancy rates, migration, land availability, household headship rates by age-sex groups etc. (Bell, 1983). But apart from a brief attempt in the late 1970s to illustrate and examine more compact and less compact forms of metropolitan development, the forecasts have taken the form of a best-estimate trend projection. There is little examination of different assumptions regarding, for example, the scale and location of public housing construction or the timing and magnitude of releases of major areas for development. On the other hand, Sydney has provided examples of prescriptive and arbitrary policy pronouncements without adequate information about their feasibility. The New South Wales government set an overall target of 12,000 new medium-density dwellings per year in Sydney for the next five years in 1982, to promote urban consolidation. This represented between three-eighths and one-half of the total new dwellings needed each year. This total was apportioned among local government areas as targets to be achieved. Some of these targets were reasonable, but others were rather uninformed as to the potential for medium-density housing in council areas, land and building costs etc.

An illustration of how a forecasting system of the kind outlined might work in the construction, monitoring and modification of urban development policy is contained in the recent study on urban consolidation in Adelaide (Bunker and Orchard, 1982). In that exercise four predictions were constructed to represent different degrees of urban consolidation over the decade 1981–91 and compared with the best-estimate trend forecast provided by the state government's excellent population forecasting and land monitoring unit. The predictions involved the inner and middle suburbs of Adelaide where it was estimated 16,900 allotments represented the potential for future residential development. Two rates of take-up of this land over the decade were assumed – 60 per cent and 80 per cent of that capacity respectively. Based on past trends and likely future conditions, it was assumed that 80 per cent of these lots would be developed for detached cottages and 20 per cent for multi-unit dwellings. With an average of four units each for such medium-density developments, this gives an even division between detached and attached dwellings. Two different rates of dwelling demolition were calculated at 400 or 800 per year, reflecting the probable limits of activity in times of high or low redevelopment activity. Based on survey information, it was further assumed that one-third of all sites where dwellings had been demolished would be used for multi-unit dwellings, the rest being used for non-residential purposes such as road widening, commercial and industrial use, and open space. The occupancy rate of the single detached dwellings completed was assumed to be 2.8 persons per dwelling and that for multi-unit dwellings 2 persons. This gives four sets of figures varying as to the rates of take-up of land available for residential development and of redevelopment for multi-unit dwellings. Table 5 shows the results of these assumptions.

Table 5. Projection and predictions of population and dwelling stock in inner and middle suburbs of Adelaide, 1991.

|  | Dwelling stock | Population |
| --- | --- | --- |
| Best estimate projection | 250,400 | 593,600 |
| Prediction 1 | 253,450 | 599,200 |
| Prediction 2 | 254,800 | 600,400 |
| Prediction 3 | 258,850 | 612,150 |
| Prediction 4 | 260,200 | 613,350 |

Source: Bunker and Orchard, 1982, p. 57.

The projection of population total shown in table 5 is a best-estimate assuming there are no policy inputs to stimulate urban consolidation. The predictions assume policy initiatives to encourage urban consolidation, particularly in accelerating the rate of development of vacant land. The best-estimate projection is used as a yardstick in the manner used in structure planning in Gloucestershire (Breheny and Roberts, 1980). As the 1981 population of the area covered in table 5 was almost 602,000, it will be seen that the more optimistic predictions of the effect of consolidation policies need to be achieved merely to retain existing levels of population.

An important methodological point emerges here. The planning process frequently generates alternative futures, selects one, or a combination of those originally formulated, and then implements that chosen strategy. In the case of the Adelaide study it was pointed out that a large number of influences affect the distribution of population in the metropolitan area. Only some of these are under the control of government: rating systems for land, charging policies for the connection of water supply and sewerage and their operation, transport pricing, zoning, residential development standards etc. (Department of Housing and Urban Development, US, 1980). Of these, some are exercised in a way that is at best neutral in their contribution to urban consolidation and some are quite unhelpful. The Adelaide study resisted the conclusion that urban consolidation was so important an objective in metropolitan development that the state government would coordinate and align policy influences of all kinds to ensure this. Instead it assumed that the government would make some attempts to encourage consolidation and that the impact of these initiatives could be monitored and related to the predictions established in the study, which in turn were generated within explicit statements of the capacity of the urban mosaic to absorb consolidation. If the state government desired a higher rate or degree of consolidation it could pull more of its policy levers to achieve that. This approach has the advantage that it recognizes the lack of understanding surrounding the impact of each policy instrument in achieving consolidation, and that even more uncertainty surrounds their combined effect. These impacts are also likely to change over time. The planning process thus becomes one of the selection of desirable population targets; adjustment of policy measures to influence consolidation as appropriate; adjustment of the desired outcome as events unfold and side-effects emerge. This approach has something of a black-box flavour about it in that causes and effects in terms of population distribution are not precisely quantified and articulated. But given the large number of influences on population distribution and densities, and the fact that some of the most important are not under the control of government, then this approach can be defended. It places reasonable bounds around alternative futures in terms of population distribution and develops information-providing and policy-adjustment processes to achieve one of those states.

At the local scale, a detailed study relevant to urban consolidation was carried out in Adelaide in early 1984. Following a decision by the state government to drop a reservation for a transport corridor, an area in the inner suburb of Hindmarsh to the north-east of the city centre became the subject of a planning study. The total area involved was about 200 hectares comprising a mixture of land uses and built form developed since the mid-nineteenth century. Because the area included the site of a major intersection proposed in the corridor, there were considerable areas of vacant and underutilized land. The study was designed to look at the possibilities for infill, redevelopment and rehabilitation. One of the major planning issues is the relationship of industrial and residential uses one to another, in the revival and reconstruction of this area following years of urban blight and decay. Accordingly four different scenarios were prepared representing different degrees of residential development. One assumed the continuation of previous land-use and zoning policies which favoured industrial extension and development to the detriment of some of the existing housing stock, much of it providing low-cost shelter. The other three

Table 6.   Population totals in scenarios with varying emphases on residential development: Hindmarsh study area, Adelaide.

| Scenario | Range of populations at Outcome of Scenario | Changes in Population since 1981 |
|---|---|---|
| A | 2,450–2,650 | −100– −300 |
| B | 3,800–4,200 | 1,050–1,450 |
| C | 4,500–5,100 | 1,750–2,350 |
| D | 6,750–8,200 | 4,000–5,450 |

Note: 1981 census population was about 2,750.
Source: Infodec, 1984, p. 72.

scenarios assumed different degrees of increased residential development following a policy statement by the government that housing was to be encouraged at the time that the planning study was initiated. The study was designed to help the final decisions about the character, location and importance of residential and industrial development. The base-line scenario, then, was a best-estimate of outcomes if there had been no policy change (i.e. a largely industrial emphasis). There followed two inter-mediate statements or scenarios showing increased housing development and a scenario showing maximum development for dwelling. The scenarios showed the areas – or modules – of land used for different purposes in different scenarios.

Table 6 shows these alternative futures. Scenario A is predicated on specified assumptions about the continued replacement of existing dwellings by industry in industrially zoned areas. Scenario B retains more dwellings in zoned industrial areas, and infill of vacant or underutilized land is dominated by residential development. Scenario C strengthens these processes even more in favour of housing and has higher residential densities for some areas than those obtaining in Scenario B. Scenario D adopts a dominantly residential character. It represents use of vacant and underutilized land almost entirely for housing purposes, redevelopment of some industrial and commercial areas for dwellings, and some redevelopment of existing dwellings where they are scattered or in poor condition, for medium-density housing.

Sensitivity analysis was then carried out to see how much the population and dwelling totals in each scenario responded to different assumptions about occupancy rates of new and existing dwellings of different types (multi-unit or detached), kinds of tenure (owner-occupied, private rental, public rental), and increased densities of development on vacant land. The results of these calculations are shown in table 6 and provide essential information about the parameters of urban consolidation.

## Summary

Urban consolidation policies are likely to have little significant influence on the characteristics of population distribution in Australian metropolitan areas, particularly in the short term. This is because of the fundamental and comprehensive influence exerted by existing built form together with changing social, economic and demographic circumstances leading to low occupancy rates for dwellings. In Sydney an examination of the scope for urban consolidation concluded that less than 3 per cent of the population at the end of the century would be affected by changes to built form designed to encourage urban consolidation. The most extreme prediction favouring consolidation in Adelaide, requiring fairly heroic policy thrusts 'represents a redistribution of population to the Central Sector of the order of three and one-half per cent of the 1991 forecast population' (Bunker and Orchard, 1982, p. 51). Nevertheless that scenario

> would mean a reduction of the order of 20% of the projected population growth on the fringes of metropolitan Adelaide or 50% of the projected population growth on the southern fringe. This would mean significant savings in social and physical infrastructure on the fringes at least in the short term and meet the social objective of increased housing choice in the more conveniently located and better serviced established urban area (Bunker and Orchard, 1982, p. 58).

The question of increased housing choice, in the light of changing demographic, social and economic conditions, is perhaps more important than the need for urban consolidation. But the two issues are related. As the Adelaide study put it: 'the urban consolidation policy, therefore, sits most comfortably in the context of the need to provide more housing choice by location, by type of dwelling and tenure' (Bunker and Orchard, 1982, p. 63). But much of that involves building small new dwellings on expensive land and modifying the processes of gentrification in some of the inner suburbs in order to retain low-cost rental housing. The Hindmarsh study suggested that the public housing authority had to be prominently involved in urban consolidation, and that some kind of zoning of mixed land use would be needed (Infodec, 1984, p. 58).

A final ironic footnote. The issue of urban consolidation has focused on the distribution of residential population. But if the issue is examined in terms of built form, then increasing density of dwellings is occurring in many areas while declining occupancy rates still cause population loss. Again, redevelopment of dwellings in inner and middle suburbs often leads to more intensive use of land for non-residential purposes. Is that urban consolidation or not?

REFERENCES

Archer, R. W. (1980) Planning for housing renewal and urban consolidation, in Archer, R. W. (ed.) *Planning for Urban Consolidation*. Sydney: Planning Research Centre, University of Sydney.

Australian Bureau of Statistics (1982) *Projections of the Population of Australia 1981 to 2021*. Canberra: ABS.

Badcock, B. A. and Cloher, D. U. (1981) Neighbourhood change in inner Adelaide 1966–76. *Urban Studies*, **18**, pp. 41–55.

Bell, M. (1983) Forecasting and Urban Programming in South Australia. Paper presented to Seminar in Forecasting and Urban Programming, Victorian Public Service Board, Melbourne.

Bracken, I. (1982) New directions in key activity forecasting. *Town Planning Review*, **53**, pp. 51–64.

Breheny, M. J. and Roberts, A. J. (1978) An integrated forecasting system for structure planning. *Town Planning Review*, **49**, pp. 306–18.

Breheny, M. J. and Roberts, A. J. (1980) Forecasting methodologies in strategic planning: a review. *Papers of the Regional Science Association*, **44**, pp. 75–89.

Bunker, R. C. (1983) *Urban Consolidation: the Experience of Sydney, Melbourne and Adelaide*. Canberra: Australian Institute of Urban Studies.

Bunker, R. C. and Orchard, L. (1982) *Urban Consolidation and Adelaide*. Canberra: Australian Institute of Urban Studies.

Cardew, R. V. (1982) Comparative costs of urban consolidation: inner and outer, in Sandercock, L. (ed.) *Urban Consolidation: the Equity Issue*. Sydney: Centre for Environmental and Urban Studies, Macquarie University.

Cardew, R. V., Langdale, J. C. and Rich, D. C. (eds.) (1982) *Why Cities Change*. Sydney: Allen and Unwin.

Department of Environment and Planning, NSW (1982) *Residential Development Standards*, Technical Bulletin 15. Sydney: DEP.

Department of Housing and Urban Development, US (1980) *Urban Infill: the Literature*. Washington: US Government Printing Office.

Department of Housing, Urban and Regional Affairs, SA (1978) *Newsheet*, December. Adelaide: DHURA.

Forster, C. (1984) *Adelaide: A Social Atlas*, Atlas of Population and Housing 1981 Census, Vol. 5. Division of National Mapping and Australian Bureau of Statistics.

Indicative Planning Council for the Housing Industry (1980) *Report on Multi-Unit Dwelling Development in Australia*. Canberra: IPC.

Infodec (1984) *Housing Demands and Opportunities, Bowden, Brompton and Ridleyton*. Report for Department of Environment and Planning, Adelaide.

Jay, C. (1978) *Towards Urban Strategies for Australia*. Canberra: Australian Institute of Urban Studies.

Melbourne and Metropolitan Board of Works (1980) *Metropolitan Strategy*. Melbourne: MMBW.

Melbourne and Metropolitan Board of Works (1981) *Metropolitan Strategy Implementation*. Melbourne: MMBW.

Melbourne and Metropolitan Board of Works (1982a) *Assessment of Residential Local Development Schemes*, Planning Guidelines No. 2. Melbourne: MMBW.

Melbourne and Metropolitan Board of Works (1982b) *Dual Occupancy*, Planning Guideline No. 1, Melbourne: MMBW.

Ministry of Housing, Victoria (1980) *Green Paper on Housing in Victoria.* Vol. 1, Melbourne: MOH.

Paterson, J. (1980) Urban consolidation: lovelier the second time round? in Archer, R. W. (ed.) *Planning for Urban Consolidation.* Sydney: Planning Research Centre, University of Sydney.

Paterson, J., Yencken, D. and Gunn, G. (1976) *A Mansion or No House: a report for UDIA on Consequences of Planning Standards and their Impact on Land and Housing.* Melbourne: Urban Development Institute of Australia.

Reed, A. and Wilmoth, D. (1983) The New South Wales Development Program. Paper presented to Seminar in Forecasting and Urban Programming, Victoria Public Service Board, Melbourne.

Sandercock, L. (1984) Planners, planning policy and recession, in Eade, R. and Eccles, D. (eds.) *Planning in a Recession.* Melbourne: Footscray Institute of Technology, pp. 25–37.

State Planning Authority, NSW (1968) *Sydney Region Outline Plan.* Sydney: SPA.

Stimson, R. J. (1982) *The Australian City.* Melbourne: Longman-Cheshire.

Town Planning Committee of South Australia (1962) *Report on the Metropolitan Area of Adelaide.* Adelaide: SA Government Printer.

Travers Morgan (1980) *Energy and Land Use.* Report for the Department of Urban and Regional Affairs, Adelaide.

Wilmoth, D. (1982) Urban consolidation and social equity, in Sandercock, L. (ed.) *Urban Consolidation: the Equity Issue.* Sydney: Centre for Environmental and Urban Studies, Macquarie University.

*Chapter 5*

# Housing Issues and Policies in Australia

CHRIS PARIS

Most Australians today are extremely well housed both in terms of contemporary world standards and local history[1,2]. Standards of provision have risen consistently since the Second World War, housing costs are low in relation to incomes and there is a very high level of owner-occupation (Neutze, 1977, 1978, 1981). Very good housing is available and affordable especially for middle- and upper-income earners (figure 1).

Despite substantial improvements in aggregate terms, however, significant minorities of households have failed to benefit proportionately. Since the early 1970s there have been signs of increasing disparities culminating during the last few years in deep and enduring housing crises for some groups. The central issue in Australian housing today, therefore, concerns the contrast between the well and cheaply housed majority and less well and expensively housed minorities (Bethune, 1984; Burke, Hancock and Newton, 1984; Carter, 1984; Kemeny, 1983*a*; Milligan, 1983; Neutze, 1981; Paris, 1984*a*, 1984*b*; Paris, Stimson and Williams, 1984).

The development of housing in Australia must be located within the distinctive local history of economic development and state formation. Assumptions and models cannot simply be imported from Britain, Western Europe or North America. Australia developed from a series of British colonial possessions in the nineteeth century, with virtually no local manufacturing working class until well into the twentieth century, but *throughout* as a dependent, albeit fully capitalist, society (Berry, 1983, 1984; Denoon, 1983; Head, 1983).

This chapter attempts to bring together critical historical perspectives on Australian society and a review of the development of housing within that society. It is an overview and a highly personal account. Others might have

Figure 1.   New upper middle-class housing. This advertisement typifies the current marketing of high-quality new housing. A building society and a group of builders have co-operated in attracting potential customers through a nice package. (*Source: The Sun*, Friday November 30, 1984, reproduced with permission of the St George Building Society Ltd and the Knightsbridge Consortium)

expanded on topics which, for the sake of brevity, only get passing mention here, such as federalism and housing finance. I am particularly interested in exploring the relationship between two analytically separate processes: (i) the production of distinctive residential environments and (ii) the development of distinctive social relations of housing. The discussion of these two processes leads to a review of the overall housing situation in Australia based on the 1981 census. The snap-shot provided by the 1981 census was always somewhat blurred and already is fading at the edges. Its focus is sharpened by an examination of some issues which have been prominent in local housing debates. Market processes and state policies are discussed in relation to the three main tenures (home ownership, private renting and public renting) and brief mention is made of two other topics: the 'feminization' of housing poverty and the largely unexplored question of growing (albeit differential) obsolesence of parts of the housing stock. I conclude with some comments on government and housing.

## Housing in Australian Society

Australian economic history can be conceptualized as a series of rapid booms and equally rapid busts within an economy expanding and developing overall. The growth of population has been fuelled by successive waves of immigrants, at first predominantly of British stock but of more varied origin since the Second World War. Successive phases of economic development can be identified, albeit crudely: pastoralism dominated up to 1850s, to be accompanied during the second half of the nineteenth century by mining booms, rapid urban growth and early local manufacturing (usually processing of raw materials or small-scale production for local consumption). Major savage depressions in the 1890s and 1930s interrupted both the growth of local manufacturing and also waves of immigration. These changes have had crucial significance for the development of the built environment and of housing in particular; cycles of rapid construction alternating with stagnation have today left a legacy of older dwellings in distinct age bands.

The form of the modern state was struck with federation in 1901 when formerly separate colonies became states collectively creating a Commonwealth: the federal nation of Australia. With some changes that form of federal nation state has persisted and Commonwealth-State relations have been of crucial importance affecting both the content and style of public policy formulation and implementation concerning all aspects of housing (see contributions to Head, 1983). Local government is of less importance, by and large, and the public housing authorities, developed mainly after World War Two, are state government authorities.

Since the Second World War Australia has moved substantially away from British neo-colonial influence to be drawn increasingly into the US-dominated Pacific and world economies. As Crough and Wheelwright commented (1982, p. 179), with reference to empire loyalty:

> The acid test of such loyalty is willingness of the rulers to send the young men of the country to fight for a new emperor; Australia's rulers passed this test with flying colours in the Vietnam War.

High levels of population concentration in the major cities were established already by 1900. Metropolitan dominance continued and even intensified until the late 1970s. Despite the continuing importance of both agricultural production (particularly to trading balances) and the resource boom in the 1970s, the Australian population is highly concentrated mainly in two major metropolitan areas (centred on Sydney and Melbourne) and a handful of state capitals (Burnley, 1980; Logan, Whitelaw and McKay, 1981).

Since the early 1970s Australia's critical susceptibility to changes in global economic processes has been revealed (see in particular, Crough and Wheelwright, 1982; McQueen 1982). Manufacturing employment has been decimated, economic growth reduced and immigration cut back (Stilwell, 1980). Unemployment now appears permanent and a new generation of unemployed youth has been excluded from the paid labour force.

Even so, *most* Australian households have not been affected by recession since the mid-1970s. A white settler-capitalist society (Denoon, 1983) has grown up after the forced displacement of an aboriginal population. An economy dominated by massive overall growth, comprising periodic booms and busts, has been accompanied by the creation of a complex modern federal state. These wider processes of rapid change and development have set the context and shaped the contents of the development of Australian housing from earliest settlement through the issues and problems of the 1980s.

## The Production of Distinctive Residential Environments

Australian homes exhibited great contrasts during the nineteenth century. Rude cottages of timber and bark, colonial mansions of brick and stone, rough tents and 'humpies', port-side makeshift slums and solid bourgeois stone terraces coexisted in the ever-expanding colonies. Only the most substantial remain today plus a few cottages lovingly preserved by local historical societies or leisure entrepreneurs.

Building materials were dictated by local availability, and regional styles emerged in terms of materials and dwelling types. Most distinctive has been the use of timber and tin roofs, combined with stilts in Queensland 'high-set' houses (see photograph number 8). Verandahs became increasingly common as protection from the harsh sun and for summer 'sleepouts'. Wooden structures predominated. Many were never more than temporary; even so they constituted the only available shelter for the emerging industrial working classes. The mass urban housing of Victorian working-class districts owed little to health and sanitation movements (see Cannon, 1975). Stone was a popular material for more substantial dwellings in Adelaide, brick was more frequently used in Sydney, but wood predominated overall.

By the 1870s 'every capital city had settled to a quiet respectable society of neat private houses' (Boyd, 1978 edn, p. 47.) The coming of railways led to rapid suburban expansion in the 1880s as Sydney and Melbourne grew nearly 75 per cent in a decade. As Boyd remarked in 1952 (1978 edn, p. 54):

East of Melbourne in 1882, Camberwell, Canterbury and Surrey Hills . . . to become the proudest centres of pure suburbia, were opened in market gardens and dairy frames beside the Box Hill railway. Adelaide's suburbs . . . spread over the plain . . . There were no more green belts; just houses, streets and houses, headed for mountains and the sea.

The 'public transport cities' of the late nineteenth and early twentieth century were soon lost amongst low-density suburban expansion. By the late 1920s there were already more widespread modern features with increasing proportions of brick construction, fewer great houses but a smaller proportion of rustic hovels. Despite improved standards for some, the Depression also brought evictions for others, a growth in mortgage failures and mass homelessness.

On the eve of the Second World War Australia contained a series of distinctive house/environment relations. Inner metropolitan areas comprised mixtures of one or two storey terraces and detached dwellings – all at densities much lower than their European contemporaries. Wide ranging suburbs of predominantly detached wooden dwellings surrounded the more densely settled urban cores. Brick was becoming more common:

By 1939 many suburbs were entirely given over to brick. Perth and Adelaide were using brick or stone only. Before this there had been a natural economic segregation (*sic*) of the two principal structural methods. Weatherboards never appeared in rich streets, bricks seldom in poor streets (Boyd, 1978 edn, p. 114).

Country towns – some, like Bendigo and Ballarat, already settling down after the racy growth and subsequent solid respectability of the goldrushes – were scattered around the hinterlands. Few such towns were to grow much more except as outer suburbs themselves of dominant metropolises. Others, based on pastoralism, whilst remaining locally significant, have subsequently lost economic momentum as well as their young people to the major metropolitan areas.

Depression and war combined virtually to halt housing production between 1929 and 1945. Subsequently, however, pent-up demand was carried along with the back-packs and mixed memories of returning armies. The natural growth of the existing population was further swollen by massive immigration. The high priority given to rapid housing production could not meet demand, so that despite record production in 1950, 'many thousands still lived in unsatisfactory accommodation; in temporary, converted army camps, in tents, in caravans and with inlaws' (Boyd, 1978 edn, p. 115).

Shortages of materials and skilled building labour were crucial (Freeland, 1982 edn, ch. 13). There was a growth of do-it-yourself house-building and rapid increase in the use of fibro-cement as a building material (especially in Sydney) between 1945 and 1955. Most early post-war dwellings were single-storey detached houses: about half were timber and one-third brick

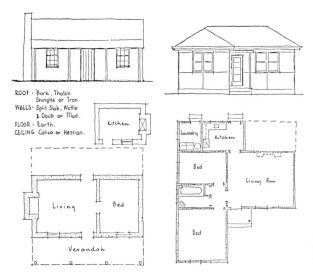

ROOF · Bark, Thatch
       Shingles or Iron.
WALLS· Split Slab, Wattle
       & Daub or Mud.
FLOOR · Earth.
CEILING Calico or Hessian.

Figure 2.  Settlers' cottages: 100 years apart. These are both settlers' dwellings, but the one on the left is a nineteenth-century cottage in a rural area and that on the right is an early post-war minium private house in outer suburban Sydney. The latter cost $1,250 and the land price was $200. These drawings correspond to photographs 1 on page 100 and 4 on page 101. (*Source:* Peter Harrison)

(though the proportions varied from state to state). Peter Harrison's drawings (figure 2) nicely illustrate the advance from the days of rural settlers to early post-war suburban settlers. As in the pre-war period, most production was in the hands of small building firms. Some contractors were already on the way to becoming big builders but the era of the 'volume' house builders and integrated multi-national building and construction firms had barely dawned during the 1950s in Australia. Until about 1960, development was almost invariably of single-storey, low-density detached single-family houses. Housing production expanded rapidly from 1945 to 1952, levelling off at about 80,000 dwellings a year during the 1950s with a drop to below 70,000 in 1957.

The total production of dwellings increased substantially throughout the 1960s (with a slight down hiccup in 1962 and 1963) to a peak of more than 150,000 dwellings in 1973/74. This period saw the growth of bigger house-building firms as well as the birth and death of countless others. Subcontracting became entrenched (Hutton, 1970). Some bigger firms diversified to become major conglomerates during the 1970s. Many firms, big and small, crashed during the property bust of the mid-1970s (Daly, 1982).

Most dwellings still were detached houses at low densities, with two major developments during the 1960s. Firstly, brick became the dominant building material: of outer walls at least. Solid 'double brick' construction had largely given way to a single outer layer of 'brick veneer'. By the 1970s over 80 per cent of all dwellings completed had brick outer walls. Even so, brick dwellings did not exceed 50 per cent of the total dwelling stock until the early 1970s. The second major innovation during the 1960s was the growth of flats, especially blocks of 'units', almost wholly in capital cities and mainly in Sydney and Melbourne.

The sheer size of cities became monumental, Sydney being developed overall at a tenth the density of Paris. Detached brick-veneered suburbia became the hallmark of the 1960s as regional variants on Australian vernacular domestic architecture were lost amongst seas of near-identical 'individual homes' (Allport, 1983; Spearritt, 1978).

Diverse new forms of higher density housing combined with the legacy of previous building cycles and continuing urban-rural variations in economic growth, building materials and dwelling types. In sum this produced a diverse residential built environment by 1981. As table 1 shows, brick was far less common in rural areas and country towns. Flats were particularly concentrated in the largest urban centres. The old stock, frequently terraced, by no means necessarily thereby the poorer stock, was concentrated in metropolitan centres, country towns and isolated rural locations. Gentrification had already transformed some older inner-city districts with widespread rehabilitation of many older terraces (Kendig, 1979, 1984a;

Table 1. All private dwellings, type of dwellings by material by outer walls, urban-rural variations, Australia, 1981 (expressed as percentages by region).

| Dwelling | Brick, brick veneer stone and concrete | Timber | Fibro, asbestos | Other not elsewhere included | Total |
|---|---|---|---|---|---|
| Major urban areas[1] | | | | | |
| Houses[2] | 52 | 17 | 8 | 1 | 78 |
| Flats[3] | 19 | 1 | *[7] | * | 20 |
| Other, not stated[4] | 1 | * | * | 2 | 2 |
| Total | 72 | 17 | 8 | 3 | 100 |
| | | | | n=3,271,350 | |
| Other urban areas[5] | | | | | |
| Houses | 38 | 26 | 20 | 3 | 87 |
| Flats | 7 | 1 | 1 | * | 10 |
| Other, not stated | 1 | * | * | 1 | 3 |
| Total | 46 | 27 | 22 | 5 | 100 |
| | | | | n=1,157,643 | |
| Rural areas[6] | | | | | |
| Houses | 32 | 34 | 23 | 4 | 93 |
| Flats | * | * | * | * | 1 |
| Other, not stated | * | 1 | * | 5 | 6 |
| Total | 33 | 35 | 23 | 9 | 100 |
| | | | | n=709,655 | |
| Australia | | | | | |
| Houses | 46 | 21 | 13 | 2 | 82 |
| Flats | 14 | 1 | * | * | 15 |
| Other, not stated | 1 | * | 1 | 2 | 3 |
| Total | 61 | 22 | 13 | 4 | 100 |
| | | | | n=5,138,650 | |

1. Centres with a population of more than 100,000.
2. Includes separate houses, semi-detached housing and row/terrace housing.
3. Includes other medium density housing and flats over 3 storeys.
4. Includes caravan/houseboat etc., improvised homes and dwellings/non-dwellings combined.
5. Urban centres with a population of 1,000 to 99,000.
6. Bounded rural localities and rural balance of the state or territory.
7. *refers to figures less than 0.49 per cent.
Source: Australian Bureau of Statistics (1983) table 72, p. 121–22.

Newman, Annandale and Duxbury, 1984). Similar *processes*, indeed, also are operating today in less spatially-specific ways, as 'yuppies' reconvert former mansions back to residential from institutional uses, or as 'historic' older settlements and major cities are (re-)colonized by young affluent home-owners (for example, the older port of Fremantle near Perth). Sydney harbour, one of the most beautiful in the world, has been massively developed for the rich and middle classes. Old assumptions about the universality of processes of residential change have to be revised in the light of such developments: gentrification being almost the precise opposite of 'traditional' patterns of change (Hamnett, 1984*a*; Smith, 1982). Meanwhile, inevitably, slum formation is displaced in space and through the dwelling stock.

Other new urban residential forms proliferated during the 1970s associated particularly with coastal development (resort/tourist/retirement complexes as in the Gold Coast, south of Brisbane), with the rapid growth in 'second homes' and with the move towards 'retirement villages' (Mullins, 1984). Speculation and over-investment caused booms and busts as ever; by 1983 it was a common saying amongst real estate agents that the main difference between herpes and a Gold Coast unit was that you could give herpes away. By 1986 the Gold Coast rental market was booming again. The more flamboyant new developments, however, represent the top side of the affluence stone. Continued recession and its differential effects in terms of unemployment and the distribution of wealth have had other effects. Lifting the affluence stone reveals rapid deterioration of access to housing for hundreds of thousands of Australians, the growth of permanent caravan living, increased sharing of cheaper private rented accommodation, the closure of boarding houses and the re-emergence of large-scale homelessness (particularly amongst the young).

## Distinctive Social Relations of Housing

Concern for the distribution of housing turns our attention away from purely physical characteristics of the residential built environment towards distinctive local social relations of housing. Most striking for all commentators is the very high rate of homeownership (Burke, Hancock and Newton, 1984; Neutze, 1977, 1978; Kemeny, 1981, 1983*a*; Williams, 1984).

Whereas half of all Australian households were owner-occupiers in 1911, most were in non-metropolitan locations and 90 per cent were outright owners (see table 2). The novel growth of mortgaged urban homeownership after the First World War was abruptly checked by the Depression and the Second World War. Real incomes fell during the 1930s, saving became impossible and many mortgages were foreclosed; the war entailed a virtual cessation of construction.

Pent-up demand was combined with returning service peoples' aspir-

Table 2. Households and tenure, Australia 1911–1981 (expressed as a percentage)[1,2].

| Tenure | 1911 | 1947 | 1954 | Year of Census 1966 | 1971 | 1976 | 1981 |
|---|---|---|---|---|---|---|---|
| Outright owner | 45 | 45 | 48 | na | na | 32 | 33 |
| Purchaser | 4 | 8 | 15 | na | na | 35 | 33 |
| All owners/ purchasers[3] | 49 | 53 | 63 | 71 | 67 | 67 | 68 |
| Public tenant[4] | 0 | na[6] | 4 | 5 | 6 | 5 | 5 |
| Other tenant[5] | 45 | 43 | 30 | 21 | 22 | 20 | 20 |
| Other/not stated | 5 | 4 | 3 | 3 | 6 | 8 | 8 |
| Total (000) | 894 | 1,874 | 2,343 | 3,152 | 3,671 | 4,141 | 4,699 |

1. Columns do not always balance due to rounding.
2. 1911–76 data refer to dwellings, 1981 data refer to households.
3. Including owner/purchaser undefined.
4. Including tenants of government housing authorities.
5. Includes tenants of other government authorities.
6. Included with 'other tenant'.
Source: Burke et al.(1984) table 1.2, p. 3.

ations and, during the 1950s, conservative government policies. Mortgaged homeownership grew very rapidly during the 1950s and early 1960s as suburban sprawl encircled all major cities (table 2). The growth of homeownership slowed down during the late 1960s and the proportion of mortgaged homeownership fell slightly during the 1970s. By this time, of course, the number of outright owners in metropolitan areas would have been rising anyway as mortgages taken out in the 1950s and 1960s were being paid off. During the 1960s increased owner-occupation of flats and 'units' resulted from the changing legal status of individual units within flat blocks. 'Strata title' was created by acts of state parliaments and flat-block subdivision began. Owner-occupation today accounts for nearly a third of all flats; it is much higher in some locations (for example middle-class areas with good Sydney Harbour views) but still accounts for only a small proportion of all owner-occupied dwellings (see table 3).

Private rental housing was in decline during the 1950s. Rent control (temporary in most cases), the advantaged status of homeownership and the growth of public housing all appeared to consign private renting to history. This changed in the 1960s as there was a new wave of investment in private renting, especially with the construction of three-storey flats in the (then) middle and outer suburbs. Aimed at an affluent youth market and providing temporary accommodation for incoming migrants during an age of prosperity, these flats are well described by Freeland (1982 edn, pp. 295–98):

> They were speculative ventures. The arrangements varied but the normal practice was for a builder, who did his own designing, to finance his scheme with a high-priced loan. This forced him to build quickly, filling the building with lessees as soon as possible, at which stage having thereby proved its financial viability he sold the building, repaid his costly loan and took his profit. Flats built this way were aimed at taking advantage of a new market created by the general affluence that existed in which, for the first time in

history, the seventeen to twenty-three year old age group had fat pay packets . . .

Because of their speculative nature and their youthful and temporary market the three-storeyed suburban blocks of flats put their money where it counted. Aesthetically they were base and crude . . . all the worst in popular taste of their time. They were jerry-built and had the barest minimum of finishes.

The boom of flat construction for rental tailed off during the early 1970s. Even with the enormous growth of flats, the majority of private tenants always did and still do live in houses. Until the 1950s they were predominantly in inner-urban areas, but by 1981 there were significant proportions of private tenants throughout Australian cities even in the most distant outer suburbs (Core Consultants, 1983).

Since the early 1970s private rental housing has become increasingly problematic. The share of households in the sector has remained at about 20 per cent but this conceals complex problems discussed below.

Public housing grew rapidly from a very low base in 1945 and by the mid-1970s had contributed some 10 per cent of all post-war construction. About half had been sold, though the proportion and type has varied between states (Kemeny, 1983a; Paris, Stimson and Williams, 1984). The public sector performed two major tasks during the 1950s and 1960s. Firstly, housing was provided for general access, mainly to working-class families. Secondly, public housing authorities provided housing for in-coming migrants especially industrial workers, as part of the states' strategy to attract manufacturing investment (this second function was more important outside the historic economic core states of New South Wales and Victoria).

With some notable exceptions, public housing authorities rarely acted as urban renewal agencies. Where they did such activities sometimes mir-rored examples of high-rise, high-density public housing projects in Britain or the United States. Some of the most oppressive built environments in Australia were constructed in this way, particularly by the Victorian and New South Wales Housing Commissions. Elsewhere there were few such monstrosities; but the problems were far less pressing elsewhere, too. More damaging, perhaps, was the obsessive determination of conservative state governments in Victoria to sell off the best public housing. This has left public tenants in that state with the least desirable dwelling types (though often in inner-city locations which have better amenities and services than some owner-occupied outer suburbs!).

Public housing has never constituted more than 5 per cent of the total stock, though the proportion of public housing varies considerably between states (highest in South Australia and very low in Victoria and Queensland). The varying balance reflects construction programmes and sales policies both of which have been strongly influenced by the priorities of different state governments. Broadly speaking the Australian Labor Party (ALP) state governments have been more in favour of retaining and expanding public stocks, though a simple ALP/non-ALP dichotomy does not always work, for example, South Australian conservatives have at times favoured interventionist policies more than the ALP elsewhere.

There can be no doubting the extent to which policies of federal and state governments stimulated the growth of homeownership after the Second World War, though debate still surrounds the motives, intentions and expectations of politicians and their advisors. There is still controversy, too, over the effects of such policies (Kemeny, 1981, 1983a, 1983b; Mullins, 1981a, 1981b, 1983; Orchard, 1984; Williams, 1984). I am broadly in agreement with Kemeny's argument (1983a) that the sponsorship of home-ownership implied a choice regarding patterns of public/private expenditure that go wider than housing alone, as expenditure on housing crowded out other social provision or urban infrastructure. Hence 'mono-tenurial' housing policies have significantly damaged the scope for public or other forms of social rental housing.

Kemeny (1983a) suggested four adverse effects of the dominance of home-ownership in Australia. Firstly, housing is maldistributed through individual and household life-cycles and 'is redistributed from those in more need to those in less need' (p. 91). Secondly, tenures become systematically class-divided: rather than cutting across existing class structures housing tenures become 'class-specific'. Homeownership policy has used 'housing tenures as a means of allocating housing in class terms' (p. 94). Thirdly, Kemeny noted the positive relationship between privatized lifestyles and the sponsorship of homeownership:

> Privatised urban structures are . . . in part related to the combination of detached houseownership and a weak welfare state, in which public urban infrastructural facilities are underdeveloped (p. 97).

The poor provision of public infrastructure had been noted by others, especially Stretton (1970) who remains a strong advocate of the benefits of homeownership (Stretton, 1982). Poorly provided public infrastructure, however, has not been just a phenomenon of the 1950s and 1960s. Boyd noted that half of the new suburban houses built between 1945 and 1950 'would be without water, electricity, sewerage, gas or telephone services, without roads, footpaths or drainage for many years' (1978 edn, p. 119). He had remarked earlier that 'comfortable villas' in the 1860s faced 'Rutted unmade roads which were impassable swamps after rain . . .' (p. 47). Kemeny's main novel contribution has been to emphasize that large owner-occupied dwellings, a tenure form sponsored by the state, built at low densities, can be seen as part of a 'package' substituting (i) privatized consumption for public consumption and (ii) homeownership for secure income support in old age. Finally, Kemeny argued that the development of owner-occupation and home-centred privatized lifestyles crucially affect the role of women in terms both of access to the paid labour force and of the domestic division of labour. This has been more fully developed elsewhere, especially Allport (1983) and Harman (1984). Kemeny has called for major policy reorientation towards 'tenure-neutrality' (1983*a*). This has generally been taken up by the ALP, albeit more in principle, so far, than in practice.

There are many points of detail and analysis over which I take issue with Kemeny. One example is his argument that there was an 'underlying trend' away from mortgaged homeownership between 1933 and 1947. This does not adequately consider the effects of depression and war. The notion that homeownership was sponsored by governments is certainly true, but it was also highly desired by working people who did not want to spend their lives making landlords rich! Overall, though, Kemeny's work has been of great importance in revitalizing scholarly debate about housing within Australian society and proposing tenure-neutrality as a positive principle for the reorientation of policies.

## The Overall Picture of Australian Housing at the 1981 Census

There are many problems with the 1981 census, not the least of which is its bizarre definition of dwellings. An 'occupied private dwelling' was defined as 'the premises occupied by a household on census night'. Hence:

> It is important to remember that the census definition of a private dwelling means that the total number of dwellings may be more than the total number of known structures in any given area (Australian Bureau of Statistics, 1982, p. 1).

The unusual conception of 'dwellings' makes the use of the census for many housing studies rather problematic! Moreover, boarding houses and caravans in caravan parks do not count as 'private dwellings', making it extremely hard to say much about two of the most knotty current housing problems. Other minor follies need not concern us too much here, though readers are advised at all times to treat dwelling statistics based on the 1981 census with a large dose of healthy scepticism.

What the census does show satisfactorily is diversity within the contemporary housing system. Table 3 compares dwelling types to tenure and some clear variations were observable. Owner-occupiers were most likely to live in houses; fewer than 10 per cent of owner-occupiers live in flats though this accounts for about 30 per cent of flats. Public tenants tended generally to live in houses rather than flats. Some variations not shown here included the high proportion of Victorian public tenants living in high-rise (nearly one-quarter live in flats over three storeys) and the high proportion of public tenants in South Australia in semi-detached housing known locally as 'double-units' (60 per cent). Most flats were rented privately though more private tenants overall lived in houses. The table

Table 3.   Dwelling types and tenure of households occupying private dwellings, Australia, 1981 (percentages)[1].

| Nature of Occupancy | Houses[2] | Flats[3] | Type of Dwelling Other[4] | Not Stated | Total |
|---|---|---|---|---|---|
| Owner-occupation[5] | 63 | 4 | 1 | 1 | 68 |
| Public tenants[6] | 5 | 2 | *8 | *8 | 6 |
| Private tenants[7] | 10 | 8 | *8 | *8 | 19 |
| Other/not stated | 5 | 1 | * | 1 | 7 |
| Total | 83 | 15 | 1 | | 100 |
| | | | | | n=4,668,909 |

1. Columns do not always balance due to rounding.
2. Includes separate houses, semi-detached houses and row/terrace housing.
3. Includes other medium density housing and flats over 3 storeys.
4. Includes caravan/houseboat etc., improvised homes and dwellings/non-dwellings combined.
5. Includes outright owners, purchasers and owners/purchasers undefined.
6. Includes tenants of housing authorities and tenants of other government agencies.
7. Includes tenants of other landlords and landlord not stated.
8. *refers to figures less than 0.49 per cent.
Source: Australian Bureau of Statistics (1983) table 66, p. 114.

Table 4.   Housing costs: rough overall comparisons by tenure, Australia, 1981 (number of households[1] in thousands).

| Weekly Cost (A$)[2] | Public tenants | Private tenants | Tenure[3] Owner- purchasers | Owners | Total |
|---|---|---|---|---|---|
| <49 | 260 | 398 | 716 | 1,549 | 2,923 |
| 50–99 | 24 | 405 | 605 | 0 | 1,033 |
| >100 | 1 | 50 | 167 | 0 | 218 |
| Not stated | 8 | 19 | 55 | na | 82 |
| Total | 292 | 872 | 1,543 | 1,549 | 4,256 |

1. Excluding those households where nature of occupancy was classified as owner-purchaser undefined, other/not elsewhere included and occupancy not stated.
2. This overstates mortgage repayments as we have divided monthly repayments by four.
3. Public tenants and private tenants defined as in table 3.
Source: Australian Bureau of Statistics (1983) tables 68 and 69, p. 116.

does not show household variations. Briefly we can say that private tenants were generally younger (though not all were young) and more often single people or small households. Owners were older, especially outright owners and the overall proportion of households who are owners increased by age.

In general, there was not much difference in aggregate terms between the housing costs of home-purchasers and tenants, though the latter were generally poorer. Table 4 contains a very rough comparison between purchasers and tenants in terms of numbers of household by income group with stated household expenditure on housing. This overstates mortgage costs which, given the data available, had to be divided by four to approximate to the weekly rent figures. Public tenants paid the least of all tenants and purchasers. Owner-purchasers and private tenants had a similar distribution: about 45 per cent of each paid under A$50 per week, about 46 per cent of private tenants and 40 per cent of purchasers paid A$50–99. The

Table 5. Number of bedrooms by number of occupants, Australia, 1981 (expressed as a percentage by number of bedrooms).

| Number of Bedrooms | Number of Occupants | | | | | | |
|---|---|---|---|---|---|---|---|
| | 1 | 2 | 3 | 4 | 5 | 6+ | Total |
| <1 | 64 | 29 | 4 | 2 | 1 | 1 | 100 |
| 2 | 28 | 44 | 15 | 9 | 3 | 1 | 100 |
| 3 | 9 | 26 | 20 | 26 | 13 | 6 | 100 |
| 4 | 5 | 13 | 15 | 25 | 24 | 19 | 100 |
| 5 | 5 | 10 | 11 | 17 | 21 | 36 | 100 |
| >6 | 10 | 12 | 11 | 14 | 15 | 39 | 100 |
| Not stated | 35 | 30 | 15 | 12 | 5 | 4 | 100 |
| Total | 18 | 29 | 17 | 19 | 10 | 6 | 100 |

Source: Australian Bureau of Statistics (1983) table 75, p. 25.

group with the lowest costs – outright owners – accounted for over a third of all households. Whereas the latter often have greater repair costs, it is clear that their regular housing costs are incomparably less than the other groups. As inflation and continued house price and rent increases since 1981 will have widened the gaps, we can conclude that a majority of owners have low housing costs (often, in real terms, declining costs) whereas tenants and first-time buyers have much higher costs.

The well-housed majority, moreover, is often 'bedroom-rich'. Table 5 looks at bedrooms and household size. On average there is a good match: closer examination shows that many households (especially small households) have two or more 'spare' bedrooms whilst others are overcrowded. Not shown in this table – though it should not come as any surprise – is the relationship of bedroom availability to tenure: tenants are overcrowded and owner-occupiers have surplus rooms. The paradoxes of housing poverty in a rich country must now be examined further.

## Issues and Policies into the 1980s

Tenure is central to current housing issues and policies in Australia. The overall balance of tenures in 1981 clearly resembled the aggregate characteristics of the United States more much closely than the United Kingdom. There was a very small public sector increasingly conceptualized as 'welfare' housing. Homeownership was dominant though there was virtually no continuing growth in the proportion of homeowning households. Mass mortgaged homeownership was very largely a post-war phenomenon, particularly having expanded during the 1950s and 1960s. Its expansion has been limited since the 1960s both by the decreasing affordability of homeownership and by increasing youth household headship. There remained a large private rental sector, albeit comprising diverse elements.

Government policies had been very important in producing the tenure system between 1945 and 1981. Many critics during the late 1970s and early 1980s, indeed, argued that the very government policies which had contributed to the growth of homeownership were also having unaccepatable adverse consequences for the whole of the housing system (Carter, 1980, 1983; Kemeny, 1981, 1982, 1983a; Milligan, 1983; Neutze, 1978, 1981). Housing activists, particularly Australian Shelter, were joined by the Catholic Commission for Justice and Peace, trade unions, the Australian Labor Party and other organizations in debating growing housing problems at a national conference in Sydney in September 1982. This was widely attended and helped relocate housing as an item on the national political agenda, where it became a major plank in the ALP, opposition platform and, after the ALP election victory in February 1983, the federal government programme.

The essence of much criticism was distilled by Kemeny in his argument that 'monotenurial' housing policies had restricted the growth of public and non-profit sectors in Australia leaving large numbers of lower income tenants dependent on the private rental sector. Hence the choices facing households are so restricted that 'competition for the favoured tenure leads to class-sorting and one-way inter-tenural movement' (Kemeny 1983a, p. 93). He presented the argument as a tendency, not as an iron law. In societies where homeownership is systemmatically favoured, he argued, owner-occupation will tend to be the tenure for the wealthy and for professionals and managers, whereas 'private and public renting form residual tenures over-represented by the poor and by semi-skilled manual workers. Housing tenures thereby became "class-specific"' (loc. cit.). In my review of private rental housing in Australia I concluded by referring to 'growing polarisation' between households who are 'well-housed, in work, usually owner-occupiers' and those 'badly and expensively housed, often with incomes in the form of pensions or benefits, who are usually renters' (Paris, 1984a, p. 197). These arguments are similar to those made by some British housing analysts, particularly Ball (1982), Harloe (1982, 1984) and Hamnett (1984b). Major differences between Britain and Australia, however, include the much larger public sector in the former and relative buoyancy of private renting in the 1960s in Australia.

Three major developments in Australia since the mid-1970s have tended to confirm the polarization thesis, though the idea that tenures are class-divided requires some qualification. Firstly, during the later 1970s, federal government policies had a major effect on limiting the already modest public housing sector (Paris, Stimson and Williams, 1984; 1985). Secondly, continued support for homeownership failed significantly to increase its share largely due to wider economic factors. Thirdly, the combination of government policies and diverse market changes led increasingly to an enduring crisis facing private tenants.

The move from a public housing approach to a welfare housing philosophy during the late 1970s reflected both changing federal government priorities and also increasing proportions of poor applicants to state housing authorities. The Fraser Liberal-National Country Party coalition changed the emphasis of public housing in two ways. Firstly, using the rhetorical claim that many 'wealthy' tenants kept out truly needy households there was a change in the basis of rent setting. State housing authorities had to move towards charging 'market' rents thereby stimulating out-movement of wealthy tenants. Rent reductions were to be available for needy tenants. Based at best on the revelations in a major inquiry into poverty which showed many poorer private tenants than public tenants (Committee of Inquiry into Povery, 1975), the existence of rich public tenants was always chimerical. By the early 1980s it was a complete nonsense. Rapidly escalating proportions of incoming public tenants and, indeed, of all public tenants were eligible for rent reduction. Charging market rents had been a symbolic gesture. The 1975 inquiry noted that there were more poor/very poor private tenants than existing public dwellings – even if all public tenants were moved on there was still an overall shortage in 1975!

The Fraser government also cut back ruthlessly on the expenditure on public housing. Expenditure is managed mainly by state government housing authorities but funded largely by the Commonwealth. The terms and conditions are negotiated periodically and embodied in Commonwealth-State Housing Agreements (see Paris, Stimson and Williams, 1984). Commonwealth support for public housing fell from A$366 million in 1974–75 to A$107 million in 1981–82 (at constant 1974–75 dollar prices, Carter, 1983). This was matched by a rapid drop in public sector completions, from 19,700 in 1975–76 to 9,330 in 1981–82. This occurred during a period of recession with rising unemployment and increasing costs of owner-occupation (due to land costs, higher interest rates and general house price inflation). The waiting lists for public housing increased and there was a rapid growth in the population of 'emergency' housing allocations.

The extreme case of the collapse of public housing was in Canberra. The Australian Capital Territory is administered directly by the Commonwealth government: hence there is no state-level 'buffer' between its policies and the locality. Despite growing housing shortages and high private rents, only one public dwelling was completed in 1980–81 for a population of nearly a quarter of a million people. With a mainly new housing stock and high planning standards there is virtually no low-cost private rental accommodation in Canberra. Despite a high level of flat construction 'over the border' in Queanbeyan, New South Wales, there is now a severe housing crisis for low-income groups in the national capital – this most planned of all Australian cities! (Paul, 1983; Committee of Inquiry into Homelessness and Inadequate Housing in the ACT and Surrounding Regions, 1984).

Home purchase has been assisted in diverse ways during the post-war period (Kemeny, 1983a; Neutze, 1977, 1978, 1981; Williams, 1984). By the late 1970s the main mechanisms directly assisting home purchase included 'home savings grants' (tax-free on a dollar-for-dollar ratio to saving to A$2,500 with 'family' bonuses), advantageous mortgages through housing authorities, continuing sale of public housing and also low interest mortgages for ex-service people. The Fraser government even introduced some tax relief for home purchasers as well as making 'emergency' assistance available for purchasers troubled by interest rate increases. Commonwealth government policies also helped purchasers indirectly by 'providing a public framework through which private finance could be channelled into the home-ownership market' (Kemeny, 1983a, p. 19) as well as aiding all owners by not taxing imputed rent.

In spite of these advantages, homeownership did not expand proportionately during the 1970s; indeed, mortgaged homeownership may have fallen slightly as a percentage of all households. The increased household headship rate among younger people may be part of the answer, but the sheer cost of entry to homeownership is generally seen as the major problem (Burke, Hancock and Newton, 1984; Bethune, 1984; Carter, 1984; Daly, 1982). Even so, despite much media coverage of first time buyers' problems of high cost and high interest rates, it is also important to note that there was little hard evidence of a *fall* in the rate of homeownership. During the 1970s there were good reasons for thinking that the political sponsorship of home purchase had as much to do with voting strength of existing homeowners (and their anticipation of continuing capital gain) as with any deepseated desire to assist low-income home purchase (Williams, 1984). The home savings grant was paid to people who already had demonstrated a capacity to save a deposit and pay off a mortgage and hence helped intending middle-income purchasers to buy sooner rather than the poor (Neutze, 1978; Carter, 1980).

By the mid-1970s there were already clear signs that investment in private rental accommodation was declining, that large proportions of private tenants were very poor and that there would be more rather than less pressure on the sector (Australian Institute of Urban Studies, 1975; Priorities Review Staff, 1975). Between the fall of the ALP government in November 1975 and the introduction of some 'crisis assistance' funding for private tenants in 1982, however, the Commonwealth government had paid little heed to the problems of private renting. The private rental sector, of course, is too crude a label for very diverse relationships and processes (see Core Consultants, 1983; Paris 1984a, 1984b). Throughout the 1970s, though, we can argue generally that private renting became less of a transitional tenure for young households and more of a residual tenure catering for the long-term poor (see, Burke, 1983; Field, 1983). The 1981 census revealed that alarmingly high proportions of the poorest tenants in the 'other landlords' category were paying very high proportions of their low incomes in rent (Henderson, 1983; Henderson and Hough, 1984; Paris, 1984a, 1984b). Vacancy rates were low; overcrowding was much higher than in other tenures.

Despite growing problems of tenants' poverty there were some factors contributing to continued landlord investment. In particular some investors were able to tax deduct loan interest and other costs against rent. In the absence of any tax on capital gains this made rental housing investment attractive for high marginal rate tax payers who converted taxable income into an untaxed capital gain. Other types of landlord were less able to benefit. This system led to price inflation in the existing stock, but due to building costs and growing poverty amongst many tenants, did not lead to new construction. As capital gains are more secure in houses than in flats the tax system has led increasingly towards speculative investment in houses: this does provide short-term rental accommodation but at the cost of bidding up house prices, excluding would-be owner-occupiers and forcing up rents. Reforms in 1985 and 1986 reduced even these modest incentives for rental investors.

In sum these three major trends during the 1970s did lead towards greater classdivision of tenure. However, we must also consider other dimensions of current housing issues, particularly the ways in which age and gender interact with class. In Australia, as elsewhere, there is a growing debate around the issue of the 'feminization' of poverty. Female-headed households have lower incomes than male-headed households, they are less likely to be home-purchasers and more likely to be tenants. Given gender differentials in mortality rates, however, older women are more likely to be outright owners. Women's housing problems, then, are often different from those of men (Watson, 1985). In many cases they are a function of gender-differentiated access to property. In other cases women's housing problems stem from other gender differentials which become reflected in housing problems; for example, deserted mothers tend to support children and face discrimination from some landlords and real estate agents (Australian Housing Research Council, 1980). Single parents, almost entirely women, form an increasingly large proportion of applicants for and tenants of public housing (Paris, Stimson and Williams, 1984); single parents were twice as likely as any other sub-group of private tenants to be paying over 26 per cent of household income in rent (Paris, 1984a, 1984b).

Age and position within individual and household lifecycles, too, complicate the relationship between tenure and class. Kendig (1981, 1984b) has documented the importance of a lifecycle approach for understanding housing careers. The continuing third of privately renting households headed by under-30s is testimony to the continuing transitional role that private renting has played and will continue to play for many households. But there are major pitfalls in a lifecycle approach. Firstly, actual lifecycles should not be treated ahistorically. They are invariably historically situated: the *longue durée* provides enormously different contexts within which individuals and groups live out lifecycles. Hence housing opportunities and constraints have been very different for succeeding generations (Kendig, 1984c). The circumstances within which 'cycles' begin and through which they travel are shaped by diverse interacting polarities: peace/war, boom/depression, labour shortage/surplus, etc. Secondly, some commentators take point-in-time age-categories and treat these as *de facto* time series data on lifecycles: for example, taking age-categories from a census, cross-tabulating these with tenure and hence inferring historical variation from non-historical data. This 'temporal fallacy' is on a par with the classic 'ecological fallacies' and is equally worthless when it comes to the analysis of processes of change (70 year olds in 1981 have lived through two world wars, the shift of allegiance from the United Kingdom to the United States and into the latest recession; 5 year olds in 1981 inherit a different world context and will live through lifecycles under entirely different circumstances).

Despite such problems, it must be clear that lifecycles, lived within the unfolding of Australian history, intersecting with and conditioned by gender, complicate simply-conceived relations between class and tenure. As Hugo (1984) has shown, the changing demographic characteristics of Australian society have had an enormous impact upon housing issues and problems. Recent changes include declining household size, increased proportions of single-person households, childless couples and single parents and an overall ageing population. The relationship between demographic analysis and housing policy has yet to be fully explored.

Tenures in Australia may have become more 'class-divided' during the post-war period but we might need to think through the category of class a bit more and respecify it in relation to gender and age (as well as, perhaps, ethnicity). Such comments, however, are intended to qualify rather than refute the Kemeny thesis. At present there are major shortages of affordable private rental housing, long and growing waiting lists for public housing matched by growing homelessness and increasing long-term caravan living. There is rapid loss of the cheapest accommodation, especially boarding and lodging houses, with severe problems in inner-city areas (Troy, 1984), but by no means only concentrated there. Many of the worst problems are found scattered throughout middle and outer suburbia; some country towns have desperate shortages of available rental stock while others have the reverse problem of property abandonment.

No discussion of current housing in Australia would be complete without reference to at least two other issues: aboriginal housing and housing obsolescence. Aboriginal housing policies have been treated separately by governments and most white housing researchers have avoided the topic for many and varied reasons. In towns and cities it is almost invariably the case that aboriginals have least choice in the housing market, though communal practices often ameliorate their disadvantaged status. The growth of black resistance to white oppression has influenced growing concern within white communities to respect aboriginal wishes and views. Current research on aboriginal housing preferences in Northern Territory, being pioneered by Loveday and his colleagues at the Northern Australian Research Unit, too, may help overcome existing barriers.

Finally I must mention the issue which in my view has been sorely neglected: the question of obsolescence. The end of the Second World War left Australia with housing shortages and slum problems which were significant locally but small by overseas standards. The massive overall expansion of the stock, to increasingly high standards of construction and amenity, has been combined with much private redevelopment and re-habilitation of inner areas. For example, Paddington in inner Sydney was considered by planners to be ripe for comprehensive redevelopment shortly after the war. Today it is an expensive gentrified suburb exhibiting many forms of sophisticated cosmopolitan lifestyles, trendy shops and smart ethnic restaurants. Even so, about a quarter of the present Australian stock is pre-war. Some has been gentrified, some is and always has been splended. There remains, however, a sizeable element of poor older hous-ing which may degenerate very quickly (much is now over 50 years old).

In addition I must emphasize that 'post-war' does not necessarily equate always with 'good'. Much housing built between 1945 and 1955 was made of poor quality materials and hurriedly built by ill-trained workers. Much of this has subsequently been 'brickclad' – i.e. the addition of single external course of bricks – to give the appearance of more substantial construction. Some other post-war dwellings have been built down to a price, especially blocks of units thrown up in the early 1960s. As the latter become increas-ingly unattractive to better-off private tenants and hence lettable only to the poorer tenants then capital appreciation slackens, minimal repairs are cut to nothing, and new slums are formed. This is happening now, for example, in many parts of Sydney's middle ring. Some of the public housing built during the 1950s and 1960s, too, already shows signs of decay, especially the high-rise blocks built in inner Melbourne and Sydney.

In sum, there are already many signs of obsolescence within the housing stock to be considered alongside the more positive signs of improvements, such as private revitalization of some older dwellings and the growth in extensions to and modifications of even quite new dwellings. Our data are appalling: there is a desperate need for a systematic housing survey. No doubt such a survey would cost something. It may even conclude that the problems are not very great. In its absence, however, there is the danger that obsolescence will lead to slum formation and the existence of crises for which policy-makers are unprepared. At present, it appears that risk is preferable to spending the money to find out. In part, no doubt, this reflects the strong ideology that with high levels of homeownership then housing problems are more or less solved. Within privatized cities, problems of older housing become individuals' problems.

## Governments and Housing: Conclusions, New Beginnings

Government policies, in conclusion, have been of great importance in influencing the shape and components of the Australian housing system. Whilst maintaining earlier commitments to homeownership, the Liberal-National Country Party Commonwealth government 1975–1983 did little to assist other tenures and probably made things worse for those groups who were in greatest need.

Since February 1983 there has been an ALP federal government which placed housing at the centre of its policies of concensus and economic recovery. The two main initiatives in housing have been the renegotiation of the Commonwealth State Housing Agreement (CSHA) and changes to the system of aid for first time purchasers (see Bethune, 1984; Carter, 1984; Wight, 1984). Overall housing starts grew following the change of government, though three years on some slackening was apparent. Greater priority is given to public housing, but levels of financial commitment are already clearly insufficient to achieve the pre-election promise to double the public stock. I estimate that the public housing stock was about 300,000 in February 1982 (including dwellings owned by government authorities other than housing authorities). Over the three years to 1985 net additions (including acquisitions) amount to less than 50,000 dwellings. The renegotiated CSHA and forward plans for Commonwealth expenditure will not substantially lift that rate of progress. If the ALP is in power federally for the ten years from February 1983 to February 1993 it will require a massive redirection of current priorities to get the public housing stock up to 600,000 dwellings.

Little progress has been made towards tenure-neutrality. The new First Home Owners Scheme is still likely to encourage people to buy earlier in the lifecycle whilst still eligible on income grounds, rather than doing much to help life-long poorer households. Very little has been done to address problems of affordability and availability in private renting. Other policies of the Commonwealth government will have as yet uncertain effects on housing. The deregulation of finance is certain to have far-reaching consequences. So, too, will policies on immigration as well as the economy more generally.

The December 1984 federal election saw the return of the ALP government, under Bob Hawke. There was a Cabinet reshuffle and Stewart West, the left-wing member for Cunningham, New South Wales (centred on Wollongong), was transferred from Immigration and Ethnic Affairs to Housing and Construction. He must face the continuing and growing gulfs of class, age and gender within Australian housing, the enduring problems of impoverishment caused by tenure and a potentially major problem of growing obsolescence. He will be helped by the majority of states (see Carter, 1984). Non-Labor states may seek to oppose and frustrate new initiatives and there are strong vested interests opposed to change. During the late 1970s most critics blamed non-Labor governments for growing housing problems. The task for such critics today, perhaps, is to try to make positive contributions to the solution of those problems.

## Australian Dwelling Types: A Photographic Interlude

The following sequence of photographs illustrates some of the dwelling types discussed in the preceding text. Like any other selection they reflect my current interests and the range of material to hand. Notable omissions are, at one extreme, nineteenth-century huts and, at the other extreme, modern high density high-rise resort developments and caravans. I also felt that it was inappropriate and unnecessary to intrude into the limited privacy of the homeless. Dates refer to date of photograph.

1. *Nineteenth-century settler's cottage.*
'The Cottage' at Gunning, New South Wales is lovingly maintained by the Gunning Historical Society. Note the timber walls and the more modern tin roof: in the nineteenth century many such cottages had bark roofs.
(*Source*: author, 1983)

2. *Substantial federation house.*
A 'federation' house built for the Chaffey family at Mildura, Victoria. The Chaffeys were responsible for developing irrigation systems, drawing water from the River Murray, which initiated irrigated fruit and vegetable production in the area. The house is now a museum attached to the regional art gallery.
(*Source*: author, 1982)

3.  *A home for a hero.*
An early post-war detached house in Bendigo, Victoria, typical of the homes for returning soldiers financed by war service loans. Note the timber construction, typical in Victoria. Fibro or brick would have been used in New South Wales. (*Source*: M. Simms collection, *circa* 1950)

4.  *Suburban house of the 1950s.*
This particular dwelling is in Victoria but it is very similar in design to the drawing by Peter Harrison (figure 2). Note the unmade road beside the finished dwelling. The wooden construction, again, identifies this as a Victorian dwelling. (*Source*: M. Simms collection, *circa* 1955)

5.  *Gentrifiers' paradise.*
Substantial older terraces in Carlton, an inner suburb of Melbourne, Victoria. Note the lavish iron-work (often brought to Australia as ballast in ships which carried wool to the British Isles). Close to Melbourne University and the CBD such terraces have become extremely popular and expensive.
(*Source*: author, 1979)

6.  *Variations on a gentrifying theme, 1.*
Former working-class terrace housing now almost completely colonized and transformed from decay to trendy: close to Sydney Harbour, The Rocks, the CBD. (*Source*: author, 1979)

7.   *Variations on a gentrifying theme, 2.*
Action groups have been campaigning against the loss of low-cost inner-city housing since the mid-1970s. A factory wall in an inner Sydney suburb, Chippendale, provided the ideal site for their expression of views of estate agents and 'trendies'.
(*Source*: author, 1981)

8.   *A Queensland 'high-set' house.*
This is a new and well built example of a classic tropical dwelling. Raised on stilts, with weatherboard outer walls and (typically) tin roofs, this style is much rarer south of the Queensland/New South Wales border. (*Source*: author, 1979)

9.   *South Australian Housing Trust 'double-units'.*
An example of a style of public housing which is widespread in South Australia but extremely rare elsewhere. These semi-detached 'double units' are at Mt Gambier, but are typical of other SAHT dwellings in metropolitan Adelaide and elsewhere in the state. Few dwellings of this type have been sold.
(*Source*: author, 1983)

10.   *Victorian high-rise public housing.*
Massive tower blocks overwhelm their surroundings in the Melbourne suburb of Fitzroy. Built in the 1960s by the Victorian Housing Commission, they represent the limited public comprehensive redevelopment of inner areas. Generally unpopular, they typically house new migrants or those public tenants least able to exercise choice.
(*Source*: author, 1979)

11.   *New brick housing built for the South Australian Housing Trust.*
These dwellings at Mt Gambier are typical recent SAHT construction both for rental and for sale. (*Source*: author, 1983)

12.   *Mixed housing types, inner Sydney.*
Renovated nineteenth-century terraces in the Glebe Estate contrast with 1960s Sydney City Council flats. Obtained by the Commonwealth government from the Church Commissioners, the estate was a pilot scheme for inner-city public sector rehabilitation. It stands as an enclave of publicly owned rehabilitated dwellings within an advancing tide of high-cost gentrification. (*Source*: author, 1979)

13.   *A block of 'units'.*
A substantial block of units in Hobart, built to higher standards than those in the inner western suburbs of Sydney. Its location also gives it a potential for conversion into 'holiday units' – an important factor in the loss of rental accommodation.
(*Source*: author, 1983)

14.   *Detached 1960s suburban home.*
Double brick house in the Adelaide hills speculatively built in the late 1960s and sold for A$16,500 in 1969. It is typical of the better middle-income homes of the period. Like many others it has subsequently been expanded with a horizontal extension and the addition of a second floor (at a cost in 1980 of more than A$20,000). (*Source*: C. Forster collection, 1979)

15.   *High-density up-market housing.*
Located in one of the many bays of Sydney Harbour this private development contrasts dramatically with the regularity of much post-war suburbia. (*Source*: author, 1979)

16.   *Canberra on sea?*
New dwellings nestle amongst trees at Surf Beach in Eurobodalla Shire: the area around and to the south of Batemans Bay, near Canberra, is one of rapid expansion for tourism, retirement and second homes. (*Source*: author, 1981)

## NOTES

1.   I should like to thank: Jan Wells for assistance in collecting data on housing construction; Stuart Hay and David Patterson for preparing good black and white photographic prints from diverse originals; Peter Harrison for giving me his drawing and sound common sense; and the St George Building Society and the The Knightsbridge Display Village for providing figure 1.

2.   This essay has been written specially for *Built Environment* and has been revised for the present book. It represents a distillation of a book in progress on the political economy of Australian housing.

## REFERENCES

Allport, C. (1983) Women and suburban housing: post-war planning in Sydney, in Williams, P. (ed.) *Social Process and the City*. Sydney: Allen and Unwin, pp. 64–87.

Australian Bureau of Statistics (1983) *Cross Classified Characteristics of Persons and Dwellings, Australia*, ABS, Catalogue No. 2452.0.

Australian Housing Research Council (1980) *Women in Last Resort Housing*. Canberra: Department of Housing and Construction.

Australian Institute of Urban Studies (1975) *Housing for Australia*. Canberra: A.I.U.S.

Ball, M. (1982) Housing provision and the economic crisis. *Capital and Class*, **17**, pp. 60–77.

Berry, M. (1983) The Australian city in history: critique and renewal, in Sandercock, L. and Berry, M. (eds.) *Urban Political Economy*. Sydney: Allen and Unwin, pp. 3–33.

Berry, M. (1984) Urbanisation and accumulation: Australia's first long boom revisited, in Williams, P. (ed.) *Conflict and Development*. Sydney: Allen and Unwin, pp. 8–30.

Bethune, G. (1984) The New Commonwealth-State Housing Agreement. Paper given at the Australian Institute of Urban Studies annual conference, Canberra, November 1984.

Bethune, G. and Downie, M. (1982) The Australian Housing System. Paper given at the Australian-German Conference on Urban Problems and Policies, Australian National University, Canberra, September, 1982.

Boyd, R. (1978 edn) *Australia's Home*. Harmondsworth: Penguin (first published by Melbourne University Press, 1952).

Burke, T. (1983) The private rental sector: problems, prospects and policy. *Urban Policy and Research*, **1**(4), pp. 2–10.

Burke, T., Hancock, L. and Newton, P. (1984) *A Roof Over their Heads*. Melbourne: Institute of Family Studies.

Burnley, I. (1980) *The Australian Urban System*. Melbourne: Longman-Cheshire.

Cannon, M. (1975) *Life in the Cities*. Melbourne: Nelson.

Carter, R. (1980) Housing policy in the 1970s, in Scotton, R. and Ferber, H. (eds.) *Public Expenditures and Social Policy in Australia II: The First Fraser Years*. Melbourne: Longman-Cheshire, pp. 363–86.

Carter, R. (1983) Housing Policies for the Low Income Group in Australia: Recent Developments in Context and Approach. Paper presented at ANZAAS Congress, Perth, May 1983.

Carter, R. (1984) Emerging Housing Policy Issues in Australia: Deregulation, Tenure Neutrality and All That. Paper presented at AIUS Conference, Canberra, November 1984.

Committee of Inquiry into Homelessness and Inadequate Housing in the ACT and Surrounding Regions (1984) *Homelessness — A Capital Problem*. Canberra: AGPS.

Committee of Inquiry into Poverty (1975) *Poverty in Australia* (2 vols.) Canberra: Australian Government Publishing Service (AGPS).

Core Consultants (1983) *A Review of the Private Rental Housing Market in Victoria and Implications for Tenancy Law Reform* (2 vols.) Melbourne: Victorian Ministry of Housing.

Crough, G. and Wheelwright, T. (1982) *Australia: A Client State*. Melbourne: Penguin.

Daly, M. (1982) *Sydney Boom, Sydney Bust*. Sydney: Allen and Unwin.

Denoon, D. (1983) *Settler Capitalism*, Oxford: Oxford University Press.

Field, T. (1983) Pensioners who rent—problems and alternatives. *Social Security Journal*, June, pp. 23–37.

Freeland, R. (1982) *Architecture in Australia: A History*. Ringwood: Penguin.

Hamnett, C. (1984*a*) Gentrification and residential location theory: a review and assessment, in Herbert, D. and Johnston, R. (eds.) *Geography and the Urban Environment: Progress in Research and Applications*, Vol. VI. Chichester: Wiley, pp. 283–319.

Hamnett, C. (1984b) Housing the two nations: socio-tenurial polarization in England and Wales, 1961–81. *Urban Studies*, **43**, pp. 1–17.

Harloe, M. (1982) Towards the decommodification of housing? *Critical Social Policy*, **1**, pp. 39–42.

Harloe, M. (1984) Sector and class: a critical comment. *International Journal of Urban and Regional Research*, **8**(2), pp. 228–37.

Harman, L. (1984) Capitalism, patriarchy and the city, in Baldock, C. and Cass, C. (eds.) *Women, Social Welfare and the State*. Sydney: Allen and Unwin, pp. 104–29.

Head, B. (ed.) (1983) *State and Economy in Australia*. Melbourne: Oxford University Press.

Henderson, R. (1983) Rentals and poverty, *Australian Society*, **2**(8), pp. 8–9.

Henderson, R. and Hough, D. (1984) Sydney's poor get squeezed. *Australian Society*, **3**(4), pp. 6–8.

Hugo, G. (1984) Macro demographic and social trends in Australia: their implications for urban development and management, in Stimson, R. (ed.) *Urban Australia: Living in the Next Decade*. Canberra: AIUS, pp. 24–58.

Hutton, J. (1970) *Building and Construction in Australia*. Melbourne: Cheshire.

Kemeny, J. (1981) *The Myth of Home Ownership*. London: Routledge and Kegan Paul.

Kemeny, J. (1982) Public and private housing: a false distinction. *National Housing Action*, pp. 5–7.

Kemeny, J. (1983a) *The Great Australian Nightmare*. Melbourne: Georgian House.

Kemeny, J. (1983b) Economism in the new new urban sociology: a critique of Mullins' 'Theoretical perspectives on Australian Urbanisation'. *ANZJ Sociology*, **19**(3), pp. 517–27.

Kendig, H. (1979) *New Life for Old Suburbs*. Sydney: Allen and Unwin.

Kendig, H. (1981) *Buying and Renting: Household Moves in Adelaide*. Canberra: AIUS.

Kendig, H. (1984a) Gentrification in Australia, in Palen, J. and London, B. (eds.) *Gentrification, Displacement and Neighbourhood Revitalisation*. Albany: Suny Press.

Kendig, H. (1984b) Housing careers, life cycle and residential mobility: implications for the housing market. *Urban Studies*, **21**, pp. 271–83.

Kendig, H. (1984c) Housing tenure and generational equity. *Ageing and Society*, **4**(3), pp. 249–72.

Logan, M., Whitelaw, J. and McKay, J. (1981) *Urbanization: the Australian Experience*. Melbourne: Shillington House.

McQueen, H. (1982) *Gone Tomorrow: Australia in the 80s*. Melbourne: Angus and Robertson.

Milligan, V. (1983) The state and housing: questions of social policy and social change, in Graycar, A. (ed.) *Retreat from the Welfare State*. Sydney: Allen and Unwin, pp. 101–22.

Mullins, P. (1981a) Theoretical perspectives on Australian urbanisation: I. Material components in the reproduction of Australian labour power. *ANZJ Sociology*, **17**(1), pp. 665–76.

Mullins, P. (1981b) Theoretical perspectives on Australian urbanisation: II. Social components in the reproduction of Australian labour power. *ANZJ Sociology*, **17**(3), pp. 35–43.

Mullins, P. (1983) Theory and Australian urbanisation: a comment on Kemeny's remarks. *ANZJ Sociology*, **19**(3), pp. 528–33.

Mullins, P. (1984) Hedonism and real estate: resort tourism and Gold Coast development, in Williams, P. (ed.) *Conflict and Development*. Sydney: Allen and Unwin, pp. 31–50.

Neutze, M. (1977) *Urban Development in Australia*. Sydney: Allen and Unwin.

Neutze, M. (1978) *Australian Urban Policy*. Sydney: Allen and Unwin.

Neutze, M. (1981) Housing, in Troy, P. (ed.) *Equity in the City*. Sydney: Allen and Unwin, pp. 104–22.

Newman, P., Annandale, D, and Duxbury, L. (1984) The rise and decline of the inner city? *Urban Policy and Research*, **2**(1), pp. 7–17.

Orchard, A. (1984) Ideas for Australian housing: Stretton and his critics, in Williams, P. (ed.) *Conflict and Development*. Sydney: Allen and Unwin, pp. 119–33.

Paris, C. (1984*a*) Private rental housing in Australia. *Environment and Planning A*, **16**, pp. 1079–98.

Paris, C. (1984*b*) *Affordable and Available Housing: The Role of the Private Rental Sector*. Canberra: AIUS.

Paris, C., Stimson, R. and Williams, P. (1984) *Public Housing and Market Rents in South Australia*. Canberra: Australian Housing Research Council.

Paris, C., Stimson, R. and Williams, P. (1985) From public housing to welfare housing. *Australian Journal of Social Issues*, **20**(2), pp. 105–17.

Paul, L. (1983) The Australian Welfare State: An Examination of Public Housing Policies, with particular reference to the Australian Capital Territory. Unpublished honours thesis, Department of Sociology, Faculty of Arts, Australian National University.

Priorities Review Staff (1975) *Report on Housing*. Canberra: AGPS.

Smith, N. (1982) Gentrification and uneven development. *Economic Geography*, **58**(2), pp. 139–55.

Spearitt, P. (1978) *Sydney Since the Twenties*. Sydney: Hale and Iremonger.

Stilwell, F. (1980) *Economic Crisis, Cities and Regions*. Sydney: Pergamon.

Stretton, H. (1970) *Ideas for Australian Cities*. Adelaide: Orphan Books.

Stretton, H. (1982) Housing: An Investment for All. Paper presented at the National Housing Conference, Sydney, September, 1982.

Troy, P. (1984) *Low Income Housing in the Inner City*. Canberra: Urban Research Unit, Australian National University.

Watson, S. (1985) The Production and Reproduction of Patriarchal Relations in the Australian Housing System. Paper presented at the First National Women's Housing Conference, Adelaide, March 1985.

Wight, B. (1984) The First Home Owners Scheme: Experience to Date. Paper presented at the AIUS Conference, November 1984, Canberra.

Williams, P. (1984) The politics of property: home ownership in Australia, in Halligan, J. and Paris, C. (eds.) *Australian Urban Politics*. Melbourne: Longman-Cheshire.

*Chapter 6*

# Transport in Australia's Cities

DEREK SCRAFTON and MARGARET STARRS

By its nature transport should be dynamic, yet the industry supplying transport to many of the world's cities is extraordinarily traditional, even stick-in-the-mud, with agencies jealously guarding what they have come to expect to be their right to funds to construct roads and bridges, private bus and taxi companies tightly protected against potential competition, and railways trying to balance technological innovation and outdated labour practices.

Australian urban transport provides a high level of service to the private car driver and passenger, to the bus, tram, ferry and suburban train rider, and to the freight and service industries moving about its major cities. But the high cost of providing this service is one of the serious financial issues facing Australians, costs which are partly due to an inability to respond to the need for change in the transport system, or at best responding slowly and inadequately.

Indeed, there has been an unwillingness in Australia to accept that change will occur in the nation's urban transport networks, whether the people, the governments, the builders, operators and equipment suppliers like it or not. It may be possible for one or more of these agencies to influence the pace of change, but the change is inevitable: shifts of emphasis between modes, new facilities replacing old, new work practices, greater efficiency, different requirements from a changing population and so on.

Of particular concern is the way in which 'solutions' to urban transport 'problems' have often been perceived only within the context of a single mode or without reference to the dynamic and inter-related nature of the land-use/transport system. If more successful approaches to transport problems are to be determined, both transport problems and possible solutions must be viewed in a broader comprehensive manner.

This chapter describes the urban transport systems existing in Australia's major metropolitan areas (Sydney, Melbourne, Brisbane, Perth, Adelaide, Canberra and Hobart) and some aspects of urban transport in smaller towns; the urban transport task; current issues in urban transport; and the need for and possible character of urban transport in the future.

## Urban Transport Services

*Urban Road Systems*

The bulk of the passenger and freight urban transport task in Australia is carried in privately owned and operated rubber-tyred vehicles operating on roads constructed and maintained by local and state governments, using finance from local, state and federal sources. The states are responsible for most of the extensive networks of urban arterial roads in the major metropolitan areas and for the limited number of urban freeways found in some of the state capital cities. (Slightly different jurisdictional responsibility prevails in the federal territories.) Local governments provide and maintain the widespread urban local and collector road system in Australia, which services the extensive low-density suburbs that characterize Australian cities.

Table 1. Arterial road network characteristics for major Australian cities in 1981.

| | Length (km) | | Daily Travel (veh-km × $10^6$) | | Mean daily travel per person (km) | Average no. of travelling lanes |
|---|---|---|---|---|---|---|
| | Freeway | Other Arterials | Freeway | Other Arterials | | |
| Sydney | 29 | 1455 | 0.9 | 30.2 | 10.6 | 2.3 |
| Melbourne | 83 | 1705 | 3.4 | 29.1 | 13.9 | 3.6 |
| Brisbane | 17 | 697 | 0.8 | 11.0 | 12.2 | 3.3 |
| Perth | 20 | 1042 | 1.3 | 13.5 | 17.5 | 2.9 |
| Adelaide | — | 675 | — | 11.4 | 12.3 | 3.4 |
| Hobart | — | 106 | — | 1.5 | 9.7 | 2.6 |
| Canberra | 11 | 94 | 0.2 | 3.2 | 16.9 | 3.3 |

*Source*: NAASRA (1984).

Melbourne has clearly the largest urban arterial road network of any of the major cities in Australia, ranking highest by: length of freeway, length of arterial roads in general, and average number of travelling lanes. The last measure is considered by National Association of Australian State Road Authorities (NAASRA, 1984, p. 25) to be a general indicator of road space in peak traffic periods. Sydney has the second longest arterial network but has a lower average number of travelling lanes than the remaining cities, reflected in poor peak operating conditions in Sydney.

Melbourne and Sydney are characterized by approximately equal volumes of daily travel which are well in excess of the other cities, Perth having the third highest level of travel. The difference between cities is far less pronounced in respect of the mean daily distance travelled per person. The interesting aspects are that the average distance travelled in Sydney (the largest city) is lower than for all cities except Hobart, there is a significant difference between Melbourne and Sydney (the two largest cities), whilst Perth and Canberra exhibit much larger values than the other cities.

Although there is a reasonable number of performance indicators available for urban roads, many relate to particular components of a road network and are not appropriate general indicators for a network as a whole. Unfortunately, the quantity and quality of information available on network-wide indicators is limited; NAASRA (1984) and the Bureau of Transport Economics (BTE, 1984b) are the most recent sources.

A useful indicator reported by NAASRA was measured travel speed for three cities: Sydney, Melbourne and Adelaide. These values are presented in Table 2. (The road lengths surveyed comprised 33 per cent, 24 per cent and 38 per cent of each network respectively.)

Table 2. 1981 Morning peak travel speeds.

|  | Peak Travel Speed (km/hr)[1] | Percentage of Roads with Peak Speed | | |
|  |  | Under 20 km/hr | 21 to 40 km/hr | Over 40 km/hr |
| --- | --- | --- | --- | --- |
| Sydney | 41 | 11 | 42 | 47 |
| Melbourne | 42 | 7 | 35 | 58 |
| Adelaide | 47 | 3 | 31 | 66 |

Note: 1. Travel distance weighted mean.
Source: NAASRA (1984).

The level of service in Adelaide is clearly higher than in the larger cities of Melbourne and Sydney. Although figures are not available for the other capital cities, their level of service is considered to be more in line with that of Adelaide than of Sydney or Melbourne. The comparison assists in evaluating the relative merits of allocating public funds between the Australian states, but actual allocations and spending have not necessarily reflected this perspective.

The road accident figures for Australian urban areas are another indicator of performance of urban roads, albeit one which is socially and politically sensitive. BTE (1984b) reports that in 1980 over 75 per cent of urban fatal road accidents occurred in the three eastern seaboard states, 40 per cent being attributable to New South Wales. A clearer indication of the relative accident rates between the mainland states is given by the fatal accident rate per 100 million VKT. The rate has declined over the period between 1975 and 1981 from approximately 2.5 accidents per 100 million VKT to approximately 2 accidents per 100 million VKT. (Tasmania's rate is higher.)

The level of amenity on the local road system is a significant indicator of non-traffic performance. The local roads in Australian cities, as elsewhere in the world, are characterized by conflict between their traffic function and property access functions. Most established residential areas in Australian cities were designed and established on the classical hierarchical approach to road classification in which the collector road category performs both the traffic and property access functions. Consequently, collector roads tend to carry significant volumes of both through and local traffic, resulting in a general loss of residential area amenity. The problem is far from resolved; progress is being made in all states and some local governments have made major changes to their systems, but it will be some time before a satisfactory level of amenity is reached in residential streets, defined in terms of 'peace' and safety.

*Urban Transit Systems*

Private carriers account for almost all of the urban freight transport in Australia, but there are large public bodies and private companies providing urban passenger transport, mainly with buses. Private and public sectors maintain fleets of service vehicles from the small traders' fleets to very large utilities' operations. Suburban rail services are important in funnelling the CBD traffic in Sydney and Melbourne, but less significant in Brisbane, Adelaide and Perth. The inner suburbs of Melbourne are the location of the largest tram system outside of Europe, and a residual single tram line and new guided bus route are useful adjuncts to the Adelaide urban public transport system. The ferry routes across and along Sydney Harbour are well known and important; smaller ferry routes also provide public transport across the Brisbane and Swan (Perth) rivers.

An unusual feature of Australian urban public transport is the role of the state governments in providing, licensing and/or subsidizing services. The exception is in Brisbane, where the city council (the only Australian metropolitan-wide elected civic authority) runs the bus services, but even there the complementary suburban electric trains are run by the state through Queensland Railways. In Sydney and Melbourne the inner suburban rail services use downtown tunnels to provide subway-type operations similar to European S-bahn operations. There are no Australian equivalents to U-bahn or rapid transit services found in other world cities.

Public transport in Australian provincial towns and cities is based on bus systems, some of which are provided by state authorities (e.g. Launceston,

Newcastle) but the majority by private bus companies. In a few towns the local councils provide the service (e.g. Whyalla) or contribute to operating costs through subsidies (e.g. Mount Gambier). State governments also provide subsidies to public passenger transport services in provincial towns.

## Sydney

The suburban rail services in the Sydney conurbation are provided by the State Rail Authority (SRA of NSW) with a network which runs some 168 km northwards to the provincial city of Newcastle, south 83 km to Wollongong, and 127 km west to the Blue Mountains. Bus services are provided by the Urban Transit Authority (UTA) and numerous private bus operators; approximately 38 per cent of bus-km were operated by private buses in New South Wales in 1983/84. The UTA also provides the bus services in Newcastle. Ferry services on Sydney Harbour are mainly provided by the UTA, although a few small privately-owned ferries also exist.

The passenger journey numbers on government provided public transport services shown in table 2 include Wollongong (rail) and Newcastle (rail, bus and ferry) as well as Sydney; no data are available on the split between these cities. Approximately equal numbers of passengers are carried on UTA bus and rail services, while ferries account for almost 4 per cent of passengers. Private buses carried a further 68.1m passengers in 1981 in Sydney and Newcastle.

Sydney's rail services are almost all electrified and operate with double-deck trains. Inter-urban services to Newcastle were electrified in 1984 and to Wollongong in 1986. The UTA ferry fleet comprised fifteen ships and five hydrofoils while the bus fleet comprised 1719 buses (including 192 buses in Newcastle). The private bus fleet in Sydney comprised 1572 buses, approximately the same size as the UTA fleet (Dodgson, 1985). There is no direct government subsidy of bus services in Sydney, although student contracts provide an important source of carriers' revenue.

## Melbourne

Government owned passenger transport in Melbourne is operated by the Metropolitan Transit Authority (MTA). Rail, tram, and bus services are provided. There are also a large number of private bus operators in the Melbourne suburbs; these carriers receive operating and capital subsidies from the Victorian state government.

Urban rail services are electrified and operated with single-deck cars. There are over 300 km of track in the network. The largest passenger carrying component of the Melbourne transit system are the trams, most of which run on-street. Since 1975 the fleet has gradually been upgraded, although a significant proportion of trams that were built before 1956 still remain. The tram routes serve mainly the near-city established suburbs,

Table 3 summarizes the most recently available data on metropolitan public passenger transport systems.

Table 3.    Passenger journeys and kilometres operated by city and mode, 1983/84[1]

| City | Passenger Journeys ('000) | Kilometres Operated (m) |
|---|---|---|
| *Sydney* | | |
| SRA Rail[2] | 198,065 | 24.2 |
| UTA Bus[3] | 187,675 | 65.9 |
| UTA Ferry[3] | 17,381 | n.a. |
| Private Bus | 68,100[4] | 40.0 |
| Private Ferry | n.a. | n.a. |
| *Melbourne* | | |
| MTA Rail | 83,000 | 14.5 |
| MTA Tram | 102,000 | 24.4 |
| MTA Bus | 20,000 | 13.5 |
| Private Bus | 55,000 | 37.7 |
| *Brisbane* | | |
| QR Rail | 35,833 | 4.9 |
| BCC Bus | 42,753 | 23.0 |
| Private Bus | 7,300[5] | 7.2 |
| Private Ferry | 1,147[4] | n.a. |
| *Perth* | | |
| Westrail Rail | 8,754 | 2.4 |
| MTT Bus | 46,712 | 32.1 |
| MTT Ferry | 439 | n.a. |
| *Adelaide* | | |
| STA Rail | 12,610 | 3.9 |
| STA Tram | 2,854 | 0.8 |
| STA Bus | 54,216 | 37.6 |
| Private Bus | n.a. | n.a. |
| *Hobart* | | |
| MTT Bus[6] | 10,600 | 7.6 |
| Private Bus | n.a. | n.a. |
| Private Ferry | n.a. | n.a. |
| *Canberra* | | |
| ACTION Bus[6] | 20,500 | 14.5 |

*Notes*: 1. *Sources*: CGC (1985), Dodgson (1985); 2. Includes Newcastle & Wollongong; 3. Includes Newcastle; 4. 1980/81; 5. 1981/82; 6. 1982/83.

but routes are still being extended, using exclusive or semi-exclusive median rights-of-way wherever possible. The MTA operated buses serve those close-in suburbs that do not have tram services while private operators provide most of the bus services in outer metropolitan areas.

In 1983/84 rail and tram services accounted for over 60 per cent of passenger journeys but only 43 per cent of km operated. In contrast private buses carried 21.1 per cent of passengers and operated 41.8 per cent of total km. This reflects the lower productivity of bus services in Melbourne, and the impact of operating bus services in lower density outer suburban areas.

*Brisbane*
Urban public transport services in Brisbane are provided by privately owned buses and a ferry, buses owned by Brisbane City Council (BCC), and Queensland government-owned trains. The state government subsidizes both local government (60 per cent of fare revenue) and private (up to 40 per cent of fare revenue) bus services (Dodgson, 1985, p. 7), while BCC also subsidizes the single ferry service across the Brisbane River.

Rail services in Queensland are being progressively electrified in the 1980s, with the Brisbane suburban electrification having been completed in 1986. Since 1978/79 rail passenger journeys have increased nearly 40 per cent, assisted by the construction of a new rail bridge across the Brisbane River linking the formerly separate rail lines on the north and south sides of the city. The BCC is the only municipal operator of bus services in the Australian capital cities, operating a fleet of nearly 600 buses, providing conventional bus services, as well as a number of fast express services from the outer suburbs (Cityxpress).

BCC buses plus the urban rail services together account for most passengers carried (91.5 per cent), with the privately operated bus services carrying only 8.5 per cent of passengers.

*Perth*
Urban public transport services in Perth are the responsibility of the Western Australian state government-owned Metropolitan Transport Trust (MTT), which operates bus and ferry services and contracts urban rail services from the Western Australian government railway (Westrail). There are no privately operated bus services in Perth.

The majority of the transport task in Perth is undertaken by the MTT's fleet of approximately 900 buses. One suburban rail line was closed in 1979 but re-opened in 1983 after an inquiry which recommended it remain closed! Planning and design work is now underway for electrification of the three rail lines in Perth.

The concentration on bus services in the Perth transit system is similar to that found in Brisbane and Adelaide, the two other medium-sized (*c.*1 million) major cities on the Australian mainland.

*Adelaide*

Public transport services in Adelaide are provided by a single South Australian government-owned body, the State Transport Authority (STA). However, four private bus operators remain serving outer metropolitan areas, particularly in the hills suburbs to the east of Adelaide. The state government purchased most of the other private bus operators in 1974, following discussions on alternative approaches to overcoming the private operators' financial problems.

The STA operated in 1984 a fleet of about 750 buses, 155 railcars and 22 tramcars (STA, 1984). There is currently under construction a busway using the German O-Bahn guidance technology ; the first stage of public operation (6 km) to the north-east suburbs opened in March 1986 (Wayte and Starrs, 1982). There are four corridor railways with several branch lines, one tram line in its own right-of-way (it was retained when street trams were replaced by buses in the late 1950s), and close to 100 bus routes, most of which radiate out from the CBD. Ten of those routes channel on to the guided busway.

Buses dominate public transport services in Adelaide with almost 80 per cent of passengers carried and 90 per cent of km operated. The one tram service shows surprising productivity with only 1.8 per cent of km operated and 4.1 per cent of passengers journeys.

*Hobart*

The Tasmanian Metropolitan Transport Trust (MTT) operates bus services in the state capital of Hobart, and in two other provincial cities, Launceston and Burnie. There are a limited number of privately operated bus services in Hobart; no government subsidy is provided. Urban rail services provided by the former Tasmanian Government Railways were withdrawn in 1974. There are also privately operated ferry services in Hobart, but they only carry a limited number of passengers since the re-opening of the Derwent Bridge, which was closed for several years following a major accident in 1975.

In 1982/83 the MTT operated a fleet of 213 buses in Hobart over a route network of 260 km, carrying 10.6m passengers and operating 7.6m km.

*Canberra*

Public transport services in Canberra are operated by the Australian Capital Territory Internal Omnibus Network (ACTION), a division of the Federal Government Department of Territories. All services in Canberra are provided by buses. The network is based on three interchanges which are linked by frequent express services, with local bus services acting as feeders to the interchanges.

In 1982/83 ACTION's fleet of 352 buses carried 20.5m passengers and operated 14.5m km. The passenger numbers are boardings (not journeys) and this combined with the interchange network inflates the number of passengers relative to other systems (Dodgson, 1985, p. 11).

*Performance*

There are a number of measures available to examine the relative performance of the publicly operated transit in Australian cities. The data are from CGC (1985) and relate to the 1983/84 financial year. Table 4 summarizes five performance measures for the five largest systems; incomplete data are available on the number of employees in rail systems so rail passengers are excluded from the passengers/employee measure, but rail data are included in all other measures.

The size of the deficit relates to the size of the city; the higher deficit in Brisbane relative to Adelaide and Perth is a function of the size of the rail systems in those cities and the higher operating costs of rail services relative to bus services.

The deficit per passenger is roughly inversely related to the size of the city. Melbourne has the lowest deficit per passenger; it is significantly lower than that in Sydney which is a larger city. Contributory factors are the higher average fare levels and lower service levels in Melbourne relative to Sydney. The low deficit per passenger in Melbourne despite lower labour productivity (passengers/employee), due to two-man operation of trams, is a direct response to the higher fares charged.

The highest deficit per passenger occurs in Perth, higher than in Adelaide and Brisbane, the two other similar sized cities. In view of the other measures in table 4 (particularly average fare and service level) the high deficit/passenger in Perth is difficult to explain; it may relate to a relatively higher cost being charged for the rail operations.

Table 4. Performance measures for the five largest capital city transit systems, 1983/84[1].

|  | Deficit[2] (A$m) | Deficit/Pax (cents) | Average Fare (cents) | Service Level[3] | Passengers/ Employee[4] |
|---|---|---|---|---|---|
| Sydney | 207.3 | 70 | 45.6 | 64.8 | 30849 |
| Melbourne | 218.4 | 56 | 52.3 | 57.5 | 24177 |
| Brisbane | 63.6 | 81 | 45.4 | 40.7 | 28636 |
| Perth | 49.1 | 83 | 39.0 | 44.1 | 22658 |
| Adelaide | 55.0 | 79 | 37.7 | 65.9 | 24727 |

*Notes*: 1. *Source*: CGC (1985).
2. Excludes capital expenditure.
3. Service km/area. Rail & tram km. multiplied by 1.2 to reflect higher level of service relative to bus.
4. Rail passengers & employees excluded.

The service level index is calculated by dividing km operated by the area served. Rail and tram km are increased by 20 per cent in the index to reflect the generally higher service levels provided by those modes relative to buses. The highest service level is provided by the STA in Adelaide, closely followed by Sydney and Melbourne.

The passengers per employee measure shows no consistent pattern with size except that it is highest for the largest system (Sydney). The Melbourne figure is low due to two-man operation of trams, as noted above. The Brisbane figure is significantly higher than for Perth and Adelaide. The Brisbane bus system is operated by a local council, and its lesser access to taxation revenues to finance deficits may force the operation to be more efficient than the state government funded systems.

## The Urban Transport Task

The population of the six state capitals and Canberra, increased 1.2 per cent per annum between 1971 and 1981.[1] Growth was higher than average in Canberra (4.4 per cent), Perth (2.5 per cent) and Brisbane (1.7 per cent). The lowest growth rate of 0.9 per cent occurred in the two largest cities (Sydney and Melbourne) and in the smallest state capital, Hobart. The growth rate for Adelaide was equal to the national average (1.2 per cent). In most cities much faster population growth has been experienced in the outer suburban areas, compensated elsewhere in the older established areas; in some inner suburbs population numbers actually declined. The geographical change in the distribution of the population can be expected to increase average travel times to the CBD for all forms of transport, and probably decrease the share of trips by public transport as it is generally more difficult to serve dispersed populations with orthodox public transport modes.

Demand for travel in urban areas is highest in the mornings and afternoons, with the volumes in these peak periods determining the capacity required in the road and public transport systems. Public transport demand is higher in the morning than the afternoon due to the closer correspondence of work and school start times than finish times. The demand for road space, on the other hand, is greater in the afternoon peak. The central city areas remain the largest single destination in peak times, although their relative importance has declined as population and employment have become more dispersed. This decline in the importance of central city areas has resulted in major shifts during the last decade in mode choice for journey to work at a metropolitan level, with more people travelling by car to decentralized locations at the expense of public transport. However, central areas continue to attract more work trips by public transport than car. The proportions travelling by public transport to central areas remained relatively constant between 1976 and 1981. Despite the importance of public transport for work trips to central areas, 80 per cent of all trips in urban areas are made by car.

Vehicle ownership in Australian cities has been growing at 2 per cent per annum in recent years. In 1981 16.5 per cent of households owned no car, down from 22.5 per cent in 1971. There has been an increasing trend for households to own two or more cars (25.9 per cent in 1971 to 36.2 per cent in 1981). Vehicle usage (in terms of km/annum) has increased faster than vehicle ownership, at 3.5 per cent per annum for the capital cities. Growth rates were above average in Darwin (8.8 per cent), Brisbane (6.7 per cent), Hobart (6.0 per cent) and Perth (4.8 per cent). Except for Hobart, these cities experienced above average population growth.

Growth in road traffic levels in most capital cities has been catered for by some freeway construction, major arterial road improvements and traffic management schemes. Where capacity has been increased, traffic volumes generally expand quickly to fill new capacity, particularly in central areas. There has been little change in travel times on the road system during peak times since 1961, but the peaks have spread somewhat, perhaps indicating some deterioration in service levels (BTE, 1984a, pp. 37–8).

Usage of government public transport has remained fairly constant since 1976. There were some exceptions due to major improvements or organizational changes. Trips per head in the six state capitals and Canberra fell from 99 (1976) to 94 (1981), but these averages conceal differences between the cities. Melbourne, Brisbane, Perth and Hobart experienced declines while Sydney, Adelaide and Canberra experienced increases. Vehicle kilometres operated increased in all cities, except Melbourne which remained constant over the same period. Most government-owned transit systems increased the number of route kilometres served over the same period, although data are not complete.

Insufficient data are available on privately operated public transport to undertake similar analysis and no government public transport systems publish data on the task undertaken in peak periods.

## Public Sector Finance for Transport

This section deals with roads and with publicly owned and operated public transport services as there is a paucity of data relating to those operated by the private sector despite the fact that they are all strictly regulated, and some are subsidized with public funds.

Table 5 shows the changes in urban road expenditure for each of the six states, ACT and Northern Territory between 1974/5 and 1983/4.

Expenditure on both urban arterial roads and urban local roads declined in real terms between 1974/75 and 1983/84. Expenditure on urban arterial road construction fell by 28 per cent while maintenance expenditure increased by 8 per cent. Expenditure on urban local road construction

Table 5. Percentage change in expenditure on urban roads, 1974/75 to 1983/84.

| State | Urban Arterials | Urban Locals | Total Urban |
|---|---|---|---|
| New South Wales | −11.9 | 16.7 | 1.0 |
| Victoria | −33.4 | 75.1 | −5.3 |
| Queensland | −37.6 | 27.3 | −7.2 |
| South Australia | −19.6 | 17.9 | −2.5 |
| Western Australia | 7.0 | 2.7 | 5.3 |
| Tasmania | 0.5 | 13.0 | 5.4 |
| Northern Territory | 35.7 | −81.0 | −59.1 |
| Australian Capital Territory | −71.9 | −72.3 | −72.1 |
| Totals | −23.2 | −27.5 | −24.9 |

Source: BTE (1985) and unpublished BTE figures for 1983/84.

Table 6. Cost recovery rates for urban public transport, 1982/83 and 1983/84.

| City | Mode | 1982/83 | 1983/84 |
|---|---|---|---|
| Sydney | Bus & Ferry | 35 | 39.3[1] |
| | Rail | 34 | |
| Melbourne | Bus & Tram | 38 | 52.8 |
| | Rail | 34 | |
| Brisbane | Bus | 38 | 34.9 |
| | Rail | 22 | |
| Adelaide | Bus & Tram | 22 | 31.2 |
| | Rail | 13 | |
| Perth | Bus & Ferry | 35 | 32.3 |
| | Rail | 14 | |
| Hobart | Bus | 35 | 33.6 |
| Canberra | Bus | 28 | n.s. |
| Darwin | Bus | n.s.[2] | 10.6 |

Notes: 1. Includes Newcastle (rail, bus, ferry) and Wollongong (rail).
2. Not stated.
Sources: 1982/3 – Dogdson, 1985, p. 13 (includes capital).
1983/84 – CGC, 1985, p. 18 (excludes capital).

increased only marginally (4 per cent) whilst a major increase of 46 per cent occurred in maintenance. Road expenditure has increased markedly since 1981/82 with the introduction of the Australian Bicentennial Roads Development Program, thus the trend reported in table 5 is less marked than the decline which occurred in the decade prior to 1981/82.

Until the early 1970s most government bus and tram undertakings came close to breaking even, while rail systems made fairly modest deficits. Since then, however, deficits on most systems have increased despite creative accounting such as abolition of debt repayments and increased payments for concession reimbursements.

Urban public transport deficits were estimated (Dodgson, 1985) to total A$793.5m in 1982/83 for the six state capitals, Canberra and Newcastle. In 1983/84 the Commonwealth Grants Commission reported deficits of A$669.1m for the six state capitals, Darwin and Newcastle (CGC, 1985, Vol. II). The CGC did not include capital payments in its deficit calculations.

Table 6 shows that cost recovery rates varied between 10.6 per cent in Darwin and 52.8 per cent in Melbourne in 1983/84. These figures exclude capital charges. When capital charges are included (1982/83 figures) the cost recovery rates decrease significantly. In general rail recovery rates are lower than for bus services, although in the two largest cities, Sydney and Melbourne, the recovery rates for bus and rail are similar.

## Current Issues

A willingness to recognize urban transport as a topic with a comprehensive solution is the first step in tackling the problems facing the industry in Australia. It seems to be easier and more convenient to ignore the relativity between provision of roads, provision of urban public transport, and their relationships to demand, and continue to deal with each as a separate issue.

The basic finding is that public roads plus privately owned and operated transport account for over 80 per cent of passenger, freight and service trips at a much lower expenditure than public transport. Carriage of road freight by public enterprises is almost negligible. However, there are significant numbers of service trips made by publicly-owned vehicles (e.g. electricity and water utility fleets). As already explained, there are extensive publicly-owned passenger transport systems, but they are comparatively expensive to operate.

Without an integrated supply/demand overview, determination of the optimum level of investment in transport infrastructure remains elusive. Australians will continue to expect roads to be built ahead of need, without reference to an optimum level of service. New road capacity tends to be used as soon as it is built, so that the level of service remains the same; although more trips may be made, there is no direct relationship to either need or the significance of the level of service.

Much has been written and said (and some modelling has been undertaken) on the interaction of land use and transport. Clearly, the use of public transport declines as activities are decentralized. The rectilinear street networks in most Australian cities cater well for non-radial transport trips by motor vehicles, and keep service and freight traffic away from the central cities. In the case of private transport, sprawling outer suburban home and work activities reflect in higher transport costs, but similar trends in public transport costs have not been passed on to users, partly because the relationship is not so clear. To what extent should other increasing costs, such as maintenance of inefficient labour practices or higher head office overheads, be laid at the door of longer distance passengers, who may have been encouraged to locate in outer areas by other government policies?

In practice transit fares have been held down to compensate for hapless land-use planning policies. As an extreme example, in several Australian capital cities the needy and carless have been relocated in distant suburbs partly because land is cheap and others avoid public housing in these areas – out of sight and out of mind, offset only by lower transit fares!

Although the continual calls for more and better roads and more and better transit services might suggest otherwise, the supply of transport in Australian cities has improved considerably in recent years, but at a cost. Excess capacity exists in the public transport industry and there are opportunities for modal rationalization and integration. Unfortunately progress is slow as it requires the redistribution of resources and services from declining markets to areas of increasing demands. The solutions are complicated in some cities by the growing outer areas being served by private operators. One technique is for government to take over the private operators; improved services will be assured, but the cost problem will equally certainly be exacerbated (Kain, 1983).

Whatever course of action is taken to fit better the service level to demand for both roads and public passenger transport in the different Australian cities, and recognizing that the solutions for one city may not be those for another, there are some common threads. Sydney and Melbourne are the big-city pair, Brisbane, Perth and Adelaide can learn from one another, and the smaller cities are a distinctive grouping. Seeking value for money expended for transport is an approach that can be applied in all cities: how can we reduce costs in a non-competitive market? Are transit services and roads being provided at minimum costs?

Obviously, redistribution is as difficult in transport as it is in other fields (Herber, 1985), but it is no excuse for doing nothing or continuing with the status quo when some obvious solutions are available. For example, taxis could be used to provide services on nights and weekends when bus and train services cannot be justified. Private buses could be used to alleviate the peaks for government systems. And road funds are not being allocated to the areas with the highest economic benefits (BTE, 1984a, p. 48).

The impediments to such changes often are institutional and political. To overcome such hurdles more and rigorous evaluation of the social benefits of alternative transport delivery is required, putting together road construction and maintenance costs, the costs of congestion, assistance to those without access to private vehicles, and so on. Unfortunately capital solutions to perceived problems tend to have more attraction than provision of funds for analysis of costs and needs.

## The Future

Will there be major change in urban transport in Australia? Or will we have more of the same?

The physical infrastructure already in existence will continue as the basis of the capital city transport systems. The size and character of the vehicles using the arterials, local roads and rail lines will change, but the rights-of-way will continue to be occupied by roads in all cities and tracked systems in the larger areas. 'New' systems will be introduced in some locations (such as the Adelaide O-Bahn and the Sydney monorail), but the greatest expense will go towards extending the existing networks to serve developing suburbs and on maintaining the stock of roads and railways.

The cities' transport links to their hinterlands and external connections will influence the priority accorded to local developments. The new road connections to Brisbane Airport and the landside facilities required to service the second Sydney Airport are good examples. On the other hand, we can anticipate that resources will in future not be diverted away from important urban projects to less economically justified ones such as rural local roads or major rail or port facilities that merely duplicate transport infrastructure already in place. Such has been the experience in Australian transport in recent years.

While the transport facilities will look the same, their role will change considerably in the near future. More effective use of taxis and cars, greater application of paratransit, considered use of alternatives to the use of private cars for CBD-bound trips, better design to encourage more cycling and walking for local trips, and planning the future shape and form of Australian cities to minimize transport requirements and costs, are all possibilities for change in the near and medium-term future (see, for example, *Search*, 1979). The extent to which they will be adopted will vary, given the size, shape, topographic characteristics and political structure of the capital cities. It may well be the smaller communities that are the vanguard of innovation. What is certain is that the handicaps to adoption are institutional, not technical.

In summary, the accent in urban transport has been on supply for too long. A switch to transport facilities which reflect the demand for services is a basic requirement in Australia, underpinned by more realistic land-use planning which does not leave (by default) accessibility at the bottom of a totem pole of priorities in which the availability of cheap land and not-so-cheap water is at the top. Under such a process, people are left to fend for themselves in first finding work and services and then sorting out their transport access.

Two influences which will encourage innovation are high costs of the existing public transport systems, which will force a move away from the fixed route bus and rail systems where they can no longer be justified

(Scrafton, 1985, p. 41) and the complementary moves within those systems to greater internal efficiency. Improved analytical techniques and a better understanding of the costs of transport are other developments that will force the individual, cities and governments to ensure that the *status quo* will not provide a long-term answer to the transport problems of Australian cities.

NOTE

1. In 1984 the Bureau of Transport Economics prepared a background paper on urban passenger transport for a seminar it hosted as a contribution to a Transport Outlook Conference (Morris & Puttaswany unpub.). The paper included a comparison of travel patterns in cities since 1971; this section draws heavily on that paper.

REFERENCES

Bureau of Transport Economics (BTE) (1984*a*) Assessment of the Australian Road System. BTE Report 56. Canberra: AGPS.

Bureau of Transport Economics (BTE) (1984*b*) Assessment of the Australian Road System: Operational Characteristcs. BTE Information Paper 10. Canberra: AGPS.

Bureau of Transport Economics (BTE) (1985) Australian Road Financing Statistics 1974–75 to 1983–84. BTE Information Paper 14. Canberra: AGPS.

Commonwealth Grants Commission (CGC) (1985) *Report on Tax Sharing Relativities 1985*. Vol. II: *Appendices and Consultant Reports*. Canberra: AGPS.

Dodgson, J. S. (1985) Benefits of Urban Transport Subsidies in Australia. BTE Occasional Paper 71. Canberra: AGPS.

Herber, B. P. (1985) *Poor Persons and Poor Governments*. CRFFR Research Monograph 42. Canberra: Australian National University Centre for Research on Federal Financial Relations.

Kain, P. G. (1983) Government and Urban Transport: The Adelaide Experience. Centre for South Australian Economic Studies, Occasional Paper No. 6.

Morris, G. and Puttaswany, C. (1984) Statistical Overview of Urban Passenger Transport 1976–1983. BTE, Canberra, unpublished.

National Association of State Road Authorities (NAASRA) (1984) The NAASRA Roads Study, 1984. Urban Arterial Roads Report, and Local Roads Report.

Scrafton, D. (1985) *Transport Policy & Strategic Planning*. Adelaide: Director-General of Transport.

*Search* (1979) (Journal of the Australian & New Zealand Association for the Advancement of Science) **10**. (Special Edition on Urban Transport containing five essays on urban transport policy, research, planning and energy issues).

State Transport Authority (1984) *Annual Report 1983/4*. Adelaide: Government Printer.

Wayte, F. A. and Starrs, M. M. (1982) Adelaide's O-Bahn busway experiment. *Built Environment*, 8(3), pp. 197–204.

ACKNOWLEDGEMENT
The authors acknowledge the assistance of Peter Tisato in commenting on a first draft.

# Chapter 7

# 'Like a Building Condemned': Planning in an Old Industrial Region

LEONIE SANDERCOCK and PETER MELSER

Once upon a time, in most 'developed' societies, urban planners could take economic growth for granted. They did not spend time trying to understand the continuous processes of growth and change, or analysing how resources flow through the economy or how to enlarge or redirect those flows. This reflected nations which assumed that the motors of economic growth could keep turning, and that no special steps were required to create and foster productive enterprise, jobs and earnings, or to link industrial development to the development of housing, transport, education and other sectors of an urban economy. Peace, full employment, Keynesian macro-economic management tools, and the welfare state were expected to solve the nation's main social and economic problems.

In property owning democracies, planning has traditionally meant controlling private development through a limited bag of technical tricks – zoning and floor space ratios and densities, for example. Or, during the more innovative period of national urban policy under the Whitlam government in Australia, the Department of Urban and Regional Development's approach to urban problems was to spend money – on programmes like area improvement, inner-city renewal, land purchasing. But these sorts of approaches can only operate during periods of urban and economic growth, when the horse to be steered by the reins of planning controls is going somewhere, and when levels of economic growth seem able to support a large public sector. Planning languishes when there is no forward movement. Planners' powers have been mainly negative; they can, sometimes, prohibit development, but there is little they can do to stimulate it when the motive to invest fails.

The agenda for the 1980s and beyond cannot be a carbon copy of these past assumptions. Planning needs to address what happens when the growth machine stops, or changes direction.

\* \* \*

Once upon a time, many urban planners were dreamers, visionaries, reformers, improvers, Thinkers about the Good Society. Then they became a 'profession'. They struggled to carve out a niche for themselves in the bureaucratic power structure with the creation of separate planning departments in the public service. Planning legislation was enacted, and planners claimed that planning was a distinctive operation based on unique knowledge and operational skills. A professional institute was created, entry qualifications defined, closed shop arrangements negotiated with public sector employers and a system of 'recognizing' tertiary courses was developed. In the more or less uniform course content, emphasis was on physical planning, regulation of land use and development. Little emphasis was given to social issues like urban poverty or regional inequality, and no attention at all to the debate about what constitutes a Good City or a Good Society.

\* \* \*

And there was a time when Wollongong's built environment, shaped by agricultural and mining capital, was a string of villages and farms and mines loosely dotting the slopes of the escarpment and nestling in the narrow basin between the range and the ocean. And then industrial capital came to the town – iron and steel industries, metal foundries and all their associates. An immigration policy after World War Two encouraged unskilled workers to come and provide the labour. In the long boom period, the iron and steel industries grew at a rate of ten per cent each year.

As a consequence, population, industries related to steel, and employment also boomed. The population of the Wollongong Statistical District tripled between 1947 and 1981. A city of workers' suburbs, primitive in their social infrastructure, took the place of the string of cosy villages.

> Wollongong, the City, is a vain, vain woman,
>> continually reducing.
> At the plain edge, the excess succumbs to the salt
>> treatment,
> while, off to the west, houses in fits of
>> depression,
> shout suicides down the mountain.
> As the city approaches the Range, it snags and
>> unravels.
> The suburbs sulk like defeat in the confines of
>> the Basin.

('Behind Dapto')

Public money provided hostels for migrants, then large public housing estates for those at the bottom of the heap. It built schools, which gave the migrants' kids a basic education. But public money never provided a decent transport system, or community facilities. If ever a region cried out for 'area improvement programmes' this one did. Yet it was systematically ignored for twenty years by a state Labor government (1945–65), and again neglected – compared with the attention lavished on Melbourne and Sydney's 'deprived western suburbs' – by the federal Labor government of 1972–75.

This company town (for it is a town largely shaped by The Broken Hill Proprietary Company Ltd (BHP), controller of the iron and steel industries and most of its subsidiaries) has suffered all of the problems but none of the advantages of smaller, more remote company towns. It has suffered the social and environmental effects of a powerful company's presence, indeed dominance, of the region, but has not enjoyed the private provision of social and communal facilities that company towns must provide in order to attract labour when they're in more remote locations.

So 'the Gong' has been a tough, no frills, workers' town. But now the boom days are gone, and jobs disappearing.

> The suburbs are anxious, like a parent after mid-
> night.
> . . .
> The City is malcontent, tense like a eunuch.
> It stands under drizzle and does not contemplate
> purpose.
> . . .
> The City braces itself like a building condemned:

('Air-raid: The Future')

\*     \*     \*

So times change. Capitalism evolves (somebody has called it a 'moving target'), and spatial arrangements change with capitalism's changing requirements for production. Capitalism is the chief architect of urban space. The international capitalist economy is undergoing a phase of restructuring which has involved mergers, takeovers, rationalizing of production processes, shedding of labour, technological change, shifts in the location of plant and an ever increasing mobility of capital.

Just one of the more notorious effects of footloose capital shifting investments between localities, cities, regions and nations has been job loss and destruction of once thriving communities, particularly in the old industrial regions. Coal-mining, steel producing and shipbuilding towns and villages in Wales, Scotland, north-east England, northern France, the 'frostbelt' of north-east United States, and in Australia, Wollongong, and Whyalla, have been devastated. Their narrow economic bases have left them particularly vulnerable to disinvestment, changing energy prices, competition from the newly emerging industrializers of the Third World and techno-logical changes. *Capitalists investing in 3rd W, results in a frckup of the towns*

Their physical environments, forged in the pre-history of environmental and planning regulations, are not attractive to the 'sunrise' industries. In Wollongong, *like Wagon which they have "created".*

> Easterlies purl and then gust up under the
>     escarpment,
> exploding with dust and picking out iron from
>     the cloud-clover
> Southerlies mean suspended matter,
> acid gases, and brown sounds on the radio:
> (the pollution reports are intoned as regular
>     items)
>
> ('The City of Sinuses')

Most of the old industrial towns in decline could be described in the way Fitzpatrick has Wollongong.

> There is shit in the streets
> There is shit over rooftops and suburbs
> it is sloshed against Works buildings,
> nudging around pylons and scaffolding,
> it is straddling the sheer walls of Keira
> and the shank walls of Ousley,
> it is shackling the city.
>
> ('Illawara Gothic')

Doubly devastated, then, are these areas where the labour force has been decimated and the built and natural environment despoiled. What does the future hold for these places?

> Wollongong, City of Sinuses:
> where old men lean blowing into street corners,
> and Emphysema, the city's cousin,
> hides out in the coal yards and mines dotting the
>     slopes . . .
> and the workers nearing forty
> run despairing along the arterials,
> their faces collapsing slowly apart like
>     mud-slides.
>
> ('The City of Sinuses')

What happens to the men over forty who are retrenched? The families who can't keep up house repayments when one or two of its earners' incomes stops? The adolescents with no job prospects? What happens to the derelict factories and mines and warehouses? Whose problem is it? The local councils? State Government? National Government? What can any of these levels of government do? And is it a problem for economic planners, educationalists, social planners, trade unions?

*Obviously says that no one group can be "socialist". It is too complex. One swallow will not make a summer.*

The ambivalent promise of transition prevails. And bureaucrats scan the horizons in search of the future. How should public policy respond – at national, regional and local level – to a future of jobless growth and uneven spatial development? In our research in progress we are seeking answers to this and other questions by focusing on the problems of Wollongong, an old industrial city of 225,000 people, which grew rapidly in the post Second World War long boom and is now, not quite as rapidly, in decline.

In this paper we want to outline the dilemmas of restructuring and transition, and the choices – where there are any – for workers, local communities and policy-makers. Not the least of the challenges this poses is how urban planners can contribute to thinking about the policies for *managing the transition*.

*     *     *

Wollongong is a relatively self-contained one-industry town. It is just 60 miles down the coast from Sydney, yet only 5 per cent of the resident labour force work outside Wollongong, and less than 2 per cent of people who work there live outside it.

An iron and steel plant operated by BHP Steel International Group's Slab and Plate Products Division is located around the man-made harbour at Port Kembla, on a once beautiful headland across the basin from the escarpment. The steel works absorbed labour voraciously in the post-war boom, reaching its peak workforce of some 23,000 in the 1970s. Government-assisted migrants from Britain, Southern Europe and Latin America were fed into 'The Works' which, in 1971, offered one-third of Wollongong's employment. Manufacturing and coal mining together contributed half of all jobs in the city. From 1947 to 1961 overseas born residents made up 40 per cent of the population increase, and in recent years, despite the economic downturn, migrants from Lebanon, Vietnam and elsewhere in South East Asia have continued to settle in Wollongong.

Since 1971, employment in Wollongong has been slowly diversifying, with growth in the professions, clerical and sales occupations. (Sixty per cent of the new jobs in the economy between 1971 and 1981 were taken by women, in clerical, sales and service occupations.) Yet in 1981 AIS, with over 20,000 employees, still provided almost 25 per cent of Wollongong's jobs. The metals sector as a whole provides more than one-third of all jobs, and more than 60 per cent of these are blue collar.

Overseas migration declined sharply in the late 1960s, since when natural increase, mostly to migrant couples, has been the major contributor to population growth. Overseas migrants and their children now make up 51 per cent of Wollongong's population and this changed pattern of growth has particular significance for the present crisis. For many of the people who have made up this natural increase, these children of migrants, are now entering the labour market and facing particular difficulties in finding jobs.

> Inhabitants of the iron city
> come hard from the mould:
> they are graven as steel
> and caked with a fine talc ore.
>
> They breathe iron filings
> and bring forth case-steel children
> and are clothed with a weariness
> that shifts with the turning of the year.
>
> They are continually changing shifts
> (the Gates are Renewal)
> and move in sooling mob
> through the streets and the business centres.
>
> Their forging and hammering
> is transferred to their time behind the wheel:
> they drive like a shaft of sheet-steel
> bent towards the chewing mill
> . . .
> They are insular, like boredom:
> no one ventures further than The Headlands or
>     The 'Rail.

Fitzpatrick's poem *The Iron People* captures the purpose of this town. Work. Production. Growth. Industry. Hard work in a hard-edged built environment, incongruously softened only by a spectacular natural setting. All the more undermining and demoralizing then, when jobs begin to disappear, which happened in 1982. Early that year registered unemployment was 7,700. By December 1983 the official unemployment rate had trebled to more than 21 per cent, or 21,000 people.

Economic recession, increasing overseas competition and technological change have meant the loss of an enormous number of manufacturing jobs in Wollongong and elsewhere. Nationally, more than 100,000 manufacturing jobs were lost between June 1982 and June 1983, 32,000 of them in Sydney. But in Wollongong the impact of jobs lost is much greater because manufacturing has provided 35 per cent of all jobs, compared to only 18 per cent elsewhere. AIS alone eliminated 6,570 places between June 1982 and December 1983 and the coal industry lost 2,000 jobs. The rapid loss of jobs has been matched by an even larger increase in unemployment as young people continue to enter the labour force. And there is considerable 'hidden unemployment' among women. If the workforce participation rates of women in Wollongong were the same as those in Sydney, for example, there would be an extra 7,750 people in the labour force. Knowing that there is no work for them (and, when married, not entitled to unemployment benefit) most women who want to work simply don't bother registering as unemployed.

This is a deteriorating situation. The length of time that people stay unemployed is increasing. In February 1983, 24 per cent of those unemployed had been without a job for more than a year. By May 1984, this proportion had increased to almost half (47 per cent) and is continuing to grow. People presently without jobs, including young people entering the workforce as well as people who have been laid off, face a prospect of very lengthy, even permanent unemployment, unless the economic situation changes.

Younger workers in the manufacturing sector are hardest hit; manual or blue collar workers are affected more than white collar; and unemployment is concentrated, spatially, in those areas where younger manual workers live. Neighbourhoods with more recently constructed Housing Commission houses have the largest concentrations of unemployment. The unemployment rates in different suburbs in table 1 reflect the concentrations of younger manual workers, and also young people as a whole, within each suburb. Unemployment rates are also higher for young people newly entering the labour force than for any other age group. The proportion of

Table 1.   Unemployment in selected Wollongong suburbs.

| | 1981 Population | 1981 Labourforce | November 1984 corrected unemployment* | Unemployed as % of workforce |
|---|---|---|---|---|
| *Selected Suburbs* | | | | |
| Wollongong | 35,011 | 17,136 | 2,987 | 17.4 |
| Cringila | 3,890 | 1,690 | 409 | 24.2 |
| Warrawong | 9,657 | 4,409 | 1,215 | 27.5 |
| Pt. Kembla | 6,762 | 3,011 | 663 | 22.0 |
| Berkeley | 4,935 | 2,308 | 941 | 40.7 |
| Austinmer | 2,543 | 1,181 | 136 | 11.5 |
| Thirroul | 5,117 | 2,179 | 393 | 18.0 |
| Bulli | 4,455 | 1,993 | 419 | 21.0 |
| Woonona | 9,105 | 3,988 | 649 | 16.3 |
| Corrimal | 17,973 | 7,926 | 1,738 | 21.9 |
| Fairy Meadow | 17,391 | 8,033 | 1,098 | 13.7 |
| Figtree | 7,695 | 7,747 | 446 | 11.9 |
| Unanderra | 11,230 | 5,028 | 710 | 14.1 |
| Dapto | 22,857 | 9,790 | 1,696 | 17.3 |
| Albion Park | 13,999 | 5,941 | 1,134 | 19.1 |
| Warilla | 25,798 | 11,562 | 2,966 | 25.7 |
| Wollongong LGA | 169,381 | 77,201 | 14,425 | 18.7 |
| Shellharboour LGA | 41,790 | 18,431 | 4,301 | 23.3 |
| Kiama LGA | 11,286 | 4,702 | 706 | 15.0 |
| Wollongong SD | 22,457 | 100,334 | 19,433 | 19.4 |

*The official unemployment rate is created to reduce unemployment. 'Corrected' figures are the result of multiplying of unemployment beneficiaries by the ratio of officially registered unemployed to beneficiaries at peak periods. A change in the number of beneficiaries gives a truer indication of change in the unemployment rate. People ineligible for the benefit quickly cease visits to the unemployment office and are therefore taken off the register even though they remain unemployed.
*Source:* Australian Bureau of Statistics, 1981 Census; CES, Employment Data.

people aged 15–19 who are unemployed ranges between 20 and 35 per cent in most suburbs, occasionally higher, as in Berkeley.

These figures describe the magnitude of the unemployment in Wollongong, but do not evoke the meaning of the experience in people's lives, or how they try to cope as victims of this vicious restructuring process. To try to understand that meaning and experience we have been interviewing retrenched steelworkers and coal miners, youths unable to get work since they left school, women retrenched from clothing factories, and the families of these people. What follows is based on these interviews.

> The first of a week's night shifts . . .
> The hours will drag like a terrible desolation.
> It is the beginning of a beginning that has no
>     end,
> Only greys, begrudgingly, between pitches.
> In the military-grey yards and at the furnaces
> The indigenes talk of *The Night Shift* and grin
>     knowing grins
> . . .
>
> They like to pretend that, one day, it will all be
>     different:
> . . .
>
> Inside the works-yard men sit in the dirt.
> They practice not talking.
> They wear the faces of those who are always
>     waiting
> But they do not think about it.
> The whistle looks for breath to sound the End of
>     Shifts:
> Some have already moved off

('Dog Watch')

The abrupt retrenchments in late 1982 were met with a mix of stunned shock and exhilaration. While public officials, public service staff, unionists and others recognized what the sharp contraction in employment would mean, many retrenched workers saw their layoff as a liberating release from a life routine of drudgery. Most of the first people laid off expected to get a new job whenever they chose. Ernie and Grace Shaw reported the cycle they went through with retrenchment. Their A$6,000 retrenchment payment enabled them to pay off their car and other accumulated debts, to take a two week holiday in a Queensland resort and manage through Christmas with still some money in reserve. The Shaws rent a house in one of the Housing Commission's new subdivisions. Ernie reported feeling relief at being away from his job and having the opportunity to develop hobbies and spend time at home.

For the first few weeks being released from work was exciting and invigorating. Ernie fixed up the backyard, took care of things around the house, and felt absorbed by work in his family surroundings. The change occurred quite quickly as the money was spent. The dole money didn't go as far as expected. Unemployment soured as he realized it was not going to be easy to find a job. Ernie tried for several jobs and was not accepted, and in a more intense search went knocking on factory doors. He wrote his name and background on countless forms, which became demoralizing with repetition. More disturbing was the derision, comments like 'you must be joking, we haven't got any work', which Ernie started to feel as a more personal rejection.

The lack of choice about whether or not to work, and the increasing sense of rejection, changed a sense of freedom into one of entrapment. Initially, the role swap – his wife Grace had found casual work 'off the books' for A$20 per day – had been exciting, but now he 'learnt what women complain about, being closed in by four walls'. Ernie didn't have enough housework to do and when it was finished he felt trapped. Grace had taken the car and it was a long way to walk to the shops. The journey was too boring to walk, especially when the trip had no real purpose.

Distance is magnified by poverty – and the cost of petrol and the cost and time involved in bus trips. Younger single people responded differently from Ernie. Dave, in his early twenties, would walk quite long distances, oblivious to how long it would take him. Dave had nothing in particular to do anyway, and unlike Ernie, had no fixed home; he stayed with a brother, his mother, or one of several friends. But in his travels he did not range outside the five suburbs to the south of Lake Illawarra.

For neither Dave nor Ernie did areas of detached housing with centrally located shops offer a satisfactory environment for their daily lives. The environment in fact increased their isolation and difficulty in staying active; things triggered by their demoralization and unemployment.

Even with a home, Ernie had no real place since he lacked a job and a sense of social function. The recurrent description of men like Ernie is that they are 'under the wife's feet'. Married couples quickly conclude that they cannot be together twenty four hours a day.

Young people without families would seem to be in a better position to cope with unemployment. They have no children to support, they are more mobile, and more apparently able to take advantage of the beach and other opportunities for recreation. Their experience of unemployment seems somewhat different. Young people, especially those who have recently left school, often don't have enough of an established role in life to maintain, or develop, strong identities. Moving from school to work, in our culture, is associated with initiation into adulthood, a rite of passage to independence and respect as a full member of the community. With those options cut off there is no clear model around which a young person can shape an adult identity. Long hours of sleep and television are the reported solution for many. Many of these still have childhood, in the form of parental support, and a family home, to hold on to.

When this breaks down, as it often does through conflict or the movement of parents to a retirement area, these young people are left more adrift. Many young people speak of nervous breakdowns, many are shaking continuously during interviews. The longer the unemployment, the clearer the signs of personal disintegration. Many people, before their twenty-first birthday, seem unemployable.

> Out-of-shift workers stand dazed in the avenues.
> They scratch at their singlets and frown
> And do not go further than the corner.
> They walk back through their single, iron gates.
> Dropping the latches carefully in place behind
>     them,
> And go up into their cluttered living rooms
> where they sit with the TV on,
> Loud, and Everlasting Present.

('Air-raid: The Future')

\* \* \*

In examining the response to economic restructuring and unemployment by government, community and unions, what seems to be most striking is the fragmented and uncoordinated nature of these efforts. The federal government especially has failed to mount a coherent programme to address Wollongong's problems. Retrenched workers are offered retraining but this is not linked to any industry plan or job creation effort. Relocation assistance does not provide an effective incentive for people to move out of Wollongong. The Steel Regions Assistance Plan is a piecemeal package of unrelated projects. The Labor government offers short-term jobs through the Community Employment Programme (CEP), thereby reducing unemployment in the very short term, but having no impact on the problem in the longer term. Community-based efforts such as the Community Youth Support Scheme (CYSS), neighbourhood centres and refuges get some support from local and state government but are chronically under-resourced and treated as peripheral by all levels of government.

The left has no alternative economic strategy, either on the national stage, or locally. They scorn suggestions of a high-tech or leisure-led recovery for the region, preferring to talk of re-vitalizing the manufacturing sector. Good, but how? There may be something too nostalgic and self-interested in this left 'line'. A hangover emotion that says that only industrial workers are real workers: and a fear that their own base of support (traditionally in the heavy industry unions) will disappear if Wollongong becomes a High Tech Town or Leisure Coast.

Like 'the left', trade unions' responses tend to be too caught up with old battles, outworn responses. Unions need to develop more forward looking responses than sit-ins and strikes to protect threatened jobs. But why should they, when governments and industry offer them so little in the way of redundancy and retraining packages?

If the left and the unions seem overly concerned with protecting the remnants of the old industrial working class, that in itself needs to be understood in the context of the local 'boosters', hell-bent on reforming Wollongong's 'image' as a dirty steel town. Their vision – expressed politically through the Lord Mayor, an Independent, who is now also the state member of parliament for the area – is for luxury hotels and marinas attracting tourists and sunrise industries attracting professionals into the town, reviving the land and housing market and cleaning up the environment. The assumption that such schemes would boost employment, especially for retrenched steelworkers and coalminers, seems a little pie-in-the-sky. But it is a convenient rallying cry for business interests hoping to raid the public purse.

The unspoken but insidious side of this dream is that the industrial working class will then quietly move away, except for those who are 'presentable' enough to be re-trained as barmen, chefs, hotel cleaners. This boosterism is a middle-class vision whose effect would be to rid a working-class town of its working class.

At least there is a *local* vision, albeit unpalatable to some. Neither state nor federal government have applied their separate or collective minds to the general problem of regional imbalance in the Australian economy, or more specifically to Wollongong's future. Apart, that is, from the usual election throwaways – promises of big capital works projects, but unlinked to industry plans or regional economic analysis.

In late 1982 two researchers within the New South Wales Department of Environment and Planning produced a one hundred page report for the state government's Advisory Committee on Employment, on prospects for employment generation in the region. It was buried for six months, then released in diluted form, but few of its chief recommendations have been taken up. These included recommendations for a Regional Economic Plan for the Illawarra; designation of the region as a special target economic development region; the establishment of an Illawarra Regional Economic Development Commission (with overall responsibility for economic development and job creation using both public and private funds) and a Regional Technology Centre; new forms of assistance for small enterprise establishment (including a small enterprise Venture Capital Fund); and the formation of a human resource council to improve the skill formation processes in the region. The authors argued that the productive capacity of the region lies in the development of its labour force from manual and relatively low skilled to knowledge and skill intensive, noting that presently 66.2 per cent of the population over the age of fifteen have *no qualifications at all*. And they concluded with suggestions for financing economic development and employment generation in the region (Larcombe and Blakely, 1982).

Why has nothing come of this innovative and provocative study, even as the basis of further study? Is it because both NSW and federal Labor governments have been too distracted by a host of (media-manufactured) 'scandals' and 'affairs'? Or, is it because, in calling for joint action from federal, state and local governments and from a multitude of federal and state departments, the report was asking the impossible – co-operation between different levels of government?

*  *  *

How, then, do we move from a description of what is, to some offering as to how things might or ought to be? What assumptions about the present and future underpin our thinking about alternatives? After we have spelt out these assumptions we will proceed by asking, first, how much might be achieved at the purely local level, and then map out some of the bigger issues which we feel cannot be avoided so long as we focus only on the local community.

Our starting point is the proposition that the most likely economic future for this country is one of *jobless growth*. This is supported by most of the literature on the employment effects of technological change and on the nature of global capital reorganization (Jones, 1982; Jenkins and Sherman, 1979; Gorz, 1982). This literature also argues that future employment opportunities will increasingly lie in jobs with decreasing skill requirements. (There will be more jobs for janitors, for example, in the next decade than jobs created in all of the 'high tech' sunrise industries). But to say that this is inevitable is to say that technological change is immune to human intervention, which is clearly nonsense. And yet there has been no successful sustained resistance to technological change in two centuries past (Rumberger, 1984; Nora and Minc, 1980; Sweet, 1984).

Some governments have handled the problems related to the introduction of technological change and industrial restructuring more successfully than others (from the point of view of the affected workforce) and we must learn from those successes – Scandinavian, West German, Japanese, (Sandercock, 1983; Ford, 1983; Ford et al., 1984).

Because there is a very important socio-spatial component to the restructuring process – that is, it affects real people in real places, but some much more drastically than others – it seems not good enough to concentrate on national economic policy and assume that any benefits will (eventually. . .) trickle down to depressed regions.

Yet it is this very reality (of apparent national neglect of hard hit localities) that, in many countries, has produced concern and action at the local level on economic development and employment issues.

What kinds of responses have local authorities been coming up with? In the United States, true to tradition, the favoured responses have been Community Development Corporations, non-profit, but designed to nurture small local business start-ups, and public-private partnerships. The literature reports considerable success (Sarkissian, 1983; Committee for Economic Development, 1982).

Some US states have also been prepared to support local communities' lobbying for departure taxes on firms withdrawing investment, the obverse side of which is the more familiar story of local agencies offering incentives to firms which bring investment to a locality. Local planning agencies often perform a central role in such 'deals', turning a blind eye to non-conforming land uses or promoting, converting or re-zoning sites for new uses. Sadly, in their efforts to outbid each other for new investment and employment creation, some local authorities have shown scant regard either for their neighbours/competitors or for the prospective local workforce and residents (Hudson and Plum, 1984).

A three-dimensional planning policy that links local manpower planning activity with local labour market analyses with a local enterprise board or development agency has been evolving in Britain and America (Cooke, 1983), but the yield of these policies by way of employment gains is meagre compared to the magnitude of the problems in some areas.

There are lessons to be learned. Firstly, the room for manoeuvre open to local government for local economic initiatives is critically constrained by national government attitudes to economic policy. Central government credit and interest rate policies may conflict with the needs and intentions of local government activities. And if the attitudes of central government involve an acceptance of the logic of capitalist development and the market as the principal economic steering mechanism – especially when this involves deliberately opening a national economy to the forces of international competition – then the scope that remains for local initiatives that break with this rationality is pretty limited (Hudson and Plum, 1984).

There is, too, in this desperate struggle between localities to sell their areas to capital, a real danger that the focus of attention will be shifted away from questions like 'why is national unemployment so high?', or 'what is happening to Australian manufacturing industry?', to those of how best to secure a share of such investment as *is* on offer for one's own area. In this way competition between areas and between working people living in them will be reinforced as an 'inevitable' or 'normal' aspect of everyday life. So it is vital that local planners recognize the class implications of these local strategies for economic development.

Which is not to say that *nothing* can be done at local level – rather, that in the absence of appropriate, co-ordinated local, state and national policies being developed, what can be done will be limited and probably defensive in character, reacting to the wreckage produced within a local area by capitalist strategies for accumulation.

So what kinds of national policies need to be developed to help Wollongong?

Certainly the future of the Wollongong economy is inseparable from the future of manufacturing industry in Australia. We need more debate about what kind of manufacturing sector (if any) we want, and how it might be revitalized. At one level this is the old familiar debate about protection levels, tariffs, subsidies, etc. But it should be seen more as a debate about national economic planning and Australia's relationship to the world economy. If we had some national economic development goals (like France, Japan, Scandanavia, West Germany over the past decades) we could contemplate allocating capital to high-priority sectors and locations. In Japan the (increasingly envied) Ministry of International Trade and Industry (MITI) uses 'administrative guidance' to bring about structural adjustment in the Japanese economy. In Sweden the government has access to investment capital in the form of socialized (social security) savings – accumulated on behalf of future pensioners – for national economic planning purposes.

At another level this is a debate about manpower planning, education and training, and skill formation processes. Ford (1982,1984) has argued that some western societies have allowed workers to be deskilled as a result of technological changes (United States, United Kingdom, Australia) while others have used the opportunitiy more positively to re-train and multi-skill workers (Japan, Sweden).

Smith (1980) has proposed massive changes to our education system to match the long-run structural shift to a services-based economy. The unemployed school leavers that we talked to in Wollongong have three words to describe their experience of school – 'waste of time'.

A debate has just begun to emerge in Australia around technology and the future of education. Some pose it as the 'education for life' (as opposed to work) issue. Others see it as a green light for techno-freaks to take over schools. Saner voices talk of the need to re-think the work ethos or of 'demystifying work' and encouraging early retirement, job-sharing, shorter working weeks/years/lifetimes, even of opting out. All of these are very important questions. But in Wollongong one thing is certain. Those who lose their jobs, or have never been able to get one, seem to lose all purpose and meaning in their lives. One middle-aged retrenched coal miner told us he'd gladly work for nothing, if they'd let him. Twenty year olds tell us, mutely, of utter aimlessness without work.

Perhaps the question we all need to be addressing then, at the level of government policy and of personal life, is 'which work, in which economy, for which member(s) of the household, and for how long?' But for individuals to give creative answers to these questions (or community groups or trade unions) needs changes to the welfare system, taxation system, schooling, and so on.

And ultimately, because it is unlikely after this present shake-out of the system that there will be enough jobs to go around, we must face some tough decisions about redistributing either work or income, or preferably some mix of both. The effect of our present reward structure is to pile the costs of structural change almost entirely on those who are locked out of the work-place. A guaranteed minimum income for workers for whom there is no work may well be the price the working community has to pay to buy political and social stability, not to mention a sense of decency.

And finally, to return to the beginning, to planners and the urban environment. Not all workers discarded by capital are free to move to areas that offer better prospects.

> Those people immobilised by circumstance, and jobless for long periods, cannot be expected to put up indefinitely with impoverished, nondescript and desolate residential environments . . . . When workers spent most of their working life in a factory, down the mine, or on the land, they were less concerned about living spaces bereft of amenities. One of the real challenges ahead of advanced capitalist societies, and not just their urban and social planners, is to create the conditions and opportunities that will give as much meaning as possible to the daily lives of people out of work within cities (Badcock, 1984, p. 337).

That is a challenge not only to the imaginations and sensitivities of local planners but also to those controllers of national resources, to invent a long-term national development plan which might smooth out the gross regional imbalances that arise if capital is given open slather to invest and disinvest where it will.

We think planners can make a contribution, but that their past tools are increasingly part of the problem. Definitely not the solution. It seems likely that if planners do not deal with these issues, a new profession or set of professions will emerge to do so.

It ought to be clear by now that any solution to the problems found in capitalist cities and regions must be a broadly based strategy that addresses structural change in its entirety. Perhaps we are calling for an end to demarcation disputes between economic, social, urban and education planners and between levels of government and different government departments. We are certainly calling for an end to cynicism, despair, factional suspicions and infighting, and a beginning for hard-headed yet visionary and holistic thinking about coherent alternatives to the present mish-mash of *ad hoc* responses to Australia's economic transformation.

The time to begin is yesterday.

NOTE

All of the poetry quoted in this paper is from the volume *Wollongong Poems* by Coral Fitzpatrick (Hale and Iremonger, Sydney, 1984). The particular poem is indicated in brackets after each quote.

REFERENCES

Badcock, B. (1984) *Unfairly Structured Cities*. Oxford: Blackwell.

Committee for Economic Development (1982) *Public-Private Partnership: An Opportunity for Urban Communities*. New York: Committee for Economic Development.

Cooke, P. (1983) *Theories of Planning and Spatial Development*. London: Hutchinson.

Ford, G. W. (1982) Human resource development in Australia and the balance of skills. *Journal of Industrial Relations*, September.

Ford, G. W. (1983) Japan as a learning society. *Work and People*, **9**(1).

Ford, G. W. (1984) Australia at risk: an underskilled and vulnerable society, in Eastwood, J., Reeves, J. and Ryan, J. (eds.) *Labour Essays 1984*. Melbourne: Drummond.

Ford, B., Easther, M. and Brewer, A. (1984) *Japanese Employment and Employee Relations: An Annotated Bibliography*. Canberra: Australian Government Publishing Service.

Gorz, A. (1982) *Farewell to the Working Class*. London: Pluto Press.

Hudson, R. and Plum, V. (1984) Deconcentration or decentralisation? Local government and the possibilities for local control of local economies. Revised version of paper prepared for the Congress of the Association of Greek Regionalists, Athens, 1983. Available from R. Hudson, University of Durham.

Jenkins, C. and Sherman, B. (1979) *The Collapse of Work*. London: Eyre Methuen

Jones, B. (1982) *Sleepers, Wake!* Melbourne: Oxford University Press.

Larcombe, G. and Blakely, E. (1982) *Employment in the Illawarra. Prospects for Empoyment Generation*. Report to the NSW Advisory Committee on Employment, Sydney, Department of Environment and Planning.

Nora, S. and Minc, A. (1980) *The Computerisation of Society*. Cambridge: MIT Press.

Rumberger, R. (1984) The Potential Impact of Technology on the Skill Requirements of Future Jobs. Paper presented to US-Australia Joint Seminar, Monash University, September 1984.

Sandercock, L. (1983) Work & Play: the architect, the bee, and the space invader, in McLaren, J. (ed.) *A Nation Apart*. Melbourne: Longman-Cheshire.

Sarkissian, W. (1983) *Employment Creation Through Community Economic Development: Selected Readings*. Sydney: Social Impacts Publications.

Smith, S. L. (1980) *Schooling, More or Less*. Milton, Qld: Jacaranda.

Sweet, R. (1984) Australian Trends in Job Skill Requirements. Paper presented to US-Australia Joint Seminar, Monash University, September, 1984.

*Chapter 8*

# Queensland:
# Planning on the Fringe

JOHN MINNERY

As the other contributions to this volume have made clear, despite all the myths, songs, poems and legends to the contrary, Australia always was and still is highly urbanized. Right from the start of its settlement, towns dominated the human landscape. The early ports clung to the edge of a largely unexplored and unwanted continent, facing outwards to Britain, the Americas and Asia rather than to the interior.

The settlement pattern within each of the states was also highly centralized. The chief port, which became the state capital, was central to the developing space economy of each of the colonies. Thus, most of the states now have over half of their population residing in their capital city. The discovery of gold in several major fields in the mid-nineteenth century boosted flagging, agriculturally-based colonial economies, and pointed the way to the importance of mineral resources in the country's future development.

In settlement pattern, as in many other characteristics, the State of Queensland is different. Queensland's population is less centralized, its resources more dispersed, and its attitude to development more strongly based on the free enterprise ethic than is the case of the other states.

Queensland lies on the fringe of Australia in at least three senses. Firstly, it lies at the edge of the main population concentration stretching from Adelaide through Melbourne and Sydney to Brisbane. Secondly, like Western Australia, it lags in industrial development, relying heavily on earnings from its rich resource endowment. The more developed states of Victoria, New South Wales and South Australia are the reverse, and have grown towards a more integrated industrial economy. As Stevenson notes, 'An important result of Australia's recent mineral development has been to increase the interdependence amongst what might be called the "inner" states [N.S.W., Victoria, S.A.] ' (Stevenson, 1977, p. 9). Thirdly, again like Western Australia, but again unlike the other states, Queensland is experiencing a rapid increase in its population, with a substantial component of this growth coming from migration from other states (Hamnett, 1984). It is thus on the developmental fringe, the frontier, of Australia.

Because of this fringe location, approaches to development and conservation in this part of Australia differ from those in the other states. Many policies in Queensland are based on non-urban values. Traditionally, non-urban political forces have been far stronger than their population base would justify.

In this chapter I will be using very wide, and loosely defined, concepts of 'resources', 'conservation' and 'environment'. Resources will include all the natural endowments of the state which can be developed in some way for financial gain; the environment will simply mean the natural and man-made surroundings within which the state's inhabitants live; and conservation will imply management and wise use rather than preservation. The intention is to discuss and draw conclusions from attitudes to these three phenomena rather than to provide a detailed description of the ways in which resource development and environmental conservation work in Queensland or Australia.

## The Australian Context

The fact that Australia is a federal state has an impact on almost all aspects of urban and regional development. In 1901 the six colonies joined to form the Commonwealth of Australia, although some did so reluctantly. The colonies gave to the new federal government certain powers (defined in Section 51 of the Constitution) but kept for themselves any powers not expressly given away. It was intended that confusion over which level of government had which powers would be kept to the minimum. As Sawer notes:

> The Australian Founders intended to create what has come to be called a 'co-ordinate' federal system, in which the two sets of authorities – central and regional – would act independently of each other, in relation to topics so defined as to reduce to a minimum the possibility of overlap or collusion (Sawer, 1975, p. 34).

But, in fact, as the examples in this chapter suggest, there is considerable overlap and confusion, particularly in areas not considered important in 1901, including environmental protection.

Local government, the third tier of government, is created entirely by state legislation. Local government has its powers defined by the states and has only minimal contact with the federal government.

Over the period from 1901 the relationships amongst the three tiers of government have altered.

> The division of powers between Australian, State and local Governments, which is contained mainly in the Australian constitution but which is constantly changing according to political pressures, legal interpretations, custom and the demands of the moment, determines the basic fields of endeavour of each level of government (Wiltshire, 1975, p. 16).

The aphorism which still best describes the situation, however, is that, 'The federal government has the money, the states have the power and local government has the problems!'

Each of the states has developed its own approaches to urban planning, conservation, the environment, urban issues and so on; although all stem from a common evolutionary ancestor in earlier British practice and legislation.

Because of these differences there is a need to distinguish amongst different types of 'planning'. There has been, in Australia as elsewhere, a tendency for town planners to claim far more for the field of 'planning' than their training or legal powers really justify. Bowman (1979) in identifying the responses of the states to environmental management identifies 'regulatory planning', 'operational planning' and 'policy planning' as three important and distinctive types, a distinction which will be followed in this chapter. The importance of this distincition is that different agencies deal with these different aspects of planning.

In Queensland, policy planning is largely *ad hoc*, unco-ordinated and decided upon by State Cabinet whilst much of operational planning is the responsibility of the Coordinator-General's section of the State Premier's Department. Until recently, the Co-ordinator-General was in charge of a separate department although directly responsible to the Premier. Recently this department was totally absorbed into the Premier's Department. Regulatory planning is largely the responsibility of local authorities overseen by the Department of Local Government, responsible to the Minister for Local Government, Main Roads and Racing!

## The Queensland Context

Queensland is the least centralized of the mainland states in population terms. In 1981, for example, only 47.8 per cent of the state's population lived in the Brisbane Statistical Division, compared with up to 72.5 per cent in the capital cities of the other mainland states.

This lack of centralization has been claimed as the result of a deliberate policy of active decentralization by the state government. However, the basis for the spread of population was set in the nineteenth century with the development of a string of coastal ports, each land-linked only to its

Table 1.    South-East Queensland in the State.

| *Proportion of the State's . . .* | | | | |
| Population (1980) | Establishments | Manufacturing (1979/80) | | |
| | | Employment | Wages | Value Added |
| 59% | 65% | 68% | 66% | 62% |

*Source:* Derived from *Queensland Yearbook*, 1982.

hinterland. Brisbane was at first merely one of these ports, which grew more rapidly because of the resources in its hinterland, its easier connections to the south, and its administrative function. In the other states the capital port was the centre of a web of land communications, linking it to and allowing it to dominate the rest of the state.

The Brisbane region is now moving towards the same concentration of population and production as occurs in the other states. Although the capital city has only 48 per cent of the state's population, the 'south-east corner', the urban area it dominates, has 59 per cent of the state population and contains over 60 per cent of the manufacturing (see table 1).

There is, thus, a dichotomy between the rhetoric and the reality in describing the state's development pattern, a division which influences official attitudes to policies regarding the environment and conservation. Government has, in the past, paid far more attention to the problems of the non-urban sector than to the towns and cities. Its attitudes to development and conservation have been structured to suit this non-urban environment rather than the towns.

Allied to this is the powerful impact of Queensland's 'cinderella' status amongst Australian states. 'Northern Italians like to claim that Italy ends at Rome. In a similar way, many Australians living along the south eastern rim of the continent would argue that Australia ends at Brisbane – if not at the NSW border' (Bowman, 1979, p. 43).

This attitude is apparent at all levels and in surprising places. For example, although Brisbane is the third largest city in the country the traditional focus for Australian urban studies has been the southern cities of Sydney, Melbourne and Adelaide, with the possible inclusion of Canberra as an example of a planned city. Serious academic analysis which includes Brisbane is relatively recent.

Until the 1950s the state's economy relied heavily upon agricultural and grazing production with little manufacturing output or mineral exploitation. Its development in the 1960s and 1970s was fuelled by the discovery and exploitation of vast mineral deposits, particularly coal but also bauxite, copper, gold, silver, and uranium.

This in turn has had two effects. The most immediate is the reliance on mineral development and export for government revenue. The power over the control of mineral resources in Australia rests with the states. As there is no specific reference to minerals in the Australian constitution 'the effect was to retain for the states, virtually unchanged, the powers over the disposition of their mineral resources which they had enjoyed prior to federation' (Stevenson, 1977, p. 14). 'Because ownership of minerals under the ground is distinct from ownership of the land on the surface, the Crown [in this case the state] can retain title to minerals even when the land is privately owned' (Stevenson, 1977, p. 15).

Queensland levies royalties on minerals, as do the other states; but it also effectively subsidizes farmers and development by forcing mining companies to finance railways from their production areas to export points. The policy has evolved over time, implemented through *ad hoc* legislation, but effectively the state government requires the company to put up the finance for the state to build the rail line. Following this, the state repays the company from the rail charges paid for the use of the line. Obviously one user of the line (often at first the only one) is the mining company.

The exploitation of mineral resources is thus quite fundamental to the state's economy. 'Conservation for future use has not been an important objective of state governments, because it conflicts directly with the principal objectives of maximizing output and maximizing government revenues' (Stevenson, 1977, p. 20).

The second but less direct effect of mineral exploitation was the development of a frontier ethos, more pronounced in Queensland and Western Australia but echoing earlier attitudes in the other states. Frontiersmen are, on the one hand, proud of their rugged individuality, their toughness, their ability to tame the wild forces of nature. Yet on the other hand, the frontier is a zone in transition. As all readers of Westerns will know, eventually the frontier is tamed and civilization gains a firm foothold. Queensland currently is in a position which probably parallels that of the American West just after the last gun-toting outlaws were hung. It has changed from being totally enthusiastic about its frontier status to seeking single-mindedly to prove to the rest of the country that it has grown up, that it is now as 'advanced' as anywhere else in Australia.

Until quite recently this was reflected in an inordinate pride in the visible symbols of development: in skyscrapers, new hotels, new office blocks and the like, particularly if these were in the same faceless international style seen in Sydney, New York or London. The historic buildings, which often were destroyed in the process, were not valued. In part this was because they represented an immature, unmodern past; in part it was because, as Brisbane was first settled in 1824/25 by convicts who were too hardened to be kept at Sydney, there was nothing of the long proud tradition which has sustained historical preservation movements in cities such as Adelaide.

In the last few years much of this has changed, at least amongst the urban middle class. Official and unofficial attitudes have changed to the extent that, for example, the Brisbane City Council has produced a Heritage Trail booklet and stuck yellow arrows on footpaths to indicate a heritage trail through the centre of Brisbane. Two older buildings are being retained and refurbished as part of a redeveloped state government pre- cinct in the central city. But this follows only a few years after shameful demolition, in the dark of the night, of a National Trust listed hotel owned by the state government and whose site is now part of that same precinct.

Government attitudes are made by politicians. In the Queensland Cabi- net of eighteen only two are listed as having tertiary education in the 1984 Queensland Government Directory. Most are farmers, graziers and businessmen. The majority are from rural electorates.

Within the state, as is the case elsewhere in Australia, both the state and local government have responsibility for environmental conservation in urban and non-urban areas. Local authorities in Queensland were given a general grant of powers 'for the good rule and government' of their areas in 1936 in terms of the Local Government Act, as well as some specific duties. The power to make town plans, to control land subdivision and to require environmental impact statements are included within their powers, although in all cases under the eventual responsibility of the Governor in Council (effectively State Cabinet). There is as yet no heritage legislation for them to work with.

'Local' level administration in Queensland illustrates something external commentators on the Australian scene often fail to comprehend, namely the incredible effect of scale, of distance. Blainey refers to the 'tyranny of distance' (Blainey, 1966), something which is felt right down to the 'local' level.

There are 134 local authorities in Queensland, ten of them with areas greater than 50,000 km$^2$. The largest, Cook Shire, has an area of 115,341 km$^2$, larger than Belgium (30,513 km$^2$), Austria (83,850 km$^2$) or the Repub- lic of Ireland (70,283 km$^2$); larger than the states of Tennessee (109,411 km$^2$), Maine (86,026 km$^2$), or Virginia (105,715 km$^2$). It is roughly half the size of the United Kingdom (244,019 km$^2$). Yet the resources available to these larger shires bear no resemblance to those of the areas they are here compared with. Table 2 lists the ten most extensive local authorities in Queensland, as well as Brisbane City Council, and some relevant indi- cators. These local authorities are shown on figure 1.

Clearly not all the state's local authorities are as extensive as these. But although 28 of the 134 are between 0 and 99 km$^2$, 63 are between 1,000 and 9,999 km$^2$, 33 are between 10,000 and 49,999 km$^2$, and ten are over 50,000 km$^2$. All, except Brisbane City, are run by part-time councillors with a permanent administrative and technical staff[1].

Clearly both vast size and resource sparsity influence the policy approaches of councils. For example, the costs of maintaining a road system in a sparsely settled shire are out of proportion to its resources, and although the state government effectively subsidizes them through its main roads programmes much of the cost must be borne by local communi-

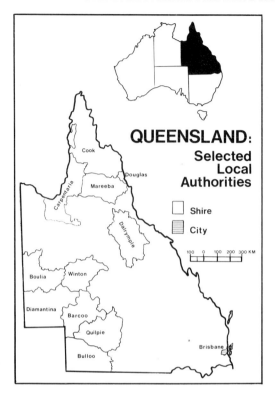

QUEENSLAND:
Selected
Local
Authorities

☐ Shire

▤ City

100  0  100  200  300 KM

Table 2.   Queensland's largest local authorities.

|  | Area (km²) | Population (est. 1983) | All Receipts ($'000) (1981–2) | Rates and Charges ($'000) (1981–82) | Number of Councillors (1982) |
|---|---|---|---|---|---|
| Cook Shire(*) | 115,341 | 7,460 | 2,370 | 330 | 7 |
| Diamantina Shire | 94,690 | 320 | 1,203 | 190 | 7 |
| Bulloo Shire | 73,620 | 500 | 1,562 | 353 | 5 |
| Carpentaria Shire | 68,272 | 3,240 | 2,719 | 553 | 9 |
| Dalrymple Shire | 67,782 | 3,650 | 4,665 | 937 | 9 |
| Quilpie Shire | 67,482 | 1,380 | 2,110 | 436 | 10 |
| Barcoo Shire | 61,910 | 610 | 995 | 130 | 10 |
| Boulia Shire | 61,176 | 640 | 1,247 | 310 | 8 |
| Winton Shire | 53,820 | 1,920 | 2,219 | 800 | 10 |
| Mareeba Shire | 52,585 | 15,050 | 6,371 | 2,662 | 9 |
| Brisbane City | 1,220 | 740,130 | 323,297 | 214,836 | 21 |

*Sources:* Australian Bureau of Statistics (1984), and Queensland: Department of Local Government (1983)
(*) see Note 1.

ties. Local authorities thus tend to encourage development of all kinds, as a way of expanding their resource base through rates revenues.

In this they are like local authorities in other places; but here development policies are more intense, more urgent and more directly linked to 'grass roots' functions than elsewhere. If development incentives are offered as a means of maintaining bridges in a setting where roads are almost literally lifelines then those opposing development are not favourably received.

These attitudes are taken on board by state parliamentarians in two ways. Firstly, they maintain contact with local electoral opinion. And secondly, a number of state politicians have served a political apprenticeship in local government. The current Minister for Local Government, Main Roads and Racing was, for example, the Chairman of Albert Shire, near Brisbane.

The unique position of Brisbane City needs to be noted. It was formed as a unitary local authority in 1925 (the only unitary local authority in Australia, covering almost the whole metropolitan area) and has its own City of Brisbane Town Plan Act and City of Brisbane Act.

Throughout Queensland local authorities have the responsibility for the provision of water, sewerage and local roads, as well as the responsibility for regulatory planning. But, 'Alone amongst the Australian states, Queensland has neither a planning authority nor a separately constituted environmental control agency at the state level. Responsibility for the oversight of statutory planning rests with Local Government Department . . .' (Bowman, 1979, pp. 44–45). So, on the one hand, Queensland local authorities have a greater local responsibility for what is normally understood as 'town planning' than do local authorities in the other states, but, on the other hand, this responsibility increases the possibility of value-based conflicts over roles between professional town planners and the councils by whom they are employed (Minnery, 1985). Resource development and environmental protection are issues which highlight these tensions.

## Illustrative Examples

The examples presented here are not intended to be comprehensive. They do not provide the full story of what happened, or is happening, in each case. Rather they are intended to illustrate relevant aspects of the planning of resource development and environmental conservation in Queensland, to show something of the face of planning on the fringe. Two examples are presented. The first is that of Moreton Island, a large stabilized sand island just off the coast from Brisbane. In this case there were three main sets of pressures, one for the mining of the sand, one for recreation use by urban dwellers and one for the protection of a unique island environment.

The second example is that of the rainforest in the Daintree area of North Queensland. Here a unique lowland rainforest is threatened by land development and road construction. It clearly illustrates the ambiguous relationships between the three levels of government in environmental matters.

*Moreton Island*

Moreton Island is one of the largest stabilized sand islands in the world, but unfortunately it is a journey of only about an hour or so, by boat, from Brisbane. Its sand contains, in part, concentrations of heavy minerals. The sand is mined by a process something like that of dredging for alluvial gold, with the separation of light from heavy sands taking place on site. The bulk of the sand is then dumped next to the mining site. Vegetation and any topsoil are removed before mining takes place. Although this was not the practice earlier, nowadays considerable effort is expended by mining companies to reconsolidate and rehabilitate mined areas. The long-term effects of the recreational and mining pressures on the island had been the focus of a major environmental impact study, resulting in a proposed strategic plan (A.A. Heath and Partners, 1976).

Moreton Island is administered by the Brisbane City Council, and is included within the city's town plan. Brisbane's town plan, like those of the other local authorities in the state, must be initiated and approved by Council, put on public display (at which time the public can lodge objections to the proposal), then forwarded through the Minister for Local Government to the Governor in Council who may reject it, approve it, or approve it with his 'own' modifications. Once approved it has the force of law as a zoning plan, and can be amended only through the normal rezoning procedures.

Mining activities in the state fall under the Mining Act. Mining can take place only after the granting of a mining lease by the Minister for Mines and Energy.

Below and right –
views of Moreton Island.
(By courtesy of
Jim Hutchinson)

The relationship between permitted uses on mining leases and permitted uses in terms of a town planning scheme was, until 1979, unclear. Thus, when in 1975 the proposed town plan for Brisbane went on public display, Council covered itself by including those portions of Moreton Island believed to be subject to mining leases in an 'Extractive Industry' zone. Around 5,000 public objections to this proposal were received (Huxley, 1980, p. 4), out of a total of some 29,000 objections to the whole plan (Haupt, 1978, p. 47).

Somewhat taken aback by the public reaction the Council recommended to the Governor when it forwarded the plan to him that all 'Extractive Industry' land be rezoned as 'Public Open Space'. (A peculiarity of the Queensland town planning system is the hiatus between Council approval of a proposed scheme and final approval by the Governor. Legally the Council cannot amend its own proposals, even to take account of public comment, unless it re-displays the whole proposal. Council must forward its proposal, with representations on all objections, to the Governor through the Minister. Changes can be made by the Governor. Thus a situation has arisen where some Council officers forward objections to their own schemes as a mechanism for correcting drafting and other similar errors!)

Brisbane's whole town plan, including the section relating to Moreton Island, was not accepted by the Governor and was returned to the Council (a procedure which required specific state legislation, the City of Brisbane Town Plan Modification Act, 1976). After modification the town plan was again put on public display in September, 1976. In this plan, Moreton Island was zoned by Council mainly as 'Existing or Proposed Open Space' (which in the town planning scheme would not permit sand mining). The Governor in Council, however, when the plan was approved in 1978 had changed the 'Existing or Proposed Open Space' zoning to 'Non Committed' (which could allow mining).

At that stage, the relationship between mining activities and town planning controls was still ambivalent. In 1979, however, the Mining Act was amended to make it clear that where a mining lease had been granted, so long as the land was being used for mining purposes, this overrode the town planning scheme.

What the Moreton Island episode illustrated was the relative ineffectiveness of non-enforceable strategic recommendations in the face of powerful economic forces; and the very effective control over regulatory planning exercised by the state government when it wished to do so. Given government's attitude to mineral resource exploitation, conservation and environmental considerations do not have any great weight. Yet it must be remembered that the state government at all times acted within legal limits as the legitimate political representative of the people of Queensland. The dichotomy between technical planning and political planning is starkly apparent here.

By mid-1986 the situation was still unsettled. The earlier management plan for Moreton Island has not been officially adopted, although the state government claims to be using it as a guide. There has been no new sand mining, but this results from the world slump in demand for minerals rather than from protective land-use controls. Government says it has committed itself to allowing mining on not more than 5 per cent of the island. There is currently no serious pressure to get it to change its mind. If there were a surge in world demand for heavy minerals, conservationists have little doubt mining companies could persuade government to allow new mining and that the 5 per cent figure would become rubbery. Tourist pressure continues, and is seen by many to be more damaging than sand mining, but both tourist operators and the public are becoming more aware of the potential for irreversible damage.

## Daintree[2]

The major interest in the case of the Daintree rainforest is what was *not* done rather than in the actions performed.

The crucial point about Daintree is the timing: the climax events occurred

Coastal rainforest near Daintree River. (By courtesy of Glen Thomas)

less than one year after the Australian High Court had decided that the
Commonwealth government could legitimately use its external treaty
powers to prevent the construction of a dam in the Franklin River wilderness area of south-west Tasmania. A necessary step in that legal process

was the listing of the relevant parts of south-west Tasmania on the World Heritage List by the World Heritage Committee. Nominations of places are made by the relevant national government, although listing depends upon the application of objective criteria by the world body.

The problems inherent in the conjoint sovereignty which exists in a federal system are well illustrated by the Franklin Dam case. The Tasmanian government, as a legitimate representative of the people of Tasmania, wanted the dam built to supply future electricity needs predicted by the State Hydro-electricity Commission and to provide badly needed employment. The federal government, legitimately representing the people of Australia (including Tasmania), was opposed to the dam largely on environmental grounds. Eventually the two met in the High Court. The Court upheld the Commonwealth's authority in this case (see Baidya, 1983; Coper, 1983).

Yet it must be remembered that one of the reasons the former British colonies joined as a federation in 1901 rather than as a unitary state was to ensure the continuance of the relative autonomy of the state governments. States' rights are a powerful political rallying cry in Australia. All states, of whatever political colour, were disturbed by the implications of the Court's decision. In fact the full ramifications are yet to be explored.

In the Daintree rainforest area, Queensland has a natural phenomenon at least as important as that of south-west Tasmania. It is unique as a 'refugia' area of lowland rainforest containing many rare species of plants and animals (Moyal, 1984). Australia is the only OECD country with intact rainforest and this area in north Queensland is unique in many scientific, aesthetic and heritage characteristics (Borshmann, 1984a, 1984b; Hill and Graham, 1984; Moyal, 1984)

The principal focus of the conflict described here was and is an area within Douglas Shire, just north of Cairns (see figure 1). In general the rainforest is threatened by tourist development and residential land development. In particular it is threatened by the subdivision of land into lots down to one hectare in size (with consequent land clearing, the introduction of domestic, and later feral, pets, and so on), and by the natural and artificial degradation which will follow the recent bulldozing of a 35-kilometre unsurfaced road through the area.

Again, regulatory planning and the three tiers of government are involved.

Douglas Shire has a town plan, prepared by private town planning consultants and gazetted in 1981. In this plan a substantial area of forest, cleared forest and hill land was zoned 'Rural: General Farming'. On the strength of one objection the Minister required important parts of the zoning to be changed to 'Residential' (Borschmann, 1984a, p. 36). In the Queensland town planning system, once the land is appropriately zoned, non-suitability for the purpose is not legally a factor to be considered in the approval of a subdivision design, and so now large areas of the land have been subdivided for residential allotments. None of these are currently served by water, electricity or sewerage. The land concerned in this particular example is generally outside the rainforest area, but its development will put additional pressure on the rainforest. A real estate sign near Cape Tribulation proudly proclaims, 'You can buy freehold land in this Tropical Paradise'.

The unique rainforest in the area is threatened from a number of other directions also. Forest logging, directed by the State Forestry Department, affects parts within the forestry reserves (even though there is considerable doubt over the economic viability of the work). Some parts are being cleared for dairying and cattle grazing (Borschmann, 1984a).

In 1983/84 the conflicts in the area gained both a specific focus and international publicity because of the clearing of a fourwheel drive road from Cape Tribulation to Bloomfield. Emotions ran high (see, for example, the account by Billington, 1984).

The background questions to the construction of the road are well set out by Borschmann (1984a):

> This four wheel drive track has at various times been advocated as necessary for the greater defense of the Far North, as a means of rescuing stranded bushwalkers and fishermen, for securing better access to this remote region to flush out drug runners, orchid thieves, bird trappers, hippies and illegal immigrants who just happen to drop in off the coast.
> But what are the real reasons?
> Certainly the major beneficiaries will not be – as consistently claimed by Douglas Shire Chairman Cr Tony Mijo – the Aboriginal people around the Bloomfield River valley who may want to visit relatives in Mossman or Cairns. Nor is it for the benefit of the small European community – no more than a couple of dozen families – who live in the Bloomfield River district (p. 32).

Borschmann then clearly indicates that 'development' is an important consideration.

> It has long been a pet scheme of the Douglas Shire Council to 'open up' the northern portion of the Shire for development. The Council owns Degarra, a townsite surveyed earlier this century into more than seventy 0.1 hectare (1/4 acre) blocks . . . near the Wujal Wujal mission. The Lutheran Church itself may be tempted to consider the potentially lucrative value of its land there for real estate development (p. 32).

The road which provided the recent focus of national and international pressure was originally bulldozed in 1968 and again in about 1976, in both cases illegally, without survey and on the cheap. Just before much of the area was gazetted as National Park in 1979, the Douglas Shire pushed a 'pilot track' along much of the route. Council also officially gazetted the track, although as Borschmann notes, '. . . they weren't quite too sure where it was on the maps' (1984a, p. 32).

In 1983/84, the Douglas Shire bulldozed this road to make it into a more substantial high quality four-wheel drive track, to be ready for the 1988 celebrations of Australia's bicentenary. The state government amended the boundaries of the National Park (as only State Parliament has the power to declare, remove or alter National Park boundaries) so that the area traversed by the road would be outside the Park. In April 1984, the gazetted road area was expanded to a 60-metre width, and 100 metres on difficult slopes. Conservationists and 'greenies' were incensed, and set up a blockade of the road. The Queensland government and the Douglas Shire cooperated to ensure the road was built. The road is now officially open, although it is unsurfaced, subject to considerable erosion, and likely to need something like $960,000 spent on it to bring it up to satisfactory standard (Borshmann, 1984a, p. 33). In fact, four buses bogged down on it on the day it was officially opened.

Throughout the confrontation conservationists had expected the federal government to intervene. Research reports indicated that the area was of World Heritage standard, and, if recommended by the national government, it would have been declared part of the World Heritage, as was south-west Tasmania (Moyal, 1984). Even without that legal step, commentators (e.g. Ward, 1984a, 1984b) suggested that the federal government both could, and was required to, prevent the road construction. The federal government consistently refused to act without 'consensus' with the state government (Cohen, 1984). The state government was strongly supportive of the construction, as part of the development, the opening up, of a wild area. Tourism is an important money-earner in Queensland, and many land developers and tourist operators have powerful state political connections. And throughout much of 1984 there was an early federal election in the offing (it took place in December, 1984).

As mentioned before, states' rights are a powerful political rallying cry in Australia, with more force in the 'fringe' states of Western Australian, Tasmania and, of course, Queensland than elsewhere. Although the federal Labor party was expected to win a large majority of the seats in the lower house, its position in the Senate (the so-called 'States' House') and in some marginal seats was less certain. Thus, it was extremely reluctant to initiate any action which would give political ammunition to its opponents. And Queensland clearly saw itself as an opponent. It is governed by the National Party, led by Sir Johannes Bjelke-Petersen, a right-wing leader who has for years successfully used as a political strategy, and strengthened, Queensland's fear and dislike of the 'centralists down south in Canberra'. And when the centralists are also 'socialists' the dislike is even stronger. Intervention by the federal government in the Daintree issue was therefore clearly electorally dangerous.

The Daintree road has now been built. Or rather carved out of the forest. It is subject to wash-outs during heavy rains. A recent newspaper report

(*Courier Mail*, 19 July, 1986) quotes the President of the Rainforest Conservation Society, Dr Aila Keto, as saying that, 'It was claimed the road would be only a track and the forest would grow over in a canopy, but at some points the permanent major break in the forest is up to 60 m wide'. She also labelled assurances by state politicians over the road as having proved 'preposterous'. But the Douglas Shire Chairman remains adamant that the road is necessary and that it will stay open. He claims the Council has now spent $800,000 on it, and in the same newspaper report is quoted as saying, 'the more the greenies stir, the more money is going into that road'. Douglas Shire is, with neighbouring Cairns City, currently the focus of considerable tourist development. Millions of dollars are being invested, with the active support of the state government, in a range of tourist facilities aimed at attracting both international and Australian visitors.

## Conclusions

It is apparent that the political and policy approaches to resource development in Queensland are dominated by short-term considerations. It is not unexpected that such considerations should prevail at the local government level, given the essentially parochial nature of local government, the spatially confined electorate to which local authorities are responsible and the enormous problems which face the areally extensive local authorities in the state. State policies are also dominated by short-term development and economic considerations, although there is a growing divergence between the non-urban attitudes of the state's political leaders and the values of an increasingly vocal urban middle class. At the federal level, attitudes are also strongly influenced by short-term considerations, although these are constrained by the limited powers the Commonwealth has over both the country's resources and environmental policies.

Queensland is in many ways representative of the 'inner' states' attitudes some years ago (although in a period of considerable unemployment some aspects of the approaches by the other states are tending to look more like those in Queensland). Planning in Queensland is indeed planning on the fringe. Queensland also appears to be on the fringe of planning.

NOTES

1 Brisbane has twenty-one Aldermen, including the Lord Mayor. Cook Shire's elected Council was earlier removed by the state government and replaced by a full-time administrator assisted by an 'Executive Committee' of six people.

2 Some of the material used in this section is derived from a student exercise carried out by R. Fleetwood, K. Means and M. Stannard of the School of Australian Environmental Studies at Griffith University in 1983. Their contribution is gratefully acknowledged, as is that of Dr. G. McDonald.

REFERENCES

Australian Bureau of Statistics (1984) *Queensland Local Authority Areas Statistical Summary at 30 September, 1984* (Cat. No. 1306.3) Brisbane: A.B.S.

Baidya, K. N. (1983) The south-west Tasmania wilderness crisis. *Environmental Conservation*, **10**(1), pp. 59–61.

Billington, H. (1984) Graveyards and bushfires in a Daintree debacle. *Habitat (Australia)*, **12**(2), pp. 9–11.

Blainey, G. (1966) *The Tyranny of Distance: How Distance Shaped Australia's History*. Melbourne: Sun Books.

Borschmann, G. (1984*a*) *Greater Daintree: World Heritage Tropical Rainforest at Risk*. Hawthorne: Australian Conservation Foundation.

Borschmann, G. (1984*b*) The Greater Daintree: a forest of forests. *Habitat (Australia)*, **12**(4), pp. 22–26.

Bowman, M. (1979) *Australian Approaches to Environmental Management: The Response of State Planning*, 6th Publication of the Environmental Law Reform Group, Hobart: ELRG.

Cohen, B. (1984) Environment Minister explains his consensus approach to the future of Cape Tribulation. *Habitat (Australia)* **12**(4), p. 29.

Coper, M. (1983) *The Franklin Dam Case*. Sydney: Butterworth.

Hamnett, S. (1984) City profile: Brisbane. *Cities*, **1**(5), pp. 442–48.

Haupt, T. (1978) The Modified Town Plan – Brisbane. *Planner (Queensland)*, **18**(2), pp. 47–55.

Heath, A. A. and Partners (1976) *Moreton Island: Environmental Impact Study and Strategic Plan: Report to the Co-ordinator General's Department*. Brisbane: A. A. Heath and Partners.

Hill, R. and Graham, M. (1984) Greater Daintree National Park, in Mosley, J. G. and Messer, J. (eds.) *Fighting for Wilderness: Papers from the Australian Conservation Foundation's Third National Wilderness Conference, 1983*. Sydney: Fontana/ACF, pp. 7–22.

Huxley, W. S. (1980) Conservation and land use planning with special reference to National Parks in south east Queensland. *Insitution of Engineers, Queensland Division Technical Papers*, **21**(4), pp. 1–8.

Minnery, J. R. (1982) Conflict and Conflict Management in Urban Planning: the Application of General Theories to Urban Planning in the Queensland Local Government Context. Unpublished Ph.D. thesis, University of Queensland.

Minnery, J. R. (1985) Urban planners and role conflicts. *Urban Policy and Research*, **3**(1), pp. 25–30.

Moyal, A. (1984) The Daintree rainforest. *Search*. **15**(9–10), pp. 243–44.

Queensland: Department of Local Government (1983) *List of Members and Employees of Local Authorities in the State of Queensland*. Brisbane: The Department (Mimeo)

Queensland: Premier's Department (1983) *Analysis of the 1981 Census, Queensland*, Report N/S 20. Brisbane: The Department.

Queensland: Premier's Department (1984) *Population projections for Queensland, 1981–2006*, Report N/S 22. Brisbane: The Department.

*Queensland Yearbook 1982* (Ed.: May, O. M.). Brisbane: Queensland Office, Australian Bureau of Statistics.

Sawer, G. (1975) *The Australian Constitution*. Canberra: A.G.P.S.

Stevenson, G. (1977) *Mineral Resources and Australian Federalism*, Australian National University, Centre for Research on Federal Financial Relations, Research Monograph No. 17. Canberra: Australian National University.

Ward, E. (1984a) The Commonwealth has legal responsibilities for Cape tribulation. *Habitat (Australia)*, **12**(2), pp. 7–9.

Ward, E. (1984b) The Commonwealth *does* have responsibilities. *Habitat (Australia)*, **12**(4), pp. 30–31.

Wiltshire, K. W. (1975) *An Introduction to Australian Public Administration*. Melbourne: Cassell.

*Chapter 9*

# Metropolitan Planning for Sydney

DAVID WILMOTH

The aim of this chapter is to identify some of the main problems and opportunities in Sydney's long-term development, and to show how an emerging metropolitan strategy addresses these issues in method and in substance. First, the overall approach is described. Then some of the main planning issues are reviewed: economic changes, population growth, employment distribution and environmental constraints. These and other elements are being integrated into a development strategy, which is out-lined along with the policies, programmes, plans and other instruments by which the strategy is guiding action.

Among planners the question of why Sydney's development needs to be guided by a metropolitan strategy might seem unnecessary. Indeed, there is widespread concern among developers and local governments about the past neglect of metropolitan planning and the absence of a public strategy. But in the broader community such a need is by no means self-evident. Will it not involve too much money and raise expectations unduly? Will it not be a 'speculator's guide' if it is made public? Should we not stop Sydney growing or at least make its expansion harder by not planning for it? Should not the process be 'bottom up', a stapling together of local and subregional plans?

These and other questions have been raised against metropolitan plan-ning and they need to be addresed.

• There is a need for regional and sub-regional plans and programmes to have a shared long-term regional framework, to reconcile contradictions or at least provide an overall context. Certainly the objects of the state's environmental planning legislation cover this.

• The widespread social, economic and physical changes since the 1968 Sydney Region Outline Plan (SROP), and, indeed, its 1980 Review, raise the need not only for a new plan, but for a new approach. The essence of the present strategy is the evaluation of alternative structure plans at the same time as a review and reformulation of policies that help or hinder planned urban development. Together, an adopted structure plan and set of supporting policies make up the strategy.

• There are other practical needs for a strategy. The release areas identified by SROP for new urban development will virtually all be serviced and available for development by 1990, and even with higher development yields from present release areas, with lower growth and with successful urban consolidation, more land will be needed. In turn, this requires a strategy to identify, and set in priority, areas for development in the medium term.

• An indication of likely directions for long-term physical development is also needed for major public investment decisions such as the second Sydney airport or the delineation of transport corridors. A long-term strategy is also called for so that sites to meet the economic development and conservation needs of the region can be earmarked in the best locations before other uses crowd them out.

• Another important reason for a long-term strategy is that public resources are in short supply compared with the demands upon them. A regional plan can save money by ensuring that public authorities and private firms use the same planning framework and link their investments. A plan can also ensure that the most cost-effective development paths receive highest priority.

• Local governments, private industry, labour organizations, community groups and many people have direct interests in a metropolitan strategy and need to be involved in its preparation. At any one time there should be available to the public, as well as to government, an expression of policy and guidelines for the longer-term development of Sydney.

• As the economy becomes less regulated and more exposed to international competition, a metropolitan strategy for Sydney can be used nationally and internationally as a guide to investment, development and conservation opportunities.

The structure plan, when formulated as part of this metropolitan strategy, will be the third regional plan for Sydney. The first was the 1948 County of Cumberland Planning Scheme. Before then, urban planning in the region was dominated by building and local land-use regulations. The scale of urban development depended on the size of investment waves and the direction of development depended on the location of water, sewerage, tram, rail and bridge investment. The 1948 plan laid down a region-wide zoning scheme guided by a number of planning objectives, including the development of suburban centres in strategic locations, the location of medium-density housing in areas with good amenities and environment, and a greenbelt to contain urban sprawl. The plan substantially underestimated the size of post-war population growth, and development pressures eventually forced the abandonment of the greenbelt.

The 1968 Sydney Region Outline Plan provided a new means of managing expansion by identifying specific greenfield areas for urban release and setting down the order of release of these areas. Since then, a programme for co-ordinating the infrastructure and servicing requirements for urban release areas has been developed so as to gear land releases to anticipated housing and servicing demand. This rolling five-year Urban Development Programme also enables area-based capital budgets for urban expansion to be compiled. The 1980 Review of SROP adjusted the focus of the plan to changed economic and demographic circumstances. SROP overestimated growth in both respects.

The 1979 Environmental Planning and Assessment Act has enabled a number of planning policies with region-wide significance to be implemented, particularly those that have increased the range of housing choice in the existing urban area. It has also enabled a series of Regional Environmental Plans for parts of Sydney, and many Local Environmental Plans, to be formulated. However, what might appear to be sensible incremental plans could, taken together, result in highly irrational overall patterns and processes of development. The need for a metropolitan strategy has become urgent.

## Economic Change

The formulation of a metropolitan strategy has to be based on an analysis of the key planning issues concerning the regional economy. At the heart of these issues is the economic role of the Sydney-Newcastle-Wollongong conurbation. This conurbation is becoming more physically and economically integrated, and consideration of Sydney's role needs to be set in the context of this wider urban unit and the state as a whole. The Sydney region as defined here includes the Central Coast, as shown in figure 1. The Sydney region is the nation's leading metropolitan area in benchmark indicators such as population, regional production and employment. As a consequence, Sydney is also the main focus for Australia's international linkages, especially migration, air passenger and telecommunication flows, finance and tourism. In any metropolitan strategy it is important to enhance this national and international role, given international economic restructuring and strong competition from other metropolitan areas for larger shares of industry, financial activity and tourism in particular.

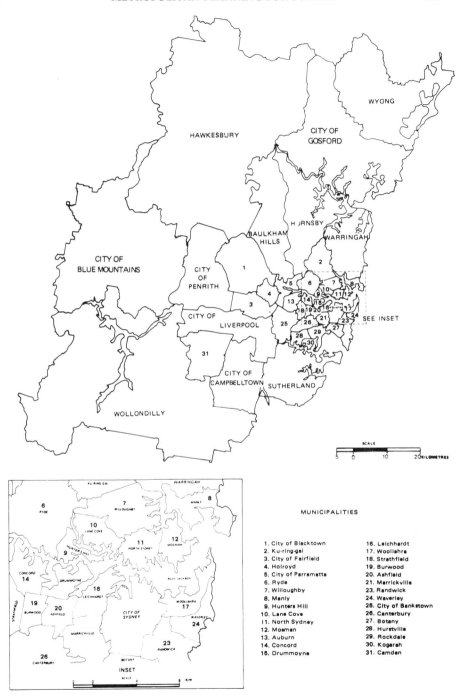

Figure 1.  Local government areas in the Sydney region.

Sydney's development is also a national issue: an efficient urban region will contribute to national efficiency.

It can be expected that Sydney will become more dominant nationally in finance, corporate management, investment and business services, as the economy shifts to closer integration with the Asia-Pacific region. Domestic financial deregulation and the greater integration of world capital and finance markets will most likely accentuate this trend. Continued prosperity would accelerate pressures for physical expansion, generate resources for high standards of urban services, and continue popular demands for high environmental standards. Less optimistic economic scenarios would tend to reduce physical growth pressures, limit the capacity of the public sector to provide services, and perhaps create pressures to lower environmental and other standards of living.

Much also depends upon how economic growth is distributed. A scenario of 'jobless growth' could combine strong economic growth with growing polarization of the population into those benefiting from an open and modernizing economy and those shut out of it for reasons of skill, location, gender or ethnic origin. Alternatively, a protected economy and an active welfare state could avoid wide economic disparities but miss out on the benefits of economic growth. These two extreme distributional scenarios are based on very different national economic and social policies and directions of the international economy. They have very different implications for the type of city that Sydney could become.

For planning, the critical economic variable is employment: the size of the workforce, the extent of unemployment and the industrial structure of employment. The proportion of Sydney's population in the workforce is expected to fall from 47.5 per cent in 1981 to around 46 per cent by the time Sydney accommodates 4.5 million people, which for reasons explained below is the planning horizon of the strategy. The lower workforce participation rate will be due to expected greater participation in full-time education and earlier retirement ages. The contrary trend of a growing female workforce participation rate can be expected to continue over the long term.

Because of the uncertain long-term outlook for the national – and therefore regional – economy, it is prudent to plan for a range of possibilities. For example, unemployment could range between 4 per cent and 12 per cent. Near-full employment would obviously enable policy to be focused more on economic production than on ameliorative employment programs, and would help to reduce intra-regional disparities in the unemployment rate. Continual structural unemployment, with an overall unemployment rate of say 7 per cent, is a more likely scenario, even with expanded economic growth. Without economic growth, and with an extended national or international recession, it is possible to imagine much higher unemployment rates. The economic and fiscal circumstances

accompanying such a scenario would greatly limit the development opportunities for Sydney. A metropolitan strategy must not contribute to slow
economic growth but it must be sufficiently robust to cope with a range of
economic possibilities. It must also find ways of encouraging equity on
territorial and population-group dimensions.

Whatever the prevailing economic conditions, the job structure of the
workforce will be very different in the future, and will affect the distribution of employment. Technological change will radically affect all industries. Manufacturing employment will be increasingly affected by
automation. However, manufacturing's share of total employment
depends on the rate of new product development in Australia, ability to
penetrate export markets, quality and cost competitiveness, and, not least,
national and state policies for job retention and industry restructuring.
From a 1981 share of 23 per cent of all employment, manufacturing's share
could drop to 15 per cent and to as low as 10 per cent by the time Sydney
reaches 4.5 million. A fairly low manufacturing share of the workforce
could still be associated with strong economic growth, but a very low
figure would likely be associated with a depressed economic scenario. A
middle figure of 12.5 per cent is assumed for most purposes. Retail,
wholesale, transport and communications industries will remain buoyant
but through productivity gains will most likely have a contracting share of
employment. Finance and business services, public administration, com-

Table 1. Employment structure of Sydney region, 1981 and 2011.

| Industry group | 1981 | Percentage of total employment 2011 Manufacturing's share | | |
| --- | --- | --- | --- | --- |
| | | high | medium | low |
| Agriculture, mining | 1.3 | 1.0 | 1.0 | 1.0 |
| Manufacturing | 23.1 | 15.0 | 12.5 | 10.0 |
| Utilities | 2.1 | 2.0 | 2.0 | 2.0 |
| Construction | 5.2 | 4.5 | 4.0 | 3.5 |
| Retail, Wholesale | 20.4 | 16.0 | 17.0 | 18.0 |
| Transport | 5.7 | 6.5 | 6.5 | 6.5 |
| Communication | 2.4 | 2.0 | 2.0 | 2.0 |
| Finance, business services | 13.0 | 19.0 | 18.5 | 18.0 |
| Public administration, defence | 5.5 | 6.0 | 6.5 | 7.0 |
| Community services | 15.6 | 17.0 | 19.0 | 21.0 |
| Personal services, recreation, tourism | 5.7 | 11.0 | 11.0 | 11.0 |
| Total | 100.0 | 100.0 | 100.0 | 100.0 |

Sources: 1981 – Australian Bureau of Statistics Census of Population and Housing;
2011 – Department of Environment and Planning, New South Wales.

munity services, personal services, recreation and tourism will expand their share of employment. Alternative future industrial structures of the workforce are shown in table 1.

Alternative economic prospects are more important to the present long-term planning period than those of the County of Cumberland Plan and the Sydney Region Outline Plan because of the apparently wider range of economic possibilities over the planning period. This time, economic factors cannot be left as exogenous forecasts: economic development policies have to be an integral part of the strategy.

## Employment Distribution

It is safe to say that employment issues will dominate Sydney's long-term well-being. The metropolitan strategy can play a significant part in ensuring that enough jobs of the right kind are available at the right places.

One option is to adopt an essentially passive response to meeting employment needs, simply providing enough industrial and commercial land and services to meet demand arising. This would involve a market-dominated employment pattern in which jobs were widely dispersed as businesses sought to minimize land costs and to seek out the suburban workforce. Sydney might gain some jobs that would otherwise locate elsewhere. However, it would mean that fewer jobs, especially office jobs, would be accessible to those relying on public transport and it would increase air pollution, energy usage and the need for road investment. Moreover, there would be no guarantee that outer suburbs with the greatest job needs would benefit by this process: current trends suggest that freestanding offices and advanced technology facilities, which house the white collar jobs needed for outer areas, in practice would be preferentially located in the middle suburbs, especially on the north shore near to executive and professional people.

An alternative option would be to locate jobs in a more concentrated pattern, making maximum use of existing transport infrastructure. A policy of promoting a limited number of large centres would help concentrate employment. At the same time the rate of job provision in outer areas, where there is a lag behind workforce growth, would need encouragement. Both of these aims would be furthered by a centres policy for outer areas, particularly to overcome the lack of white collar jobs, especially high order jobs, which now contributes to long work journeys and high unemployment in outer areas.

Other opportunities to increase jobs to meet outer-area needs lie in tourism and manufacturing. Tourism is one of the region's growth industries and outer areas have good opportunities to share in this growth via increased accommodation, convention facilities and the like. Advanced technology industries have growth potential, though there are doubts about the number of new jobs likely to be created. If more advanced technology industries halted manufacturing decline by say 2 per cent of the region's total employment, they could save or create up to 40,000 jobs.

More generally, policies to increase the rate of take-up of ordinary industrial land in outer areas can help increase the rate of job formation. This rate could increase by 25 per cent in the early years of development, with an extra 20,000 manufacturing jobs in outer areas by the time the population reaches 4.5 million. This would, however, require increased public sector involvement in areas such as marketing, finance and transport. The second major airport would also offer good employment opportunities.

In other words, there are two basic employment distribution scenarios – dispersed or *laissez-faire*, and concentrated or planned. However, even the planned option assumes that market forces will still dominate employment distribution. To enable land-use and transport requirements to be anticipated, it is necessary to define these scenarios in greater detail.

For locational purposes employment can be divided three ways: jobs near the workforce; jobs in major industrial and special use areas; and jobs in major commercial centres. In 1981 about 54 per cent of jobs were in the first category, in local shopping, service establishments, light industry, schools and other establishments mixed through residential areas. It would be unrealistic to expect a radical change to the share of jobs in the first category, even over the long term. The concentrated option is assumed to include 50 per cent of jobs distributed this way, and the dispersed option 60 per cent of jobs. Even with strong policies to redistribute outer-suburban job growth, however, these jobs will not be evenly distributed. Future new outer areas will experience long lags between workforce growth and job growth, as today's outer areas catch up. Under less optimistic economic scenarios the concept of lag might be inappropriate: the region would have areas of very high long-term unemployment. Efforts to avoid this should be central to any metropolitan strategy.

The proportion of the second category of jobs, located in major industrial and special use areas, is assumed to drop from 21 per cent in 1981 to about 20 per cent in the concentrated option and to about 17 per cent in the dispersed option, mainly to reflect the assumptions about workforce decline described above. This is likely to be partially countered by the continued growth of mixed employment areas where the distinctions between warehousing, retailing, manufacturing and office activities become more blurred.

The third category of employment distribution, the share of employment in major centres, is the one most important to the strategy. Twenty-five per cent of the Sydney region's employment was located in major centres in 1981, and this figure is assumed to grow or decline according to whether governments continue to implement a centres policy or retreat from it.

A key feature of both the County of Cumberland Planning Scheme and the Sydney Region Outline Plan – still being implemented – was the promotion of a limited number of major employment centres. The Sydney Region Outline Plan nominated Parramatta, Chatswood and Penrith as major sub-regional centres and Blacktown, Penrith and Mt. Druitt as major commercial centres in new areas. The rationale behind this policy is to minimize urban sprawl, shorten journeys to work, maximize public transport use, improve access to services and 'encourage civic consciousness and interest'.

An important strategic issue is whether centres-type employment should be concentrated or dispersed, and if concentrated, what should be the preferred pattern. A concentrated employment option would encourage over 30 per cent of jobs to locate in regional and sub-regional centres, in order to maintain the viability of the public transport system, reduce air pollution, improve access to public and private services (especially for those without a car), and encourage higher-order services to be provided than a dispersed pattern would allow. The fewer the regional and sub-regional centres designated for concentrated promotion, the greater the chance of success, but a reasonable number of centres is needed for reasons of access to jobs and services. Sydney CBD would be promoted as the major regional centre to enhance the region's economic performance and to maximize use of the rail system, but locationally it is becoming more and more eccentric. Parramatta would be strongly promoted as a second regional centre because it is central to the western half of the region, where most people will live by the time the region houses 4.5 million people. It has the best metropolitan-wide access of potential centres in the west, and it is already the biggest commercial centre there. To have an effect on employment distribution, a number of sub-regional centres would also be promoted for commercial, service, transport and residential development. Supporting policies would both encourage development in regional and sub-regional centres and discourage office and retail development outside centres.

The government through its office relocation programme, public transport programmes, roads programmes and other programmes and policies currently supports the centres policy. Several Regional Environmental Plans and Local Environmental Plans also give effect to the policy. The concentrated employment option allows higher overall accessibility to employment in Sydney, particularly for workers in the western half of the region. It assumes further action over the next twenty-five years to implement the centres policy, measures such as rezoning, development of surplus government land and airspace, transport infrastructure and service improvements, site amalgamations, design and amenity improvements, and limitations to free-standing commercial developments. It also assumes a continuing private sector interest in suburban office development.

A different distribution of employment among major centres would result if the centres policy were only weakly pursued or abandoned. A *laissez-faire* option could result in around 23 per cent of employment located in major centres, with the CBD continuing to lose employment and with private dispersal of office and retail to freestanding sites. A dispersed pattern could come about by design or by neglect as market forces are leading in this direction. The argument for dispersal is based on emerging market and technological trends and the risk that well-meaning regulation

Table 2. Sydney: alternative employment distribution in major centres.

| Centre | Employment at 3.25 million (1981)[1] | Employment at 4.5 million (2011)[2] concentrated option | Employment at 4.5 million (2011)[2] dispersed option |
|---|---|---|---|
| *Regional centres* | | | |
| Sydney CBD | 188,919 | 220,000 | 150,000 |
| North Sydney | 28,750 | 40,000 | 40,000 |
| Paramatta | 20,360 | 60,000 | 35,000 |
| *Sub-regional centres* | | | |
| Bankstown | 9,727 | 15,000 | 10,000 |
| Blacktown | 10,592 | 18,000 | 13,000 |
| Bondi Junction | 6,095 | 10,000 | 7,500 |
| Burwood | 7,355 | 10,000 | 7,500 |
| Chatswood | 9,363 | 20,000 | 20,000 |
| Campbelltown | 4,729 | 30,000 | 11,000 |
| Gosford | 5,233 | 10,000 | 6,500 |
| Hornsby | 9,637 | 15,000 | 10,000 |
| Hurstville | 6,978 | 10,000 | 7,000 |
| Liverpool | 10,904 | 20,000 | 12,000 |
| Mt. Druitt | 1,746 | 5,000 | 3,000 |
| Penrith | 3,703 | 20,000 | 11,000 |
| St. Leonards[3] | 22,983 | 20,000 | 20,000 |
| Sutherland[3] | 5,524 | 10,000 | 8,000 |
| Wyong-Tuggerah | — | 5,000 | 3,000 |
| Bringelly Sector Centre | — | 12,000 | 7,000 |
| NW Sector Centre | — | 8,000 | 5,000 |
| Total major centres | 352,598 | 558,000 | 386,500 |
| Share of total employment | 23% | 30% | 21% |

*Notes:* 1. *Source*: State Transport Study Group, 1981 Travel Survey. Figures exclude students working part-time.
2. *Source*: Department of Environment and Planning, New South Wales.
3. Includes industrial and special uses area employment outside centre but in same traffic zones.

of the location of employment could drive jobs out of Sydney or out of the state, or be overridden by market forces.

The benefits of dispersed employment accrue privately to freestanding office and retail developers and employers. However, these benefits may be costs to employees and, for reasons stated above, would be costs to the community at large. For example, extremely high costs to the State Rail Authority would be incurred if it sought to maintain service standards against declining demand. The concentrated employment option could reduce the loss of ridership in the metropolitan rail system from 28 per cent to 14 per cent, though such figures are based on some assumptions that might not hold over the longer term. Greater use of public transport and walking to centres would also enhance the quality of the environment. A concentrated pattern of employment would also enable higher-order services to be provided through the economic advantages of agglomeration. For these reasons policy of concentrating jobs in a limited number of centres is preferable. Possible distributions of employment in major centres are shown in table 2.

## Population Growth and Social Change

Sydney's share of Australia's population has been slowly declining since around 1970 at least, and its proportion of the state's population is now showing the same trend. There is a net internal out-migration from the region. But even if these trends continue, Sydney's population is expected to grow by about one million over the next twenty-five years. Many policies for Sydney's development are inseparable from those for state development. A central question here is whether policy measures can or should direct some of this increase to such areas of the state as the north coast, which are in any case expected to receive large numbers of out-migrants from Sydney over the coming decades. In other words, should Sydney's growth be encouraged, discouraged or left alone? Irrespective of policy, Sydney will keep growing. There is some limited scope to adjust rates of growth by immigration, economic and land release measures, but almost no scope, within present civil liberties, for limiting Sydney's size to any preferred level. In any case, in a changing society the idea of an optimal size for cities has little meaning.

The case for discouraging Sydney's population growth rests on claims that Sydney is too big, that its environment will deteriorate, that the social impact of rapid growth is harmful, that decentralization remains a good policy, and that other attractive parts of the state should be preferred to Sydney. Discouraging growth by economic means such as zealous regulation could take jobs out of the state and possibly the country. Discouragement of further immigration would have humanitarian disadvantages given Sydney's share of family reunion and refugee intakes, and would lose the long-term advantages of skilled labour and ethnic diversity. Discouragement by deliberately limiting land and housing would make Sydney's housing prices and the costs of living even higher than they are now, and would lead to unwarranted burdens on immobile lower-income households forced to pay high prices.

A second option is actively to encourage Sydney's population growth. Most arguments for encouraging Sydney's growth appear to rest on economic efficiency, for which the region would continue to capitalize on its advantages; presumed economies of scale as Sydney's national and international influence grows; the local advantages of continued growth, for example in the building and construction industry; and the greater up-front costs of accommodating growth elsewhere in the state. However, economic gains from size or from rates of growth are not well documented and could be illusory.

A third *laissez-faire* argument is that it is too complex for governments to take a position on a region's rate of growth, and that households and firms will sort themselves out according to individual preferences and market mechanisms. While there is some truth to this view, it ignores the biases already built into government policies and the statewide context of the Sydney region.

There could be a tendency for some state development policies to be dominated by Sydney issues, to the detriment of the rest of the state. A development strategy for Sydney must be seen as part of an even-handed statewide strategy: to locate growth by positive means at nominated areas desirable for work and recreation and which have the capacity for more people; but not to discourage growth by socially punitive constraints on Sydney designed to push people out or to discourage them from coming to Sydney. In other words, any current biases to favour growth in Sydney should be replaced by regional development policies to promote growth elsewhere, but Sydney's growth should not be penalized by negative means.

Population forecasts are notoriously inaccurate and the history of the County of Cumberland Plan and the Sydney Region Outline Plan show how difficulties can arise when plans are based on fixed-date forecasts of population. For this reason, the metropolitan strategy in preparation is based on a fixed population level for Sydney: a population threshold of 4.5 million people. Why that number? The 4 million mark is already within medium-term commitments to urban infrastructure. The 5 million mark is too far away to guide a credible strategy. The 4.5 million mark helps set other critical thresholds. Importantly, the strategy is sufficiently robust for high or low growth and for policies of decentralization or accelerated growth.

Current population projections estimate three rates of growth – high, medium and low – and on present trends Sydney will reach 4.5 million by years 2007, 2012 and 2017 respectively (see table 3). The most likely medium rate of growth therefore implies a planning horizon of twenty-five years, during which time 1.11 million extra people would need to be accommodated in the region.

Table 3. Population projections, Sydney, 1981–2011.

| Level of Growth | Population (m) | | | | | | | Year 4.5 million |
|---|---|---|---|---|---|---|---|---|
| | 1981 | 1986 | 1991 | 1996 | 2001 | 2006 | 2011 | |
| Low[1] | 3.253 | 3.351 | 3.439 | 3.439 | 3.534 | | | 2017 |
| Medium[2] | 3.253 | 3.438 | 3.653 | 3.857 | 4.059 | 4.265 | 4.46 | 2012 |
| High[1] | 3.253 | 3.446 | 3.715 | 3.973 | 4.235 | | | 2007 |

Sources: Department of Environment and Planning, New South Wales and Australian Bureau of Statistics. 1. Census enumeration. 2. Estimated resident population.

Sydney's growth depends very much on statewide and national population trends, overseas migration and internal migration in particular. Overseas migration into the region at recent statewide rates of between 20,000 and 50,000 net per annum more than compensates for internal out-migration from the region, from 6,500 to 15,000 each year. Sydney's rate of growth depends very much on overseas migration, an element that cannot be reliably forecast and which must be constantly reviewed – see table 4 for the components of Sydney's likely growth.

Table 4. Components of population growth, Sydney, 1976–2011.

| Component | Year 1976–81 Population | Percentage | Year 1981–2011 Population | Percentage |
|---|---|---|---|---|
| Natural increase | 115,200 | 85 | 768,100 | 90 |
| Overseas migration | 82,400 | 61 | 198,500 | 23 |
| Internal migration | −61,800 | −46 | −115,800 | −14 |
| Total growth | 135,800 | 100 | 850,800 | 100 |

Sources: 1976–81 – Australian Bureau of Statistics Census of Population and Housing; 1981–2011 – Department of Environment and Planning, New South Wales.

For many planning purposes the number of households is a more important forecast than the number of people. With population ageing, more divorces and more single-parent and single-person households than in the past, the average size of household has been falling and will continue to fall, from 3.05 persons per dwelling in 1981 to 2.75 in 2011. While economic conditions and the price of housing may slow this rate of

Table 5. Household forecasts, Sydney, 1981–2011.

| Level of growth | Households (m) | | | | | |
|---|---|---|---|---|---|---|
| | 1981 | 1986 | 1991 | 1996 | 2001 | 2011 |
| Low | 1.082 | 2.141 | 1.223 | 1.296 | 1.331 | |
| Medium | 1.082 | 1.230 | 1.331 | 1.431 | 1.542 | 1.620 |
| High | 1.082 | 1.182 | 1.347 | 1.516 | 1.641 | |

*Sources*: Australian Bureau of Statistics; Department of Environment and Planning, New South Wales.

decline, it is most unlikely that they would reverse the trend. Table 5 shows the household forecasts assumed for the stategy. These forecasts also need to be kept under review.

Though social change is difficult to forecast, in large measure patterns of social development depend on economic conditions and demographic trends. It is assumed that households will be smaller and more heterogenous, with single-person and lone-parent households increasing and extended households declining. It will be difficult for service agencies and the housing market to keep pace with these changes, though buoyant economic conditions and a fiscally healthy public sector would make the transition more smooth than continued depressed conditions.

Different groups will create more diverse demands on services and facilities: aged, youth, children, migrants, lone-parent households and single-person households. Continued difficult economic conditions would have a disproportionate impact on these vulnerable groups and on women. A long-term depressed economy could be expected to lead to a greater degree of social disintegration – crime, unemployment, civil disorders, mental health problems and homelessness. Moreover, these problems would be concentrated in some areas and not others.

Overall affluence would bring its own problems for social policy, even with the unlikely outcome of wealth being equitably distributed: more leisure time, changed nature of work, greater pressures on recreation resources, more cars, and market tendencies towards a dispersed urban form. A metropolitan strategy needs to anticipate and cater for likely future lifestyles.

The population can be expected to become more culturally and ethnically diverse, with many sources of overseas migration and further suburbanization of foreign-born households. Whether ethnic groups are concentrated or dispersed depends on migrant housing policies, the operation of the housing market generally and the preferences of groups for different parts of the region. Inner-city gentrification and the displacement of working-class households will spread to the middle suburbs as office jobs grow, but the pattern will be selective, leaving areas of poor housing between renovated suburbs. This and demographic and ethnic changes will continue to

challenge the public sector to avoid mismatches between traditional services provided and the needs of new groups.

Whether the class segregation of Sydney gets greater or not depends in
part on employment location, housing, zoning and land release policies
and in part on the future employment structure and the location of unemployment. At the metropolitan scale and within major sectors, equity
considerations lead to policies of social mix.

A less than rapid rate of population growth in the region – and in any
one sector – could enable services to be provided in time with urban
development, especially if economic conditions and public finances allow
adequate resources. High rates of population growth could burden local
and state government authorities beyond their capacity and make it difficult for new community identity to develop, especially if public finance is
strongly constrained over the planning period.

In order to calculate future land needed for urban development, it is
necessary to make forecasts of likely demand for dwellings. Demographic
forecasts of numbers of households may be used as measures of latent
demand for housing, but economic conditions prevent some of this latent
demand from becoming effective demand. In turn, effective demand for
housing can be turned into demand for *new* dwellings by taking demoli-
tions, non-structural dwellings (rooms, huts, etc) and vacancy rates into
account. Forecasts of the likely demand for new dwellings in the Sydney
region are shown in table 6. 654,000 more new dwellings (from 1981
figures) will be needed by the time Sydney houses 4.5 million people.

Translation of demand for new dwellings into demand for land depends
on assumptions about infill and redevelopment in established urban areas,
the proportion of attached and unattached dwellings, and the density of
housing in new areas. These are policy variables and are discussed below.
Before development policies are formulated, it is important to examine
forecasts of the condition of the environment, particularly air quality,
water quality and noise.

Table 6. Demand for new dwellings, Sydney, 1991–2011.

|  | 1991 | 1996 | 2001 | 2006 | 2011 |
|---|---|---|---|---|---|
| Occupancy rate | 2.97 | 2.90 | 2.84 | 2.77 | 2.75 |
| Total households (000) | 1230 | 1331 | 1431 | 1542 | 1620 |
| New Dwellings from | | | | | |
| 1981 (000) | 201 | 318 | 434 | 561 | 654 |

*Source*: Department of Environment and Planning, New South Wales.

## Environment

Air and water quality in Sydney has been improving. However, without special efforts the Sydney region could suffer from air, water and noise pollution as it grows. As well as improvements to future technology and increases to finance available for amelioration to maintain the rate of recent improvements, special attention will need to be paid to the location and timing of urban development and environmental planning at the earliest possible stages of decision-making.

The configuration of the Sydney air basin – surrounded by steep terrain and dissected by river basins – when combined with Sydney's climate and prevailing air flows, can allow unacceptable levels of pollutants to accumulate and recirculate during stable weather conditions. Sydney is perhaps more vulnerable than any other Australian capital city; certainly its expansion is more physically constrained than any other. Photochemical smog episodes during summer, brown haze during winter and carbon monoxide levels on congested streets all could worsen without strong control programmes. Hydrocarbon emissions and ozone levels will improve with new emission standards but could be overtaken by growth in vehicle trips. Acid gases, dust, and suspended matter could remain around present levels though controls on backyard burning will reduce the latter. Lead levels will gradually improve with the introduction of unleaded petrol. In short, even with new regulations and new technology, further urban growth could make high air pollution events more frequent and more widespread across the region. Prospects for maintaining air quality levels depend on further policies for the location and timing of urban development, slower growth of private vehicle use (perhaps through better public transport), a decline in manufacturing or further prohibition on air polluting industry within the air basin. None of these policy options are easy.

Water quality faces similar trends, with recent improvements coming under longer-term risks of deterioration. Further growth in sewerage discharge will be accommodated by sewerage outfalls and tighter controls along the two major rivers currently used for sewage disposal – Georges and Hawkesbury-Nepean Rivers. Treatment works, diversions, augmentation of existing works and submarine outfalls are all planned to cope with expected increases in point source sewerage loads. With urban growth of the scale forecast above, current strategies will need full implementation to keep water quality from deteriorating. Dry weather water quality is likely to improve in most instances, perhaps with the exception of the Hawkesbury-Nepean River which will drain most new urban areas of Sydney and which will come under some stress. Wet weather water quality is not good now and could deteriorate without stringent run-off and erosion control programmes. Land-based irrigation of effluent may prove to be a viable alternative to the installation of some nutrient removal facilities but it will require suitable vacant land areas to be set aside. Pollution from urban and rural run-off could get worse in the upper reaches of Sydney's major inland waters if urban development were to proceed there because the soils are particularly erosion-prone. A more compact form of expansion would avoid most of that risk.

The major source of noise problems in Sydney, as elsewhere, is road traffic. Other noise sources, in order of importance, are domestic appliances, aircraft, public transport, air conditioners, rail traffic, maintenance activities and industry. The impact of road traffic noise could become more widespread, even with new noise reduction technology and various policy measures for noise control. Aircraft noise is expected to continue to grow near Kingsford-Smith airport until it reaches full operational capacity some time during the metropolitan strategy's planning period. The second Sydney airport will divert some of this noise potential. Noise problems from rail are not expected to grow as the system is unlikely to expand significantly. Manufacturing districts will become quieter as fabrication technology changes and as service activities penetrate industrial zones. Recreation activities – sportsfields, stadia, raceways, powerboats, and their like – could become a growing noise problem with increases in recreation activity.

In short, technological controls will get better but alone may not keep pace with urban growth. To maintain or improve present standards a greater share of resources would need to be spent on pollution control technology, or, as a tradeoff, people would need to accept restrictions on their activities in the future. For example, recreation activities in some waterways would need to be prohibited, outdoor exercise and use of private motor vehicles on high air pollution days would need to be controlled, and noisy activities would need to be restricted at night time. This is not an attractive option.

In addition to the use of technology, the allocation of more resources and the tightening of pollution controls, land-use planning can help improve environmental quality. Metropolitan planning can reduce the risks of growing pollution by locating emission sources in areas that have the capacity to assimilate them. For example, new air emission sources could be located in well-ventilated areas, polluting water sources could be located near the coast or water-courses with spare capacity, and noise-generating land uses could be located in areas away from residential development. Whether the Sydney region has enough land with assimilative capacity to accommodate 1.25 million more people – or indeed, enough land to accommodate them at any environmental standard – is an important issue.

## Land Availability and Urban Consolidation

Sydney's expansion is strongly limited by physical, environmental, financial and other constraints. Even where there is some capacity for urban development, factors like agricultural land quality or the costs of development may make such areas unsuitable.

Some areas can be excluded from consideration by the obvious constraints of their status: existing and committed urban areas; floodplains; developed water supply catchments; wetlands; public open space (including national parks, wildlife refuges and state forests); public uses like special use corridors and liquid waste disposal sites; major conservation and heritage resources; steep terrain; and soils with extreme erosion or drainage hazards.

On top of these are less obvious constraints of alternative land uses such as potential waste disposal sites; scenic landscapes; areas with high bushfire danger; good agricultural land; areas with mineral resources; mine subsidence districts; and future airport sites. These criteria eliminate many areas from suitability for urban development and limit the capacity of other areas. Figure 2 and table 7 show what is left. The amount of land suitable for urban development that would also minimize future environmental impact is very limited indeed: most areas drain water into the Hawkesbury-Nepean River system and air into the Sydney basin. However, before accurate measures of the urban capacity of areas can be made, it is necessary to make assumptions about population distribution and density. The density of residential development in new urban areas is a major factor in determining the amount of land required for urban expansion, and to some extent the pattern of social interaction and access to services. One reason for the Sydney Region Outline Plan's underestimation of population in new release areas has been low yields in terms of dwellings per hectare. With few exceptions the gross residential density now commonly achieved is about 8 lots per hectare. A continuation of present trends would be an easy option. There is some inconclusive market evidence that in new areas medium-density housing, which would be necessary for higher densities, is unpopular, but some of this relates to the price of town houses relative to detached houses and not to density itself or house form.

A higher density of 10 lots per hectare is preferable. Lower densities result from large lot sizes and, in developing areas, from a pattern of 'leapfrogging', with expensively serviced land lying idle and with new residents isolated from social contact and community services. The public costs of providing services to low-density areas are very high, and these costs can be reduced by higher densities. So far densities around 10 lots per hectare have been attained in a few areas that have a substantial component of medium-density housing, so implementation of this part of the strategy would require policies to encourage infill development, efficient development of land and an average of 20 per cent of dwellings in multi-unit buildings. This will not prevent large-lot subdivisions from occurring, and indeed in parts of the west and south-west this would be desirable to

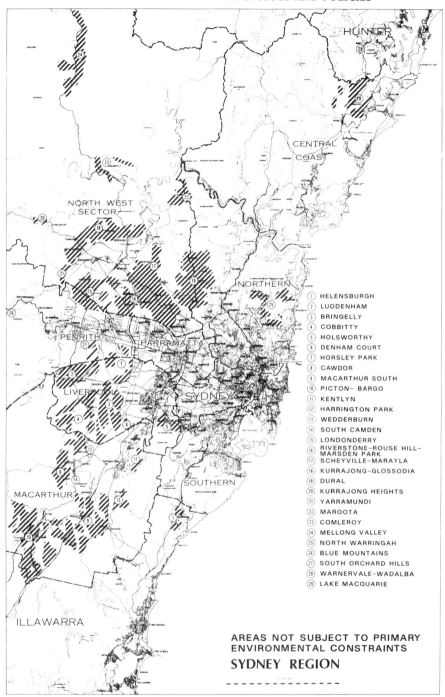

1. HELENSBURGH
2. LUDDENHAM
3. BRINGELLY
4. COBBITTY
5. HOLSWORTHY
6. DENHAM COURT
7. HORSLEY PARK
8. CAWDOR
9. MACARTHUR SOUTH
10. PICTON– BARGO
11. KENTLYN
12. HARRINGTON PARK
13. WEDDERBURN
14. SOUTH CAMDEN
15. LONDONDERRY
16. RIVERSTONE–ROUSE HILL– MARSDEN PARK
17. SCHEYVILLE–MARAYLA
18. KURRAJONG–GLOSSODIA
19. DURAL
20. KURRAJONG HEIGHTS
21. YARRAMUNDI
22. MAROOTA
23. COMLEROY
24. MELLONG VALLEY
25. NORTH WARRINGAH
26. BLUE MOUNTAINS
27. SOUTH ORCHARD HILLS
28. WARNERVALE–WADALBA
29. LAKE MACQUARIE

AREAS NOT SUBJECT TO PRIMARY
ENVIRONMENTAL CONSTRAINTS
## SYDNEY REGION

Figure 2.

Table 7. New areas capable of urban development in the Sydney region.

| Sector | Development areas | Indication developable area (ha)[1] |
|---|---|---|
| North West Sector | Riverstone, Rouse Hill, Marsden Park | 10,500 |
| | Londonderry | 3,500 |
| | Glossodia, Kurrajong | 6,700 |
| | Scheyville, Maraylya | 2,500 |
| | Sub-total | 23,200 |
| Macarthur | Macarthur South | 8,000 |
| | Holsworthy | 50 |
| | Harrington Park | 400 |
| | South Camden | 50 |
| | Picton, Bargo | 8,000 |
| | Sub-total | 16,500 |
| Bringelly | Austral, Catherine Fields, Kemps Creek, Cecil Hill | 5,200 |
| | South Orchard Hills | 700 |
| | Sub-total | 5,900 |
| Warringah | Duffy's Forest, Terry Hills, Ingleside, Warriewood, Oxford Falls | 2,000 |
| | Sub-total | 2,000 |
| Central Coast | Warnervale, Wadalba | 4,000 |
| | Sub-total | 4,000 |
| Southern & Illawarra[2] | Part of West Menai | 580 |
| | Helensburgh | 180 |
| | Sub-total | 760 |
| Total | | 52,360 |

Notes: 1. Other uses such as commercial and industrial are assumed to take up 10–15 per cent of major development areas.
2. Not defined as in Sydney region but indicates spillover accommodation.

attract executive housing. In general, though, attainment of this target density will mean smaller lot sizes.

Even with policies to ensure the efficient development of new land, not all the land in new release areas would be taken up by the time the region accommodates 4.5 million people. The resultant urban development capacities of these areas, assumed to be 90 per cent of potentials, are shown in table 8. Overall, at the higher densities there is potential for about 667,000 more residential allotments in the region, with over 500,000 of them in areas not yet committed to urban development. At the lower density of 8 lots per hectare there would be capacity for fewer than 400,000 uncommitted lots.

How much of this capacity would be needed to accommodate Sydney's expansion to 4.5 million people depends on assumptions and policy

Table 8.  Sydney region, residential lot capacity and extent of development for new areas at 4.5 million population.

| Area | Residential land capacity (no of lots)[1] | Residential land to accommodate 4.5m people[2] |
|---|---|---|
| Sydney Urban Development Program | 159,800[3] | 159,800 |
| Pt. West Menai | 4,100[3] | 4,100 |
| Helensburgh | 1,500[3] | 1,500 |
| Holsworthy | 500[3] | 500 |
| Warriewood | 400 | 400 |
| South Orchard Hills | 6,200 | 6,200 |
| Harrington Park | 3,400 | 3,400 |
| Rouse Hill-Marsden Park | 71,400 | 53,350 |
| Warnervale-Wadalba | 25,200[3] | 16,200 |
| Macarthur South | 63,000 | 37,900 |
| Bringelly-Horsley Park | 54,000 | 31,900 |
| North Warringah | 14,600 | 14,600 |
| Scheyville | 20,700 | 19,500 |
| Picton-Bargo | 63,000 | 11,600 |
| Londonderry | 22,400[3] | 0 |
| Glossodia-Kurrajong | 60,300 | 0 |
| Luddenham | 20,700 | 0 |
| Cawdor | 22,500 | 0 |
| Cobbitty | 47,700 | 0 |
| Yarramundi | 6,000 | 0 |
| Total | 667,400 | 360,950 |

Notes: 1. Residential land potential is for 'lot equivalents', i.e. total number of dwellings, generally at 10 lot equivalents. The data are current estimates only and are subject to detailed investigation. Capacity is assessed at 90 per cent of total potential because of problems of slow build-out and the difficulty of achieving maximum yield from awkwardly shaped areas.
2. Assumes multi-unit dwelling commencements at 9000 each year and density in new areas generally of 10 lots per hectare except as indicated.
3. Based on 8 lots per hectare not 10 lots per hectare, because of environmental, drainage or coal industry constraints.

choices about urban consolidation in particular. Should higher residential densities be encouraged in established areas and if so how strongly? Sydney is one of the lowest-density large cities in the world and the population density of established areas in Sydney is declining. Despite the perceived advantages of owning a detached house, even if at the urban fringe, a number of costs occur to the general community from continued urban expansion in terms of land, infrastructure, community facilities and the social effects of isolation and poor accessibility. Housing variety and prospects for meeting the needs of various groups suffer if only one form of housing is available in an area. Urban consolidation can occur through redevelopment, infill, building conversion or the retention of housing stock. Much of the initiative with urban consolidation rests with the private sector, though public sector regulations and changes to development procedures can play a part.

Multi-unit dwelling commencements offer an indirect measure of urban consolidation. A very active policy could pursue a target of more than 12,000 multi-unit dwelling commencements on average every year, double the current level of commencements. However because of limited land availability in established areas such a high level would have the effect of requiring most higher-density housing to be built in new outer urban areas rather than more accessible inner urban areas.

A more realistic indicator of an active urban consolidation policy would be around 9,000 units each year. This could be sustained over the long term, though it would represent about 40 per cent of all new housing built in the region, as compared with an average of 35 per cent over the last ten years.

Without an active set of urban consolidation policies, a more market-oriented choice could yield about 6,000 units a year. This is slightly higher than the level of commencements of attached dwellings over the last few years, but over the period of the proposed strategy, such a level would represent only 29 per cent of all new dwelling completions.

It is occasionally argued that detached housing development should be encouraged more than attached dwellings because of alleged overseas housing preferences towards lower densities and because of optimistic future affluence and consequential demands for low suburban densities. Active promotion of lower densities could take attached dwelling commencements even lower than 6,000 a year, but the cost, variety and equity disadvantages of such a policy eliminate 'urban thinning' as a serious alternative.

If urban consolidation policies were weak (say 6000 multi-unit dwellings a year) or if new residential areas attained only 8 lots per hectare, there simply would not be enough capacity in the Sydney region, as presently defined, to accommodate 4.5 million people. Of course, such a scenario would not occur without changes to densities. In established areas, the highest practicable level of urban consolidation should be pursued. An indication of this level of effort would be an average of 9,000 multi-unit dwelling commencements each year.

Several principles determine which areas should be used for new development, though there is not a wide range of choice.

• Rate of development: in any one sector, development should not exceed 3,000 lots each year, for reasons of service availability, the stresses of growth, and market acceptance.

• Variety: development should proceed in many areas rather than be concentrated in any one sector, subject to cost-effectiveness considerations.

• Simultaneity: to cater for different geographic sub-markets, a degree of concurrent growth is necessary in the four major growth sectors (North West, Macarthur South, Bringelly and Central Coast). While near-coastal development would be preferable to westward expansion for environmental, recreational and housing variety objectives, the development potential in coastal areas is low and is further limited by accessibility, affordability and cost-effectiveness constraints.

• Compactness: development should generally occur incrementally from one developed area to the next, avoiding 'leapfrogging' at the broad scale.

Based on the principles espoused above and the overall objectives of the development strategy, table 8 shows a possible sequence of development for these areas.


## Towards a Strategy

The population, economic, employment distribution and environmental issues are only four components of the structure plan options and associated policies. Clearly, alternative transport networks and modes, energy and resource use, conservation and heritage, recreation, systems of government and public finance are other important elements. There is not space to deal with them here.

Alternative structure plans and policies are designed to meet a number of objectives for Sydney's future. None are more important than economic and employment objectives, which are concerned with improving the economic performance of the larger Sydney region (consistent with state-wide efficiency) and ensuring sufficient total employment opportunities and an equitable geographic distribution of them. Equity should be an important objective on its own, relating to the social and economic structure of society as much as to the location of urban opportunities. The strategy should also ensure that there is a sufficient supply of affordable serviced land and housing to meet the region's demands, and that there is a sufficient variety of housing for the needs of all types of households. Action to eliminate community and human service backlogs and mismatches should be taken, especially in areas of new or rapidly changing urban development. Recreation facilities and parks need to be expanded and made more accessible to meet the demands of a larger, more leisure-oriented population. The conservation of important natural features and buildings will also be increasingly important in the face of lifestyle changes towards leisure and environmental pursuits. New development should be

sited and implemented so that adverse environmental effects are mini-
mized or avoided, while pollution from existing development should be
reduced. The metropolitan strategy should also plan for an adequate level
of both public and private transport access from all areas to employment
and other opportunities: at present there are great disparities in public
transport access. Adequate airport and seaport capacity to meet future
needs should also be planned for. While new arrangements for financing
urban development need to be explored, continuing resource constraints
dictate a plan that ensures public expenditure on infrastructure has maximum cost-effectiveness for the community as a whole.

The policies that help or hinder structure plans are more prone to change
than the plans themselves. Nevertheless, a metropolitan strategy has to
assume that certain policies are in place and to propose further policies, to
help implement the plan. Together, plans and policies make up the
strategy. The main policies proposed in the strategy are to do with the
patterns of urban change – spatial policies – and with the process of
planning and development.

There should be policies to promote a compact pattern of overall urban
growth, to avoid leapfrogging and to save infrastructure costs. A complementary policy of urban consolidation in new as well as established areas is
needed to reduce sprawl and infrastructure costs, and to provide greater
housing variety and better access to employment and services. A set of
policies to favour the development of selected major centres would
increase employment and service accessibility for those reliant on public
transport, reduce road transport (if not transit costs), energy usage and air
pollution. The strategy must also include the identification of key sites well
in advance of development, planned in such a way as to meet the policies
and objectives indicated above. The identification of new urban areas, and
the staging of their development so that infrastructure and service provision can be co-ordinated, is central to the strategy. The management of
urban expansion is going to be more important as housing and service
demands become more heterogeneous.

A set of policies is also required to initiate development, rather than
merely facilitate it as in more traditional metropolitan plans and strategies.
Economic development should be a primary objective of planning: unprecedented structural change to the economy makes an economic development strategy for the metropolitan region essential. Development policies
in this area could take a number of forms, including policies for promoting
advanced technology in the workplace, the establishment of sub-regional
economic development organizations where none now exist, training and
education policies targeted on urban sectors, and the creation and retention of employment in areas with surplus labour, especially new outer
suburban areas.

Policies to improve service availability and timing are also needed, with concentration on services that so far have not been well provided for, such as intermediate roads, suburban public transport and district-level community facilities. These policies may involve an agreed process for implementing new needs-based programmes and more sophisticated priority-setting processes between and within agencies. The private sector can be expected to play a larger role in human service provision, as new services become commercially viable and as other services are seen as part of a widening view of corporate responsibility. Policies to widen access to housing are also needed. These would embrace measures to preserve and increase the rental housing stock, and to make homeownership more widely available. These policies are especially important because it is quite possible that structural changes to the economy – for example, housing finance deregulation – might otherwise produce the opposite effect. A set of policies is also needed to make the conversion of land to urban use more cost-effective, possibly involving financial penalties where there is leapfrogging and idle utility-serviced land, a land pooling policy to speed up the consolidation of small rural holdings for urban development, and changes in subdivision planning standards. Pollution abatement policies will need to be expanded to accommodate the expected increase in traffic and the spread of the urban area, and energy resource constraints could again dictate strong conservation policies. Changes in the planning and development process itself could also assist the region's development and improve its quality: the Environmental Planning and Assessment Act of 1979 may well be a different entity by 2011.

Spelt out in more detail, such policies will be brought into effect by implementation programmes and other more detailed plans. Existing programmes such as the Urban Development Program, the Urban Consolidation Program, the Advanced Technology and Small Business Development Funds, the Area Assistance Schemes, Employment Assistance Fund, the Government Office Relocation Program, the Local Government Development Program, public transport re-equipment and expansion, the ocean sewer outfall programme, and various programmes to extend Sydney's parks and recreation and sporting facilities will all help to achieve different objectives of the strategy. Commonwealth and local programmes can also support, and in turn be guided by, a metropolitan strategy. However, new programmes may well be required for the region's economic well-being, employment and backlogs with service provision. Programmes and arrangements which more closely integrate the planning and development of housing, services, and employment in areas of major urban expansion would go some way towards meeting the growth problems of new urban areas. Changing the pattern of services in established urban areas to reflect social and demographic change is difficult for the public and private sector alike but has to be addressed.

Planning policies themselves will be fundamental to achieving the objectives of the metropolitan strategy. Regional Environmental Plans (REPs) are the most obvious mechanism for translating a metropolitan strategy into more detailed guidelines. REPs for each sub-region containing major new development, or major urban changes, can allow metropolitan objectives and policies to be expressed in more detailed terms, and ensure that land rezoning and development approvals conform to agreed objectives. Thus REPs could be used to give major centres preference for large commercial developments, to achieve selective urban consolidation, or to identify an arterial road network. REPs are also an effective tool for managing particular elements such as housing and regional open space objectives.

The next level of planning, embodied in Local Environmental Plans (LEPs), is appropriate for the needs of local areas within Sydney. LEPs can be used to implement metropolitan strategy where the way the strategy would work changes between areas. LEPs can also ensure that smaller-scale planning objectives, such as those concerned with subdivision standards and the promotion of innovative forms of development, are achieved in accordance with the metropolitan strategy.

Some metropolitan planning objectives would also be statewide objectives. For example the need to ensure co-ordination of services with development applies just as much to growing country towns and resort areas as to Sydney. To meet statewide objectives State Environmental Planning Policies are appropriate instruments. Other planning instruments can give effect to the metropolitan strategy. Environmental Impact Statements and Assessments, for example, can ensure that major projects go ahead in accordance with environmental objectives. Early discussion and negotiation with proponents of development, technical bulletins and other guidelines to local councils and widespread public awareness of the metropolitan strategy can all play their part.

Detailing the means of implementing a strategy at this stage would be premature: there is still a task of policy development ahead. Work on metropolitan strategy is at a stage where it would greatly benefit from wider discussion. In 1982 preliminary long-term options for Sydney's development were identified, and a smaller set of medium-term options evaluated for possible release beyond SROP release areas. The 'first cut' of a joint transport/land-use evaluation tested the long-term options. This work, along with other government agency evaluations, enabled the options to be refined. An urban policy review that came out of the 1980 SROP review helps make these options realistic in policy terms. The effect of all this work has been to widen the structure plan options under consideration. However, the need for guidelines for major investment decisions with long lead times – second Sydney Airport, for example – have required strategic planning advice in the meantime. Investment in urban development does not wait for the planners.

Tempered by current use, the metropolitan strategy that emerges should be a practical tool for managing growth and change in the region. However, its successful formulation and implementation will rely on wide public consultation. In addition to all the technical and political work, it is vital that we keep our eyes on what is the ultimate purpose of the exercise: creating the kind of urban region that best meets the needs and the hopes of the people of Sydney, in all our diversity.

NOTE

Much of this chapter is based on the work of the metropolitan planning team in the New South Wales Department of Environment and Planning, whose contribution is gratefully acknowledged. A shorter version of this paper was published as 'Metropolitan Planning in Sydney' in *Australian Planner*, 1985, Volume 23, number 3, pp. 25–37. The views expressed in this chapter are those of the author and are not necessarily those of the Department of Environment and Planning or the New South Wales Government.

# Conclusion: Who Plans and for which Goals?

STEPHEN HAMNETT

Australian federal governments have seldom pursued interventionist locational policies intended to discriminate in favour of some parts of the
country against others for the sake of distributional equity. Indeed, if one
discounts the rather modest efforts of the Ministry for Post-War Reconstruction to direct employment growth away from the major cities in the
early post-war years, then the only significant attempts by a federal
government to address national urban policy questions of this sort were
made during the life of the Labor government of Gough Whitlam between
1972 and 1975. Whitlam came to power committed to the view that the
quality of life is determined less and less by the goods which individuals
can purchase for themselves from their personal incomes and more and
more by the things which the community provides for all its members from
its resources. At the time of Whitlam's election some members of the
community were clearly receiving less than their fair share of these community goods. Large parts of the outer suburbs of the major cities were
characterized by a dearth of social facilities and physical infrastructure.
Journeys to work were increasing in length, public transport was often
inadequate and rising land prices were placing home ownership out of
reach of young families.

Maher's chapter describes how the Whitlam government set out to
address these locational inequalities by establishing a Department of Urban
and Regional Development (DURD) which was to be responsible for co-
ordinating the activities and programmes of other federal ministries in
pursuit of national urban policy goals. Some of the principal policies
introduced involved the establishment of land commissions to hold down
urban land prices; area improvement and urban renewal schemes; a drive

to provide sewerage in new outer suburban areas; and the establishment of a growth centre at Albury-Wodonga on the New South Wales-Victoria border to relieve pressure on Sydney and Melbourne.

When Whitlam's government fell in 1975, the conservative government which followed under Malcolm Fraser quickly reverted to the more traditional federal approach of limited intervention in the land and housing markets. A considerable number of books and articles which analysed the policies and achievements of DURD also appeared subsequently (for example, Jones, 1979; Lloyd and Troy, 1981). Most of these emphasized the obstacles which the Department had faced during its brief life, including rivalry with the Treasury and other functional ministries; and the difficulty of pursuing federal urban policies in the face of opposition from state governments of a different political complexion. Some went further to suggest that there are deeper structural barriers to reformist policies of the sort which the Whitlam government espoused and that solutions to the urban problems which they had identified are impossible without complete economic control of the private sector and very substantial increases in public expenditure.

The contributors to this book have shown that many of the issues which the Whitlam government attempted to tackle in the early 1970s still need to be addressed. They have also shown, however, that the context has changed significantly. During Whitlam's period of office this context was one of steady economic and population growth, with unemployment rates which were significantly lower than those of the mid-1980s. The Hawke Labor government which came to power in 1982 has been required to operate under conditions of lower economic growth, a deteriorating employment situation and a greater awareness of the nature of structural economic change, deindustrialization and the prospect of jobless growth. Its response has been to pursue corporatist industrial policies which are dominated by efficiency rather than locational concerns, with a strong emphasis on targeting industrial assistance to new areas of high technology development (McLoughlin, 1986, p. 4).

At the metropolitan level, also, planning in the mid-1980s appears to lack explicit commitment to interventionist policies in pursuit of social and spatial goals. It is characterized, instead, by an approach which emphasizes the management of urban change and the use of sophisticated monitoring systems to speed up or slow down the pace of land release and infrastructure provision according to the changing nature of demand for new housing. The research and technical studies carried out by state planning agencies are often a very high standard, but at a time when there is increasing evidence to show that Australia's metropolitan areas are becoming more polarized and unequal (Fagan, 1986; Forster, 1986), the lack of any substantial political interest in metropolitan policy-making is cause for concern. The one clear metropolitan policy idea in good currency in Australian cities at present is that of urban consolidation. Bunker's chapter shows that the pursuit of consolidation involves a number of uncertainties which are not always acknowledged by its proponents. But there are grounds for doubting, in any case, whether any state or metropolitan government currently has the willpower to take on local government and private developers to the extent that might be necessary to encourage more – and more diverse – housing within the existing built-up areas. A further disturbing tendency is the apparent willingness of state governments to set aside their existing planning policies and controls in attempts to attract new commercial developments, often by foreign investors, for the sake of job creation and other economic benefits (real or illusory). The Darling Harbour Project in Sydney, the 'Expo 88' project in Brisbane and the Victoria Centre in Melbourne are the largest of such projects, but there are several more.

It is only at the local level at present that there appears to be some innovative thinking taking place about appropriate solutions to current problems. In their chapter Sandercock and Melser note evidence of a growing concern to promote community consciousness, a greater involvement by local government in the planning and provision of human services, and considerable interest in programmes of economic self-help. These build on an awareness of initiatives in Britain and the United States to promote local economic development by designing institutional forms and policies to fit specific local circumstances. The obstacles to these sorts of initiatives are also formidable, however. Local governments in Australia often have very small populations and resources, and lack the capacity and expertise to contemplate and implement schemes for promoting economic development. Local autonomy is a fine principle, but it should not be introduced as a substitute for appropriate policies at higher levels. As Sandercock and Melser argue forcefully, unless state and federal resources are made available in some way to areas which are in the greatest need because of the changing economic structure of the country, local initiatives alone will accomplish little in those areas.

The contributors have provided a snapshot of current urban planning and policy issues in Australia in the mid-80s. They have been selective and there are clearly other important issues which might have been addressed – the policy implications of an ageing population and the special needs of ethnic minorities, including aboriginal people, in the cities, to mention but two. One encouraging feature of the field of Australian urban studies today, fortunately, is the existence of a growing library of scholarly studies of urban policy and planning issues (see McLoughlin and Huxley, 1985), to which it is hoped that this book makes a small but useful addition. Some suggestions for further reading in this field are given below. An understanding of the complexity of the urban policy process is a necessary prerequisite for rethinking the education of planners and urban policymakers. Key questions in that process in future are likely to be 'who plans? and for which goals?'.

## REFERENCES

Fagan, B. (1986) Industrial restructuring and the metropolitan fringe: growth and disadvantage in Western Sydney. *Australian Planner*, **24**(1), pp. 11–17.

Forster, C. (1986) Economic restructuring, urban policy and patterns of deprivation in Adelaide. *Australian Planner*, **24**(1), pp. 6–10.

Jones, M. A. (1979) Australian urban policy. *Politics*, **14**(2), pp. 295–303.

Lloyd, C. and Troy, P. (1981) *Innovation and Reaction: the life and death of the Federal Department of Urban and Regional Development*. London: George Allen and Unwin.

McLoughlin, J. B. and Huxley, M. (1985) Australian urban studies: the state of the art. *Built Environment*, **11**(2), pp. 143–156.

McLoughlin, P. (1986) Regional development, policy and the Commonwealth. *Australian Planner*, **24**(1), pp. 3–5.

## SUGGESTIONS FOR FURTHER READING

Burnley, I. and Forrest, J. (1985) (eds.) *Living in Cities: Urbanism and Society in Metropolitan Australia*. Sydney: George Allen and Unwin.

Maher, C. A. (1982) *Australian Cities in Transition*. Melbourne: Shillington House.

Parkin, A. (1982) *Governing the Cities: the Australian Experience in Perspective*. South Melbourne: Macmillan.

Sandercock, L. and Berry, M. (1983) *Urban Political Economy: The Australian Case*. Sydney: George Allen and Unwin.

Troy, P. N. (1981) (ed.) *Equity in the City*. Sydney: George Allen and Unwin.

# Index

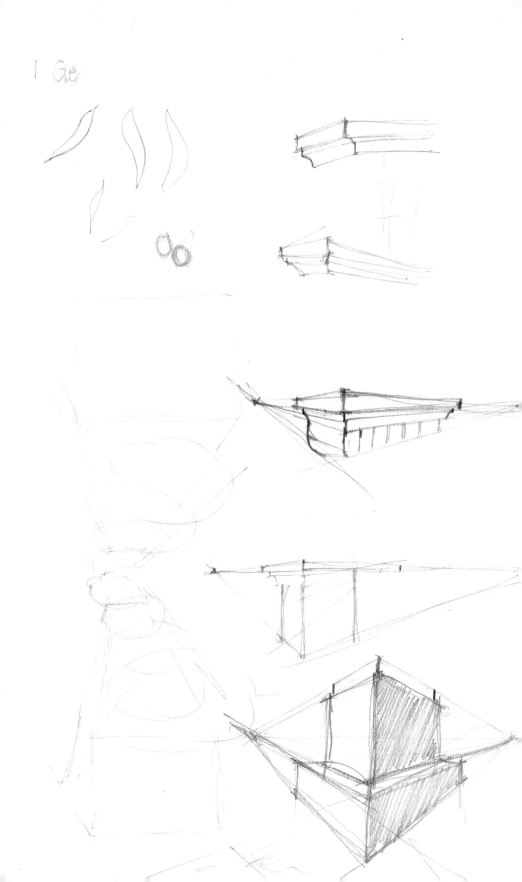